GW01017708

Along the Great North and Other Roads

GIRTFORD BRIDGE Which carried the Great North Road over the river Ivel. Millions of cyclists have ridden over it in haste and in leisure, including the artist, W.A. Ellis, winner of the North Road '24' in 1927-28-29.

Along the Great North and Other Roads

The North Road
Cycling Club
1885-1980

A. B. Smith

Alan Sutton
1981

Alan Sutton Publishing Limited
17a Brunswick Road
Gloucester

First published 1981

British Library Cataloguing in Publication Data

Smith, A.B.
Along the Great North and other roads
I. Title
796.6060421'4 GV1047.N/

ISBN 0-904387-73-9

Typesetting and origination by
Alan Sutton Publishing Limited.
Photoset Plantin 10/12
Printed in Great Britain
by Redwood Burn Limited
Trowbridge & Esher.

Contents

Foreword 11
Introduction 13
Chapter 1. The Eighties. 15
2. The Rise and Decline of the Paced Game. 27
3. The Twenty-four. 45
4. Other North Road Open Events. 83
5. North Roaders in other Clubs' Open Events and the Road Records Scene. 105
6. Other Competitive activities. 121
7. Club Life. 143
8. Our Presidents. 159
9. Addendum. 175
Appendices
1. Officers of the Club. 181
2. The Club Trophies. 183
3. Menu — Fourth Annual Dinner, 1889. 188
4. York Run Card, 1894. 191

Illustrations

Girtford Bridge, *W.A. Ellis* 2
A.J. Wilson 22
The North Road Fifty – the finish, *G. Moore* 31
The North Road Fifty – officials and press, *G. Moore* 31
Dan Albone and M.A. Holbein, *G. Moore* 34
G.P. Mills and A.J. Wilson 36
M.A. Holbein, *G. Moore* 36
T.A. Edge, *G. Moore* 36
W. Chater Lea, *'E.K.'* 36
R.L. Ede, *G. Moore* 36
The North Road '24' – 1887, *G. Moore* 47
The North Road '24' – 1891 check sheet – Wisbech 48
North Road Winners of the 'Twenty-four' Invitation Time Trial
  C. Hilhouse 1906 57
  F.H. Wingrave 1909/10 57
  W.A. Ellis 1927/8/9 58
  R.F. Mynott 1949/50 58
C. Smith taking '24' cup for tenth time 63
S.A. Mottram '24' organiser 1950-76 64
The Memorial '50' – 1931
  1st F.W. Southall, 2nd F.G. Frost, 3rd F.T. Brown
  4th G.W. Jenkins 98
F.W. Shorland, *G. Moore* 122
North Road Cycling Club – 1895 137
York Run at Askern – 1907 138

New Year run – Cross Keys, St. Neots – 1928 140

At. Gosling Stadium, Welwyn Garden City – 1967 141

Characters of the 1930s 149

K. Lovett and R. Cook 153

Tony King Memorial 154

North Road Presidents

- A.J. Wilson (with first Mrs. Wilson) 157
- T.G. King – with F.T. Bidlake 161
- F.T. Bidlake 162
- S.H. Moxham 167
- H.H. England 168
- W.C. Frankum 173
- G.E. Edwards 174

North Road Team – 1979 '24' 178

North Road Trophies

- Open events and Hadley Highstone Memorial } Appendix 2 . 184
- Club events

1889 Dinner Programme Appendix 3 189

1894 York Run Programme Appendix 4 191

To all those with whom I have
shared the social, competitive and
administrative aspects of the
club's life this book is dedicated

Foreword

To have survived for over ninety years as a continuously active cycling club, as fewer than ten clubs have done, and with an unbroken record of service to the sport, is no mean feat in a Britain which has changed so dramatically in its social structure and industrial development from iron to plastics. It is characterised by the transition from the Ordinary (high) bicycle originally built by the techniques of the blacksmith but later by highly skilled manufacturers of the slim, lightweight safety bicycle made from high-grade aircraft steels and the latest alloys. A photograph of the first run of the Club in 1886 depicts mostly Ordinaries and tricycles with only a few safety bicycles; the transition had already begun and the Ordinary gradually faded from the scene although the tricycle remained and remains a favourite of the connoisseur.

I first met the author of this book in 1924 when riding with the Hampstead Section of the Cyclists' Touring Club. He had already been a 'real' cyclist for four years while I was only in my second year. Among our companions were some older men riding tandems with wives or sweethearts, the men being noted members of the North Road Club whose feats are recorded in this book and of whom Frank Armond, who attained the age of eighty-eight on 26 March 1977, is still an active cyclist. Arthur Smith and I were apparently considered suitable recruits to this august body and early in 1925 were elected members. It was not long before we were elected to the Committee and in 1929 Arthur was appointed assistant to Frank Armond, the Racing Secretary. From that time until the outbreak of the Second World War in 1939 he was an official of the Club in one guise or another and perhaps his most valuable contribution was as Editor of the monthly *Gazette* from 1935 to September 1939. Throughout these years he was a keen tourist, an ardent and successful racing man on the road and a breaker of road records on tandem with Frank Marston. Alas, the fortunes of war decreed that Arthur, as an official of the Admiralty, should move to Bath in 1940; he never returned to London and although remaining a keen and interested member with annual pilgrimages to the Great North Road for the York Run (of which he only missed one between 1946 and 1968), the Twenty-four hours road ride and other major events he was unable to undertake any official position in the Club apart from the labour of love involved in writing this book.

Nevertheless his principal interest has remained in cycling in all its facets with its companion pastime of photography. The loss of such a capable and enthusiastic official by the North Road Club was the gain of the West Country cycling fraternity who have benefited from his talents, experience and abilities. For twenty-two years she represented the Western Counties on the Council of the Cyclists' Touring Club and was a member of the Rights and Privileges Committee for many of those years. He is Life President of the Bristol District Association of the Club. He is also a member of the Bath Cycling Club, the Wessex Road Club, the Tricycle Association, the Hereford Wheelers, the Ross-on-Wye Cycling Club and other cycling bodies and, of course, remains a Life Member of the North Road Club. For his services to cycling in the West Country he was awarded the Widmann Memorial Plaque in 1960. He also found time to break the Pembroke to London Tricycle record in 1947 with a time of fourteen hours.

In his introduction Arthur Smith has explained how he came to write this book. With his great affection for both the Club and the sport and pastime of cycling no one was better fitted for the task. The book is not only a faithful chronicle of the history of a club which has had considerable influence in the cycling game but shows how the bicycle was an instrument of social change in the ninety years from 1885. Not only the North Road Club but the whole cycling fraternity will enjoy this fascinating narrative.

W.Frankum.
President. North Road Cycling Club.
1938 — 1945
1961 — 1977.

Introduction

A second history of the North Road Cycling Club was planned as part of the celebrations of our 75th anniversary and was to have been written by our then President, Harry England. Although he looked forward eagerly to the task he explained that his other commitments would prevent him from starting on it until at least a year after the anniversary. It was designed to be a complete history from 1885 and not just a continuation of S.H. Moxham's *Fifty Years of Road Riding* and Harry envisaged chapters covering different events, in particular, changes in courses used as well as the performances achieved on them. His thinking may well have been influenced by *The Black Anfielders* which appeared in 1956.

Alas, before he embarked on the task, he died in 1961 and the Club committee asked me to accept the task. I was about to retire and had considered volunteering to ensure that I did not miss my basic eight hours a day at my office table – I haven't. The delving into ancient records; weeks spent at the British Museum Newspaper Library at Hendon, living at my sister-in-law's home at East Barnet, were entrancing and rewarding. The real task started when I tried to select the appropriate information and compress it into chapters. This proved most difficult when it came to the twenty-four – how to tell the story of nearly seventy (now seventy-seven) twenty-fours in a single chapter? It baffled me for years after, as a first exercise, I wrote a chronological story of them.

Our title (suggested by Bert Dollamore – a member since 1935 and participant in the 1937 revival of the York Run) is culled from part of the sub-title of the *North Road Gazette* – 'Founded in October, 1885 to promote fast and long distance riding on the Great North and other roads'.

Our frontispiece is one of the many sketches by Bill Ellis which enlivened the *Gazette*, particularly during the editorship of fellow Bedfordian Woodbine Haylock. The delightful caricature portraits of North Roaders prominent in the 1930s and signed 'Bux' were by then member Colin Buckland and also come from Gazettes of the later part of that decade. Those of our outstanding characters of the 1890s, by George Moore and that of Harry England by 'Lewis', are taken from the pages of *Cycling* with the consent of its current editor. I am indebted to John Boon of Bristol C.T.C. for assistance in photo-copying most of these drawings and to member Fred Sellens for copying the older photos and providing the more recent photos –

in particular for the photo of the club trophies arranged, with the assistance of Ken Davis, prior to the 1974 Annual Dinner.

I owe a debt of gratitude to three people who, in turn, have converted my difficult-to-decipher writing into neatly typed pages. The late Gladys Armond did the first two chapters; her daughter, Margaret Hay, Chapter III; and Frank Marston the remainder. I am also indebted to Cecil Paget for relieving me of the basic research for Chapter VIII – and for cheerfully authorising me to do what I liked with his draft! Greatly appreciated have been the comments and corrections on the various chapters by Derek Roberts of the Fellowship of Cycling Old Timers and Southern Veteran-Cycle Club, who kindly agreed to read through the chapters – and by members Frank Armond, Bill Frankum, Cecil Paget and, most of all, Dick Cheveley, a member since 1908. In returning one of my chapters Dick said 'if you ever complete this dreadful task it will be worthy of the Club!' I humbly hope that he is right.

Last but not least of my appreciations must be of my wife's forbearance.

Arthur Smith.

CHAPTER I.

The Eighties.

Solid men in sombre suits, wearing waistcoats looped with watchchains, chains heavy or slender, gold, silver or plated, according to the taste and status of the wearer: men crowned with bowler hats, except those (such as doctors and bank clerks) for whom the top hat was the accepted or ordained wear, or the manual worker who wore a cap — the top hatted, incidentally, usually substituted the long 'frock coat' for the jacket. All — men, women and children — were normally completely clad from top to toe (boots being normal outdoor footwear) except that the poorest might have gaps in their ragged clothes and their children went barefoot.

The ladies, bless them, although escaped from the voluminous crinoline, indicated that they were not both 'angular and flat' (vide W. S. Gilbert) by their skirts having the peculiar rearward decorative hump of the bustle — to help emphasise the slim waist just above: those skirts still swept the ground. The blanket shawl was a normal part of the costume of the poorer women — it could cover her head or be used to carry a baby, by binding it round both, and was worn by the street vendors, standing in the gutters of busy streets and displaying their wares in trays or baskets.

Such were facets of the 1880s, when Victoria had been Queen for over forty years — a mourning widow for some twenty of them — Queen of a prospering nation nevertheless just entering one of the periodic slumps which were the serious malaise of the last decades of the nineteenth century. In the newer industrial towns particularly, below the facade of prosperity was a festering layer of squalidly housed — if housed at all — poor, those at the lowest levels of employment (or unassisted unemployment) in the mines or factories. True the conscience of the nation was slowly stirring, moved by the efforts of the few social reformers, and the conditions for the 'lower orders' were slowly, very slowly, being improved. In Birmingham, under Joseph Chamberlain's radical mayoralty, a great slum clearance work coupled with the provision of adequate sanitation was achieved, ironically under powers provided by Tory Disraeli's Acts of 1875. The long strife between Disraeli and Gladstone which had enlivened — nay dominated —

politics for so long, ended in 1881 with the death of 'Dizzy', by then Lord Beaconsfield.

Coincident with the industrial slump ushering in 'the eighties' a succession of bad summers, which spoiled crops and spread disease among cattle (three million sheep died of 'rot' in 1879), combined with the rapid increase in the volume of cereal imported from North America and, a little later, of meat from Argentine and Australia, were ruining the British farming industry. This gave impetus to the emigration of workers from country to town and overseas to the Colonies or to the United States. Nevertheless over a third of the total population, then about seventeen million, were still country-dwellers.

Compulsory elementary education had, incidentally, ended child labour in mines and factories and was providing an enormous potential increase in the reading public. Tennyson, most popular of Victorian poets, was growing old: Matthew Arnold, in poetry and prose, like William Morris and John Ruskin tried to combat the materialism of the age: Thomas Hardy, in his tragic novels, was also enshrining, as in amber, the scenes and characters of the Wessex countryside: Brahms and Dvorak were composing orchestral and chamber music, now accepted as 'classical', Dvorak visiting London and conducting concerts in 1884 and 1885: by then D'Oyly Carte had built a special theatre, the first electrically lit, to house the existing and future light operas, peculiarly English, of Gilbert and Sullivan — the Savoy opened in 1882 with *Iolanthe*. In Bristol Frieze-Greene was working on the problems of cinematography, but was unable to take out his first patent until 1889. The £1 was a golden sovereign, worth twenty silver shillings and in comparison with the values of today could purchase an amazing quantity of goods.

The railways, by then past their jubilee, had reduced wheeled traffic on even the main roads to the local journeys of milord's or the squire's carriages, farmers' traps, slow farm carts and carriers' wagons: the passenger carrying coach had almost disappeared. Most people walked to and from work or between village and town on market days — and some walked many miles. Villages and country towns were still, mostly, homogeneously built of the locally available materials and their inhabitants were closely knit entities: each town, at least, had a team of independent craftsmen (blacksmith, carpenter, wheelwright, mason, tailor, saddler . . .) to cater for its needs. Village water supplies came from communal or household wells or pumps: bathrooms were unknown, baths being taken in front of kitchen or bedroom fire, less extensive washing being performed at a basin in kitchen sink or, maybe, on marble topped washstand in a bedroom.

Amid all this — between the houses of city streets or the hedges (or stone walls) of country roads and lanes — young men on bicycles, older men and courageous women on tricycles were threading their way. By 1880 the bicycle had become the high, front wheel driven, machine later known as the ordinary — and later still, to the irritation of its devotees, as the 'penny-farthing': these driving wheels were normally between fifty and sixty inches in diameter, the rider choosing the largest wheel he could bestride (in Britain the gear ratios of our bicycles are still expressed in relation to the diameter of the driving wheel of an ordinary). Increasing the bicyclist's appearance of height, the saddle of the ordinary was placed not far behind the vertical (and the handlebars) and the rider usually sat bolt upright — except when indulging in a spell of 'scorching' on the road or when racing on the track, the rider then crouched forward: this however increased the skill required to preserve the precarious balance. Whether the balance was upset by unskilful scorching or by hitting an obstacle on the rough roads it could result in the rider taking a header over the wheel (and such headers, on occasion, proved fatal) but the more agile riders learned to land on their feet! The ordinary exerted such a hold over, and gave such delight to its devotees that, for some years after the first 'dwarfs' and rear wheel driven 'safeties' appeared (about 1884), many ordinaryists were convinced that their mounts would always remain the choice of cycling athletes: some of the best racing ordinaries were built at a weight of twenty-one and a half lbs. — less well built machines suffered dangerous breakdowns resulting from bad weight trimming.

The limitations of the 'ordinary' naturally resulted in alternative designs of bicycle being developed and two types appeared at about the same time — the rear driver, and precursor of the present bicycle, and front drivers. The latter were in two broad classes, lever driven by an up and down motion of the feet and, retaining rotary pedalling, through underslung chain drives: with both the rider sat lower and further behind the front wheel, which was normally smaller in diameter than that of the 'ordinary'. The rider was thus less liable to go over the top — though he was still restricted to a single gear and had to pedal all the way — unless he transferred his feet from the pedals to the rests provided on the forks. For a few years these geared-up front drivers, which with the rear drivers were called 'safeties', achieved a certain degree of popularity and some notable rides were done on them in races and record rides. Athletic types, as well as the more sedate, also used the tricycle, despite its extra weight — in the early eighties some tricycles weighed 120 lbs. and more! — and used it very effectively. All the early practical tandems were, in fact, tandem tricycles: they were, probably, the mount most favoured by the ladies, who sat decorously on the front seat and thus, in the more popular types between the side wheels.

Although, from the beginning (and ever since) a percentage of pleasure, as distinct from utility, cyclists annoyed both their fellows and the non-cycling public by merely parading along city streets, the majority were attracted out to the country: to the sights, scents and sounds long since familiar to all but now, to many, rendered remote and strange by the spread of the towns — a spread accelerating with the twentieth century. To the early cyclists from the towns — the forerunners strangely enough of much of the individual motorised travel now taking place and resulting in so much spoliation — the countryside was an arcadian wonderland full of strange lures. The very inhabitants of the countryside then differed more in mannerisms, clothes and speech from the townsmen: there were also the signs of the changing seasons — the sight and scent of blossoms, particularly as the buds burst in the first warm days of spring: or the rustle of wind across a field of wheat or barley. And adventurous souls embarked on rides through the summer nights, beneath stars whose brilliance was undimmed by the poor, yellowish light given by their unreliable oil lamps — and there were few brighter lights outside the towns: for these night riders dawn brought the wonder of the dawn chorus of birds including, perhaps, thrush and blackbird competing with nightingale. And then there was the indescribable but evocative scent raised by the initial wetting of the road when rain starts gently — a scent which altered but retained its subtle charm with the change from dusty to tar-bound surfaces.The arrival of the cyclists did not affect the basic nature or appearance of the countryside. But, at all levels of society, individuals and groups developed and showed a strange, unreasoning dislike — even detestation — of the new fangled machines and their riders. Early cyclists were thus, on occasion, deliberately ridden down by the horsey folk or were lashed at with the horse whips, or they were attacked by roughs on foot, pulled from their machines or sticks thrust into their wheels to bring them down, or stones were thrown at them. Sometimes the victims were able to bring their aggressors before magistrates or judges and were generally successful in such actions — though on occasion magistrates or judges appeared to have so strong a bias against cycling as to interfere with true justice. A successful case reported in 1879 was that of a Mr. A. J. Wilson against a carter who deliberately turned his horse into the cyclist.

Another problem for the early cyclists was the condition of many roads. As long distance coach travel waned many rural local authorities (Justices of Peace until County Councils were established in 1888) lost interest in the maintenance of their roads — the toll system of maintenance by Turnpike Trusts had practically ended. Repairs were neglected or ill done: a favourite economy was to purchase stones for repair work in too large a size (vide John Macadam's dictum — translated by roadmen to making the mouth the gauge!) to bed down and knit together: outside the towns steam rollers (available since 1866) were little used. Surfaces could be so thick with dust and loose stones, especially after a long spell of dry weather, or so deep in mud after much rain as to be unrideable by the cyclists: but given reasonable maintenance and just the right amount of rain, the surface could be wonderful. Cyclers (as they were often called) regularly protested about the condition of roads even, in at least one instance, combining with the horsefolk to this end: as a practical measure cyclists subscribed to funds from which the roadmenders in an area were entertained, particularly near Christmas, to dinners, hoping thus to get the sympathy of the men on the job.

The professorial Frenchman Taine, visiting England some decades earlier and writing his impressions of its inhabitants, commented on the apparent need and desire of the English for extravagant physical exercise — a need he took to be one of the effects of the foggy and humid climate. Maybe the growth of cycling, after the commercial introduction of the bicycle to England at the end of the 1860s, was a response to this need. By 1878 cycling periodicals estimated that there were 60,000 cyclists and seven years later (when there were some half dozen national periodicals devoted entirely to the pastime, while the more general sporting papers, such as The Field, Athletic News, Referee and Sporting Life, included long reports of cycling activities) the estimated number had grown to 400,000. Long before this the numbers had increased sufficiently for another facet of the British character to take effect and riders had grouped themselves together in clubs. The Pickwick Bicycle Club, currently and for some decades a social club only, but maintaining an interest in the pastime, is the oldest survivor with 22 June 1870 as its foundation date: in 1889 it obtained a ruling from the National Cyclists' Union 'that no other club had established a prior claim' to being the oldest club — a ruling promptly challenged by the then Scottish C.U., which was investigating the claims of the Edinburgh Amateur Bicycle Club. A chronology published in the November 1881 issue of a monthly journal *Cycling* lists a Western A.B.C., with a secretary in Paddington, as being founded in 1869 and holding a handicap road race on, believe it or not, 29 January 1870. Maybe the Western A.B.C. did not survive until 1889 — a Wheelman's Year Book of 1882 devotes four pages to listing 'extinct clubs', to a total of about 170.

The majority of those who took to cycling had no desire to ride in a competitive way and found their pleasure in the adventure of exploration alone or with a few companions of similar age or social standing. Others younger or, perhaps, unembarassed by social standing (in a very status conscious world) found pleasure in the life of a club — on road or, in the winter, indoors at Smoking Concerts, Cinderella Dances, Balls and other gatherings: in the winter many put away their cycles. The pastime also attracted a number who found the elation of achievement either in the distance they covered or the speed at which they rode. Some, of course, desired, possibly for commercial ends, to demonstrate the efficacy of bicycle or tricycle as a means of travel: early examples being Messrs. Mayall Junior, Rowley Turner and Charles Spencer who, in 1869, rode their primitive 'boneshakers' from London to Brighton in about twelve hours.

So clubs, in their hundreds, were started, up and down the country, in different districts of the larger towns (Craven Hill, for many years housing the office of the Cyclists' Touring Club, had its Bicycle Club) and in most of the smaller towns. Many ran short races on the roads, at distances of five or ten miles, sometimes providing the method of selecting the Club Captain and Vice Captain. A few were more strenuously minded: in 1877 the London B.C. instituted, for its members only, a 100 miles race between London and Bath (or vice versa) and in 1878 the winner achieved seven hours eighteen minutes fifty-five seconds, which was regarded as best on record until 1884. In 1883 the London Tricycle Club — in those years it was not unusual for separate clubs to cater for bicycling and tricycling activities — promoted a twenty-four hour race for tricyclists which attracted seventy-four entrants of whom sixty-seven started from Caterham: it was won by T. R. Marriott, of the tricycle making firm of Marriott and Cooper, with 218¾ miles: A. J. Wilson started on a path racing trike and claimed to have been the first to arrive at Brighton, but his front wheel wasn't strong enough to withstand the road conditions and collapsed — he afterwards said he was not displeased at being thus forced to stop!

From early times a number of national bodies evolved to look after cycling affairs. The Amateur Athletic Association initially took charge of track racing and promoted national cycling championships. The Bicycle Union was established in 1878 (as was the Bicycle Touring Club) and promoted championships in 1879, but for some years afterwards the A.A.A. continued its cycling championships. The B.U. was primarily designed to cater for membership through club affiliation, but required those wishing to race to take out a licence and pay a licence fee. The B.T.C. catered only for individual membership — at an annual subscription of 2*s*. 6*d*! A Tricycle Association, to function for tricyclists as the B.U. did for bicyclists, came a little later and, amongst its activities, promoted some fifty miles championships on the road: the first of these, in 1880, was on the 'North Road' from Tally Ho! Corner to St. Ippollitts (near Hitchin) and back. This fifty mile tricycle championship was won by C. D. Vesey on the 'Rara Avis', which was an ordinary trailing a pair of back wheels and caused such a furore that the machine was banned from future tricycle events: had G. Lacy Hillier (later to become famous as bicycle 'Champion at all Distances' on the path) not arrived late and started thirteen minutes after the field the result might have been different, for Hillier finished second.

While the North Road surface pleased the tricyclists, the hills did not and the 1881 course started at Hounslow, followed the Bath Road to Maidenhead and, avoiding the turnpike gate, turned north to and through Marlow.

In 1882 that original Tricycle Association (with which the present body of that name has no other link) amalgamated with the Bicycle Union and the title National Cyclists' Union was adopted. The Bicycle Touring Club, incidentally, also became the Cyclists' Touring Club and adopted the winged wheel badge. (Later, in 1886, the N.C.U. and C.T.C. formed the Roads Improvement Association to work for the making and maintenance of better road surfaces). Also in 1882 came the apparent first road race designed to popularise a particular make of machine, in this case the Facile — initially a lever driven front driver with a front wheel forty-four or forty-two inches in diameter (smaller sizes were made) and weighing thirty-two lbs: later they were geared up to the equivalent of a large wheel ordinary. The event was a twenty-four hours race from London i.e. Anderton's Hotel in Fleet Street, to Bath and back as far as possible and was won by W. Snook with 214½ miles: along the final miles he was acclaimed by enthusiastic crowds.

In 1883 a similar event on the London to Birmingham road was won, with 220⅞ miles, by J. H. Adams, a notable performer at anything from track events to the End to End record. In 1884 the makers of the Kangaroo, another geared-up front driver but with an underslung chain drive (by 1886 it was reported to weigh 20½ pounds and be geared to sixty-four inches), responded with a 100 miles race on a new course attributed to C. H. Larrette, a cycling journalist (initially with Bell's *Life of London* until absorbed by *Sporting Life*, when he became London Editor of the *Manchester Sporting Chronicle*) and a member of the Pickwick B.C. This course started one mile west of Twyford, on the Bath Road, and went through Slough, Denham, Rickmansworth, St. Albans, Welwyn and Hitchin to Biggleswade and then up the North Road to Norman Cross Hotel, where Mrs. Brooks was a popular hostess. The event was won by George Smith of Merry Rovers C.C. in the new record of seven hours eleven minutes. In 1885 he won another 100, on the 1884 course in reverse, promoted by the Rover Co. on their rear driven safeties and the time was further improved to 7h. 5m. 16s: Edward Hale of Gainsborough C.C. (a Brixton club) was second in 7h. 17m. 2s. after spending twenty minutes at a blacksmith's having a break, resulting from a collision, repaired: later Smith was sued for failing to return the machine lent to him for this event and was accused of selling it! Also in 1885 the Rudge Co. ran a twenty-four hours race for riders of Rotary tricycles — an early single wheel drive machine having the large driving wheel on the left of the rider and two small wheels in tandem, incorporating the steering, on his right: J. H. Adams won with 232½ miles.

The Portsmouth Road, particularly as far as Ripley (and it was frequently called the Ripley Road) was probably the most popular among London cyclers. The Anchor at Ripley was famed for the welcome given to cyclists by the Dibble family: they had a visitors' book which the Misses Dibble endeavoured to persuade all visitors — whether for a meal or for a night — to sign: inevitably they failed but circa 1884 there were 6,000 signatures for the year and it was estimated that there had been at least 8,000 visits from cyclists in that year. Some even appear to have done most of their cycling on this road: the ten miles between the Angel at Ditton and the Ripley Anchor were much used for impromptu trials of speed. But Kingston police and magistrates became notorious persecutors of cyclists.

A.J. WILSON
NORTH LONDON T.C.

Some cyclists, more strenuously minded, had discovered that the Great North Road — or their variant of it from Welwyn via Hitchin to Biggleswade — was mostly in good condition and well cared for, and had found a welcome at Biggleswade from Dan Albone at his Ongley Arms or in his 'Ivel' Cycle Works — and Dan was a keen cyclist himself. Among his visitors was A. J. Wilson of Canonbury B.C. (other members of which established early unofficial records, in turn from London and Lands End to John O'Groats). The name of A. J. (or 'Faed') Wilson — 'Faed' was a self applied anagram of his affliction, since boyhood, of deafness — was constantly cropping up in the cycling press of the late 1870s and early 1880s: he was a C.T.C. member, a Vice President of North London Tricycle Club (later to become the still active North London C.C.) and a member of the N.C.U. Executive Committee. He had edited (jointly with another) a weekly *The Bicycling Times and Touring Gazette*, was author of slim volumes such as *Riding Rhymes: or every Bicycle Club its own Music Hall* and *Duffersville*, a collection of light hearted essays covering cycling life in Biggleswade. 'Faed' also competed successfully in races on home trainers, in track events and hill climbs but road riding was his prime interest and his favourite outgoings were along the North Road: he was credited with riding on every day of 1885, covering 7,000 miles in the year. During that year he was a prime mover in organising a testimonial fund to express appreciation of Dan Albone.

Quoting Faed's own words, as recorded in the *Bicycling News* of 18 June, 1886:-

> I had frequently experienced the advantage of having fast riding companions to help make the pace hot on a return journey from Biggleswade, and seeing how much more pleasantly the journey was made when a number of crack riders were with me than when I was grinding along alone, or with slow riders, the idea occurred to me that it would be beneficial to others as well as myself if some kind of organisation was arranged to ensure suitable companions being at hand on Saturday to Monday or Saturday and Sunday spins. At first I thought of merely making a list of 'scorchers' in North London and arranging to send postcards round for occasional meets and runs in company, as all the men I could think of were already members of local clubs as well as of the C.T.C.; but afterwards it occurred to me that a really well organised club could do more than this and could assist in promoting good road-riding, so that the North Road Club was the outcome. It was first proposed by me at a meeting of the subscribers to the Albone testimonial and was not fully launched until we had held three meetings, all of which were announced as *open* so that there was no trace of hole-and-corner secrecy or cliquism about it. I was asked to be captain, but refused to occupy any office except that of committee man . . .

The initial meeting culminated in one, at the then N.C.U. offices at 17 Ironmonger Lane, London, E.C. on Friday 23 October 1885 with C. H. R. Gosset of Temple B.C. in the chair: earlier in the year Gosset had achieved a twenty-four hours tricycle record of 233½ miles, albeit traversing the road between Biggleswade and Norman Cross three or four times, a practice not subsequently accepted by the N.C.U. Records Committee. At this meeting it was resolved to form a club for the purpose of encouraging and facilitating fast and long distance road riding chiefly, but not exclusively, in the Great North Road district: bicyclists or tricyclists, to be eligible for membership, must have ridden at least 100 miles in a day. A provisional committee was appointed to draft the rules, to receive the names of candidates and, subject to the receipt of twenty names, to call a general

G.P. MILLS and 'FAED' WILSON
On a Humber Tandem Trike of late 1880's

meeting to settle all details: the members of this committee were J.H. Price (Stanley C.C.), R. E. Knight (Southwark C.C.), H. J. Jones (Haverstock C.C.), E. P. Moorhouse and A. J. Wilson, the last two as North London T.C., Wilson being the provisional secretary.

Three days earlier, on 20 October, a several times postponed 'Kangaroo' 100 had been won by E. Hale (second in the 'Rover' 100) in the record time of 6h. 39m. 5s: this 100 miles event was, apparently, the first to be entirely on Fenland roads and the North Road — it started at Holbeach and went via Long Sutton, Wisbech (names to become so familiar to riders in North Road C.C. twenty-fours etc.) and Peterborough to join the North Road at Kate's Cabin whence south to Hitchin, returning to 960 yards north of the now missing forty-ninth milestone: timekeeper Larrette made Hale go on to the fiftieth milestone as an insurance against a short course: this extension took three minutes twelve seconds and proved unnecessary: first prize was a piano!

In the two months after the October meeting the proposed North Road C.C. appears to have been well supported in the cycling press — references often being coupled with 'alias The Scorchers'. The Albone testimonial fund came to fruition at Biggleswade on 8 December when Dan received a gold watch chain and the N.R.C.C.'s envisaged General Meeting took place on Monday 21 December 1885. This General Meeting was also held at the N.C.U. offices and to have power to vote, participants had to pay the proposed club's entrance fee of 5s., returnable in the event of non-election to the Club, to the honorary treasurer (pro tem) J. H. Price. At this meeting the Club was formally established with E. E. Bernhard as secretary, J.W. Day (Stanley C.C.) as Captain, with two sub-captains — Marriott (Nottingham B.C., twenty-four hours and End to End trike record holder) and O. G. ('Old Gold') Duncan (Beretta C.C.): 'Faed', Whorlow and Moorhouse (N.L.T.C.), Jones (Haverstock C.C.) and Knight (Southwark C.C.) were on the Committee — and the subscription was 10s. per annum. To quote again from the *Bicycling News* article

> Among the rank and file are Flying Furnivall, Golumpshus Guest, Finchley Brown, The Mild Melano, Notelet Nym, the Actuarial Allvey, St. Bartholomew Belding, Solemn Solomon, Facile Boothroyd, Raspberry Asbury, Climbing Hill, Queercuss Oakden, Gentle White and in the provinces are Golder, Buckingham and Oxborrow at Coventry, Rowe at Peterborough, Albone at Biggleswade, Harry Priest at Birmingham, G. P. Mills and Hugh Fraser at Liverpool and wearers of the oval badge (whose design had been proposed by 'Faed') at Sheffield, Cambridge, Barnet, St. Albans . . .

Not all of those listed by *Bicycling News* were founder members — who totalled three dozen: and some founders did not stay long, notably Teddy Hale, who was so upset by Bernhard that he resigned in 1887 — a year or two later Bernhard was in the news (and the police court) for abusing a track rider for 'loafing' in a race, abuse culminating in pulling the track-man's nose!

Despite the restriction of a qualifying ride and the competition of other roadmen's clubs starting up in 1885/1886 (such as Bath Road Club, Catford Cycling Club and Ripley R.C.) — some making special efforts to recruit the faster racing men — the N.R. grew in strength and in reputation. Its first official run, thrown open by invitation, attracted about 100 cyclers, on a wide variety of machines, to 'Tally Ho! Corner on the Barnet turnpike' at 4.30 p.m. on Saturday 27 February 1886. *The Cyclist* which had just previously been concerned about a falling interest in the game (a concern recurrent to this day) commented ' . . . the large muster reminded us of the palmy days when club musters were large and regular . . . ' *The Cyclist* report went on after enumerating some of the men present, ' . . . After a run to Shenley and a good scorch back to Barnet about forty sat down to a substantial tea at the Old Sal, T. R. Marriott in the chair. A very pleasant evening being passed with music and recitations, the start for home was made about 9.30 p.m. The run must be characterised as a great success and the majority of members seemed to be in good form for the time of year . . . The roads from Barnet through the lanes to Shenley, Well End, Radlett and St. Albans were in splendid condition . . . ' Tramlines (then carrying horse drawn trams) which later troubled us as far as Barnet for many years, had not reached as far out as Tally Ho!

Thus was the North Road Cycling Club launched and, with few exceptions, appears to have received a heartening welcome and been widely wished all success. Prior to the first official North Road run two of the leading founders — 'Faed' Wilson and 'Johnnie' Price — being regular users of the racing track at Alexandra Palace — were moving spirits in the formation there in January of The Racing Cyclists' Club and at least three other N.R. men were on the committee: its purpose was, for the track rider, similar to that of the N.R. for the road rider: it achieved some notable successes in promotion of track meetings, particularly a Queen's Jubilee Year Tournament in 1887 but did not survive that year — how much more successful were 'Faed's' ideas in the road riding sphere!

CHAPTER II.

The Rise and Decline of the Paced Game.

'Faed's' wisdom in suggesting an independent club to promote good road-riding was proved inversely by the growth of a vociferous antipathy to road racing among certain followers of the pastime in general and some leading members of the National Cyclists' Union in particular. Whether in the early years road racing was practised extensively enough to warrant the virulent attacks made on it seems doubtful: certainly in 1886 there appear to have been only five 'open' events — North Road promotions at 50 miles, 100 miles and twenty-four hours, Catford C.C.'s twenty-five miles handicap and a forty-five miles handicap promoted in the Manchester area by the periodical 'Sport and Play'. Many local clubs admittedly organised members' road races, often just outside their towns and if these took place on Sundays and on roads also used by churchgoers the public not unnaturally took exception to such activities. The 'anti's' within the cycling fraternity argued that road racing was not only illegal but unfavourable to a good public image of the pastime — but, strangely enough some of the 'anti's', notably G. Lacy Hillier and H. J. Swindley (London Editor of *The Cyclist*), could be found on the Portsmouth Road on Sundays, indulging in unofficial scorching! Initially the police seemed prepared to turn a blind eye to cycle racing on the road, though laws and bye-laws gave sufficient authority to Chief Constables to initiate action against the road racers should local pressures make this appear desirable. The campaign against road racing mostly followed two lines — expression of individual viewpoints either in the press or to Authority, or by persuading the N.C.U. to act. In the first class was a letter purporting to be from Lacy Hillier (he denied it and offered £5 reward for information leading to the identification of the author — a reward apparently never claimed) to Chief Constables of the Home Counties drawing attention to an advertisement for the first North Road C.C. open event. Another facet of the personal vendetta appeared in *The Cyclist* during April 1889: Swindley averred that at a Dinner he had met a landowner with an estate astride the North Road 'somewhere between Hitchin and Peterborough' who, on being complimented about the condition of the roads in his county, retorted 'Yes, we spend two or three thousand a year upon our roads . . . make them the best in the kingdom, with the result . . . every summer hordes of ragamuffin cyclists, who ride races and make records upon them, frighten our horses and knock down old women and children'. A. J. Wilson commented that the London editor's reactions would have been very different had the landowner lived by the Portsmouth Road, but Swindley went on to aver that Biggleswade folk now hated, as much as previously they loved, road racing: this roused Dan Albone to deny the assertion about his fellow townfolk and, moreover, to state that the landowner concerned did not oppose road racing! Lacy Hillier was provided, in October 1887, with grounds for a fierce attack when a West Road Club promoted a twenty-five miles handicap on a course between Kingston and Ripley: Seventy started, each accompanied by one or two pacemakers and were watched by a police inspector at the start and another at Cobham — however Hillier paused to praise N.R.C.C. promotions on quiet roads well away from London. Also following that West R.C. race the *Pall Mall Gazette* commented 'It is satisfactory to note that public opinion among the better class of cyclists is entirely against road racing which, but for the weakness of the N.C.U. which pretends not to recognise the racing while hall-marking the records made in road races, would long ago have been abolished'.

Pro and anti road racing views sporadically enlivened the columns of the cycling press through the years, even after police action had ended road racing, leaving, for a time, only paced record rides on the roads. Two notable North Road names thus appeared in 1897, those of G. H. Stancer and E. J. Steel. Stancer, in a pro-racing letter revealed the style later to become familiar in his years as a great leader and administrator in the pastime, while Steel favoured unpaced riding: they were members for near sixty and seventy years respectively.

In the N.C.U. sphere, a Council meeting on 9 December 1886 passed a resolution expressing 'its disapproval of the growing practice of racing on the public roads and directs the Executive 'to do its utmost to discourage road racing'. Following the furore after the West R.C. twenty-five miles handicap on 1 October 1887, the N.C.U. Records Committee was instructed not to adjudicate on or recognise future claims to road records and a Wheelmans' Paper Chase announced for later in that October by Catford C.C. was 'proclaimed' by the N.C.U. These moves led the North Road Club to circularise road clubs with a letter headed 're N.C.U. v. Road Racing' and posing several questions: 150 replies were reeived and showed that 122 did not favour the total abolition of road racing while twenty-eight did, but sixty-five:fifty was the proportion favouring abolition of open road races while sixty-seven:thirty-seven favoured limitation of open races to not less than fifty miles for scratch events and 100 miles for handicaps. Subsequently at A. J. Wilson's instance, the Club called a meeting of road clubs to consider establishing a 'Road Records Committee' to fill the hiatus left by the N.C.U.: only twenty-two clubs were represented on 11 April 1888, but the Road Records Association was formed — and has been very successful in ensuring that spurious claims get no credence. Three years later, after methods of checking in road races (to avoid riders having to dismount to sign check sheets at nominated places) and a controlling body for road racing had been prominent topics in the correspondence columns, an informal meeting at the home of Dr. E. B. Turner (N.C.U. Councillor and a Vice President), North Roaders F. T. Bidlake and A. F. Ilsley being present, agreed that a controlling association was desirable. But when S. E. Blair of Catford C.C. proposed the expansion of the R.R.A. to control road racing, his proposition was rejected, its opposers (including N.R.C.C.) feeling that the proposed body would lack effective control over individuals — if the N.C.U. would not (or could not) exercise the desired control no other body could.

April 1892 brought rumours of police opposition in Cheshire and, surprisingly, at Biggleswade — or was this latter change of heart the belated outcome of K. E. Edge's collision with a pony cart during the well supported N.R. Club Fifty of June 1890? Edge wrecked his machine, damaged his knees and was apparently not too polite to the occupants of the pony-cart. In May 1892 a Catford man died after a collision with a cart in a Club fifty miles race and various clubs, including Catford, Polytechnic and Unity, announced the abandonment of their road racing programmes for the time being. N.C.U. Manchester Centre held a special meeting to consider the best means of suppressing road racing and Catford C.C. called a meeting of London clubs to 'consider road racing': North Road Club declined the invitation, saying no reason was seen to change the Club's policy, but considering it advisable not to publish results, thus promoting the privacy of events. The majority at the Catford sponsored meeting were against any interference with their road racing by the N.C.U. It took until the end of 1897, by which time police action had ended the promotion of open road races, at least in the North Roader's country, for the N.C.U. to take decisive action, making a new rule 'No licensed rider may take part in any race or paced record attempt on the road'. At a consequential Special General Meeting the North Road Club withdrew its affiliation to the N.C.U. — some commentators thought this action precipitate.

Prior to this, despite the opposition within the cycling world, the interest in road racing had grown steadily with club promotion of 'open' events. The North Road C.C. racing programme planned for 1886 was for two races, one at 100 miles and one at twenty-four hours, open both to members, and, by invitation to non members, without limitation to any type of cycle — in fact separate awards were to be offered for rides on each type. In addition monthly programmes of club runs were envisaged, such runs being linked, where feasible, with long distance races promoted by other clubs so that North Roaders might proffer assistance in pace-making, checking etc. However the first open race promoted by the Club, the first in Britain and, probably in the world, was a fifty miles scratch race on 19 June 1886. This was well publicised in advance both by panels in the advertising columns and editorial paragraphs in the cycling press, initially stating an entry fee of 10s., later reduced to 5s. These advance notices carefully avoided any reference to route or, indeed, area in which the event would take place, but stated that special arrangements had been made for London competitors and their machines to travel by train to a station (unnamed) near the start, at a reduced fare of about 3s.

This fifty miles race attracted forty four competitors and they were started, with a crowd of about 100 cyclists (but no police) watching, from the thirty-ninth milestone north of Henlow level crossing — 'the tricyclers at 3.55 p.m., the tandemons at 4.00 p.m. and bicyclers at 4.05 p.m.'. Two misfortunes marred the race — first there was 'half a gale from the north' and the course took the riders north through Biggleswade and along the North Road to the turning point half a mile beyond the sixty-seventh milestone on Alconbury Hill, all 'splendid road' but all into the wind and only the balance back to the forty-sixth milestone (by Tingey's farm north of Biggleswade) was wind assisted. Secondly, H. E. Irons, roped in at the last moment to take the times at twenty-five miles misunderstood his instructions and also tried to turn the riders — he succeeded only with one tandem pair, Golder and Buckingham (of Coventry) on a Premier tandem tricycle, who thus finished first in 3h. 0m. 25s. (and were advertised a week later, by Premiers as the winners!) Fastest time was actually 3h. 16m. 58s. by C. E. Liles (Ripley R.C.) and A. J. Wilson on a Beeston Humber tandem trike, the mount also of second fastest Lee and Gatehouse (3h. 23m. 16s.): Golder and Buckingham's short turn must have saved them about seven miles, so they could not have been among the prizewinners — they were five minutes slower than Liles and Wilson at twenty five miles. Fastest bicycler, and third in the race, was E. Hale in 3h. 29m. 55s. on a safety, followed by O. G. Duncan on an ordinary in 3h. 31m. 22s.: hope of Golder's record of 3h. 5m. 34s. being beaten was shattered by the wind but Liles and Wilson broke the tandem tricycle record. Twenty-three machines finished, four of them tandem trikes, the slowest finisher being C. H. R. Gosset (chairman of the October foundation meeting) who took 4h. 40m. 5s. to get his tricycle round: the press was somewhat critical of the marshalling arrangements. North Roaders took five of the first six places

THE NORTH ROAD FIFTY.

The Finish

THE NORTH ROAD FIFTY.

Officials and Press go home.

A GEORGE MOORE MEMORY OF THE 1890's

while among the ordinaryists, and finishing in 4h. 2m. 18s. was a 'T. Owen': he did better off the ten minute mark, in the second open-to-all-types road event promoted. This was a twenty-five miles handicap run by Catford C.C. and Owen, riding as 'C.T.C.', was third in the race behind North Roaders G. A. Nelson (1h. 41m. 32s.) and secretary Bernhard (1h. 41m. 40s.) both off four and a half minutes and who rode together most of the way. Another North Roader, H. W. Staner (virtual scratch off four minutes) was fourth (and third fastest): riders were started in handicap order, limit men first: Owen got in front fairly early and stayed there until caught by Nelson and Bernhard. Now although one of our most active cycling veterans was, until 1969, Tom Owen, he was two or three years younger than the Club: that earlier T. Owen was also a member, but only in 1887/8.

Reports of these two events make no specific reference to pacemakers but such assistance to the racing men was a normal feature of events, whether trade sponsored or limited to club members. As the sport developed the more fortunate riders (or, said scandal, the wealthier) had relays of friends along the course to provide fresh pacers.

Apart from these two events, the 'Sport and Play' one and the North Road 100 miles and twenty-four hours races, (dealt with in later chapters), there were in 1886 quite a number of record attempts, then widely publicised in advance, particularly the succession of Land's End to John O'Groats ('End to End') rides for which assistance en route was solicited. Outstanding among these rides were the feats of young G. P. Mills: already, as a lad of seventeen, he had won the 1885 Anfield B.C. twenty-four hours race with 259 miles on an ordinary, later accepted by the N.C.U. as bicycle record. In June 1886 he again won the Anfield twenty-four hours on a bad day with 235 miles ('The Cyclist' of 16 June), in July he knocked some forty hours off the End to End bicycle record on an ordinary taking five days, one hour, forty-five minutes — it was recorded that he rode all of the seventeen uphill miles from Kendal to Shap, except for half a mile covered by a four inch layer of large stones, taking two and a quarter hours. Early in August, having moved from Liverpool to Biggleswade, he coverd 268 miles in twenty-four hours in a record ride, again on an ordinary, using a Fenland course: later in the month he improved the tricycle End to End record to five days ten hours — during this ride a detective wanted to arrest him at Exeter for stealing a bicycle at Southampton (the non-returning hirer had called himself 'G. P. Mills') and much further north, in Scotland, Mills re-started on the Garry Pass, after a thirty-five minutes stop for supper, at 10.50 p.m. when his companion wouldn't attempt to cycle but followed by horse and trap over loose and dangerous roads — these twenty-three miles took four hours ten minutes! Mills won the North Road twenty-four hours in very bad conditions on 4 September with 227miles and in the middle of the month paired up with 'Faed' Wilson for an attempt on the twenty-four hours tandem tricycle record: they were inside record figures at fifty and 100 miles but hadn't made appropriate timing arrangements for these distances — and their axle broke at 160 miles. Before September was out they went for the fifty miles record (by then held by Lee and Gatehouse) and improved it by twenty-three minutes to 2h. 46m. 3s. On 2 October Mills used an 'Ivel' rear driver safety to reduce the fifty miles bicycle record to 2h. 47m. 36s. — he started from the thirtieth milestone near Hitchin and finished at the eightieth near Peterborough, his timekeeper catching a train from Hitchin to Peterborough (a procedure followed on many subsequent attempts). Two days later he pushed the twenty-four hours record up to 295 miles on the same machine, Dan Albone reporting 'he outpaces nearly every pacemaker that tries to take him along': the N.C.U. Records Committee hadn't then completed investigation of his August record and now saw no reason to do so — the fact that one was on an 'ordinary' and the other on a 'safety' did not concern them — so the 268 miles on a solid tyred ordinary never got on the books. This was quite a year for a lad of eighteen — but he continued riding for many years and, although he turned to motoring in its early years, he remained interested and in membership of both the Anfield and North Road Clubs until his sudden death on 8 November 1945, shortly after our Diamond Jubilee Dinner.

Despite N.C.U. disapproval of road racing Catford C.C. received seventy-four 'acceptances' for the first subsequent open race, a fifty miles handicap run in May 1887, the start and course being kept secret to avoid crowds and police interference: forty-seven finished of whom G. P. Mills, riding as an Anfielder, was fastest in 2h. 54m. 15s. but only thirty-fourth in the race. A North Road club Fifty in which Mills competed (but was beaten by four seconds by Godfrey White) was reported to have attracted a crowd of 500 to the finish near Biggleswade: by then, after a kindly warning from Biggleswade's Chief Constable (via Biggleswade Cycling Club's captain) courses had been altered to avoid races passing through Biggleswade town. Apart from North Road C.C. events, the Bath Road Club (founded the previous November) promoted their first open event: although not announced in advance the course proved to be that used by the North Roaders — the Bath Roaders didn't like the surface of 'their own' road.

In the ensuing years road racing grew in popularity: the Anfielders made their twenty-four hours an open event and in 1888 the Bath Roaders promoted two fifty miles handicaps (on the North Road) while North Road Club events received such support as to have open event interest. In January 1889, London road clubs got together to agree dates for open events, avoiding clashing, and to consider measures to combat the growing practice of one man belonging to several clubs: linked with the latter, North Road C.C. introduced a new rule — 'a member of any open road racing club whose H.Q. are within thirty-five miles of London' became ineligible for the N.R.C.C. (but recently-joined Holbein was excepted from the new rule). Following the N.C.U. ban on publicised events, some clubs withdrew events from the list published after the January conference, but went ahead with their promotions, notifying clubs and riders by private circular letters: one secretary was alleged to have sent out 700 such letters! The North Road, Bath Road and Catford were of these and the Catford again promoted the first open event after the N.C.U. ultimatum — a fifty miles handicap in June which received forty-six entries of whom thirty started. But the North Roaders were worried about the number of clubs promoting events on the roads between Hitchin and Peterborough and in 1888 did not support other clubs' open races on these roads. The support for N.R. club events continued to make them as interesting as opens, attracting considerable numbers both of spectators and pacemakers — for a Club Fifty in July 1889, Holbein had five pacemakers, mostly Catford men, out for him: these events had, therefore, to be promoted with great care to avoid giving offence and thus alienating the police. The North Roaders were naturally concerned that all promotions should maintain this quality and that events should not become so numerous as to give offence by their very frequency.

A NICE BABY TO CARRY.
Dan Albone takes Holbein for a spin in the "Kid Karrier."

DAN ALBONE and HOLBEIN

True these road races did, of course, bring business to the towns and villages used as headquarters — at least to the caterers and to the blacksmiths or others capable of doing repairs to the riders' machines. Dan Albone's cycle factory must have contributed usefully to the prosperity of Biggleswade — in 1956 the town council had a commemorative tablet affixed to the house which was his 'Ongley Arms' and factory. Not that the number of men participating extensively in road racing was ever great — to be counted in hundreds rather than thousands, and those with the ability to win were few. These latter tended to congregate together, irrespective of club affiliations, for training with, as well as racing against, each other. Dan Albone's Ongley Arms and later his Ivel Hotel were, naturally, early rendezvous and for a time the George at Buckden was very popular until the departure of the good ladies who fed the riders so royally. At such places riders seemed to spend much of their free time, and some appeared to have plenty of this, making deep and lasting friendships. Others came to bask in the aura of the giants, such as 'Sam' Lewin, for long president of Bath C.C.: in his youth he was a Londoner but had relatives at Brampton, Hunts, and visited the George at Buckden, in the years of its fame, while cycling to and from Brampton, afterwards recalling the cycling notabilities met there.

Not all the open events were popular, as Anerley B.C. found when they ran an open 100 miles handicap but only received fourteen entries: they attributed this to the course being over the notoriously hilly roads south of London, instead of the flat North Road courses — and this was many decades before a national Best All Rounder contest was accused of concentrating support on 'fast' events! Another problem appeared in the Bath Road open Fifty miles handicap of September 1889 — a problem similar to that known as 'loafing' which had cost the track game much support: in this Fifty the scratch contingent caught the tandems after about thirty miles and then none was prepared to set the pace so the whole lot stopped racing, allowing Bath Roader P. T. Pyne, riding an ordinary, to be first and fastest in 3h. 11m. 6s. — North Roader J. G. H. Browne was second fastest in 3h. 16m. 25s. In the next month, after winning the North Road 100 in a sprint finish, S. F. Edge was accused of not taking his fair share of making the pace: in the ensuing correspondence 'Bath Road' Smith suggested that promoters in future road races should provide the pacemakers even if this entailed using professionals! The size of the professional class is not clear but path matches for purses of £25, £50 and more were regularly advertised and reported (even £25 was then a useful sum of money).

In contrast was a Dublin Wanderers' 100 miles event late in 1889, in which Frank Shorland, by then a North Roader, participated during a visit to Ireland. *The Cyclist* reported 'At Kildare Wayth took a bath while

MONTAGUE A. HOLBEIN,

Holder of the Twelve and Twenty-four Hours Safety Bicycle Records.

HOLBEIN ON A WHIPPET
SPRING FRAME BICYCLE

T. A. EDGE,

T. EDGE WITH HIS 'PEREGRINE'
SAFETY BICYCLE

CHATER LEA.

CHATER LEA LATER FAMED
FOR
GOOD CYCLE COMPONENTS

R. L. EDE.

R.L. EDE

Shorland waited for him, but a little further the Londoner began to ride and . . . drew away . . .'. Shorland won with a time of 9h. 26m. 23s. — perhaps it could only happen in Ireland!

Early in 1890, illustrating the interest in some quarters, the Surrey Bicycle Club was offering prizes of twenty guineas value to any member winning the North Road twenty-four hours or 100 miles races, and one valued ten guineas for a win in the Speedwell B.C. 100 miles race. Other developments appeared in 1890 North Road Fifty miles handicaps — multiple entries: i.e. from one member on various classes of machine were accepted (with a fee for each) and handicapped, the rider deciding which to ride on the day of, or prior to, the event: also the, initially, few riders of J. B. Dunlop's new pneumatic tyres or of the rival 'cushions' (thick walled tyres with a central, but not inflatable, air channel) were penalised five minutes in handicap. 'Cushions' and various types of spring frames, with cushion or solid tyred wheels, only temporarily challenged the pneumatic tyres. About this period some daring riders competed with parts of their legs bare, mostly only the knees, but were severely reprimanded for this indecency (!) — reflecting the continued desire to avoid giving offence to the non—cycling public.

In 1891 the road racing game received a great boost from the outstanding success of the English team in the first ever Bordeaux to Paris race in May. This was won by G. P.Mills in 26h. 34m. 57s., 1h. 14m. ahead of Holbein, S. F. Edge and J. E. L. Bates tieing for third place a further 2h. 23m. slower: the first two were North Roaders, while Shorland was among the pacemakers. A cup was, for the first time, offered to the winner of an open road race — by the Bath Roaders for their first open 100 miles, which, like their Fifties, was held on a North Road course: North Roaders J. M. James (alias 'Jimjams') and R. L. Ede ('The Pocket Hercules') were sixth and eighth respectively, the latter after a fall during the final sprint resulting from Ede catching his front wheel in winner 'Bath Road' Smith's rear (mounting) step. The new weekly *Cycling*, at the end of its first year ran a voting competition to place the 'Best Twelve' both of Road Racers and of Path Racers: six North Roaders won places in the roadmen's list, Mills, Holbein and Shorland being the first three in that order: Ede was seventh, T. A. Edge eighth and Bidlake tenth. Robert Todd, ex-honorary secretary and currently a Vice President of the N.C.U., took the chair at the North Road Dinner, when Police Superintendent Lawson of Peterborough was one of the principal guests.

Despite the apparently favourable atmosphere of the previous year, at a committee meeting on 23 May 1892, the North Roaders debated whether or not to hold any further fifty miles handicaps on the road but no proposition was made and fifty-five entries were handicapped for the fourth club fifty.

The second Bath Road 100 was run successfully early in September, five North Roaders getting in the first ten, Bob Ilsley being the best of these in third place. Five North Roaders also got into *Cycling's* Best Twelve Road Riders for 1892, Shorland and Holbein being first and second, T. A. Edge fourth, Bidlake eighth and J. M. James tenth. Shorland also figured in the Best Twelve Path Riders, as did Ede. In 1893 the North Road Club Fifties each received between forty and fifty entries but the Open 100 entry dropped to twenty-four. In September the start for events was moved from Hitchin to outside the Hertfordshire boundaries (in fact back to Henlow) to avoid difficulties with that county's police: and during the year it was ruled that a rider must not 'go back' from his handicap — except that a scratch man might go back to start with a rider having an 'owe' handicap.

A further move to reduce bunching was made in the 1894 'Fifties' by ruling that pacers not actually engaged in pacing must ride behind the field and all pacers were required to drop out prior to the finishing sprint — at points which varied, from event to event, between a quarter and a half mile from the finishing line. Much faster times were being achieved: in an Anerley B.C. Open Fifty Wridgway (who had become a North Roader after a quarrel with the Bath Road Club) accomplished a 'world's record' of 2h. 23m. 16s: he was one of the early wearers of the black tights and light-weight black jacket which (despite some initial opposition) became the standard garb for the road racer. North Road club Fifties continued to receive over forty entries, but the third — on 21 July 1894 — was most momentous: there were forty-two entries with Bob Ilsley on scratch while new member Arthur Chase, whose entry arrived too late for handicapping and, therefore, his inclusion in the race, was allowed to start with Bob Ilsley. These two had a neck and neck battle all the way, Chase winning the sprint for the line and finishing in 2h. 16m. 13s. — two seconds better than Ilsley, who however was the official winner of the event: both were nearly three minutes faster than Chase's existing straightaway record and Chase was regarded as having established a world's record for an out and home Fifty — his 2h. 16m. 13s. was hall marked as fifty miles record by the R.R.A. But the tricycle division, including W. W. Robertson, Bidlake and A. F. Ilsley, while being paced by J. W. Stocks (of Polytechnic C.C.) along a straight stretch of the North Road near the fifty-seventh milestone were involved in a collision with a horse and trap due to the lady driver who in her alarm at the approaching group, picked up the reins from her lap and pulled the wrong side causing the horse to veer across the road into the tricyclists' path: Bidlake went under the horse but Stocks and Ilsley got to the animal's head and steadied him, thus saving Bidlake from more serious injury than scraped and bruised arms (he was hardly recovered from a heavy fall from his bicycle in the previous fifty, when he touched a pacer's wheel). None of the occupants of the trap was physically injured but they complained to the police and the Huntingdonshire Chief Constable gave notice of his intention to suppress road racing in his county.Bidlake secured an interview with the Chief Constable but could not change his decision: the fourth Fifty was cancelled, the Chief Constable so informed and that no further Fifties would be promoted while pointing out that neither passengers nor horse were hurt in the regretted accident. The Open 100 was postponed — eventually abandoned — and the start of the twenty-four moved to near Peterborough, the course being changed at the last moment to avoid entry into Huntingdonshire: that was the last North Road C.C. paced open race on the roads and the last in North Road 'territory' for quite a few years. Some of the provincial clubs maintained a programme of club road races and the Anfield B.C. continued to run its Invitation 100 miles as a race for a number of years. Attacks on road records continued, pacing increasing and including solos, tandems, triplets and 'quads', riders going ever faster while the anti-road racing faction fulminated, painting horrifying word pictures of large groups surrounding the record rider, scorching along the roads on their brakeless machines in alarming fashion.

On the continent road racing continued, encouraged rather than opposed by the authorities and one cycling commentator facetiously suggested that the North Roaders would be holding their road races in Northern France! But in fact in 1895 and 1896 the North Road, and the other road clubs in the London area launched into the promotion of track meetings, some running open twelve hours and twenty-four hour races hoping to emulate the great successes of the 'Cuca' twenty-fours of 1892, 1893 and 1894, but, as an insurance against failure, the North Road Club became a Limited Liability company necessitating the addition of 'Ltd.' to our name. This proved a wise precaution as track events, particularly open meetings, proved fated to be run at a loss, the 1896 North Road twenty-four being specially disastrous.

A more strenuous club riding programme was arranged, with longer day runs and week-end trips to Portsmouth,Bath and Warwick added to the already traditional Peterborough and York runs, thus offering some hard riding alternative to the abandoned road races but these did not receive the support accorded to the fifty miles handicaps and riders obviously longed to return to the road game — even as some of the deserted racing headquaters longed for the return of the riders. Having aired the idea at the previous meeting, at the N.R. Committee meeting on 16 September 1895, W. Ward proposed that an unpaced fifty miles road race be promoted for members only, Bidlake seconded and the proposal was agreed. The event took place on Saturday 5 October and attracted twenty-two entries of whom J. P. K. Clark, one of the three on scratch, was started first at 2.15 p.m., the remainder being sent off at intervals of two or three minutes in order of handicap so that, in theory, there would be no overtaking: pacemakers were not allowed but the regulations did not legislate against company riding. The course avoided Huntingdonshire roads: riders were instructed not to ride on the footpath, to observe caution in overtaking other traffic, particularly in villages and to call their names to the checkers — all interesting sidelights on the times: also each machine had to be fitted with a bell. These regulations set the standard for many years. Unfortunately the weather on 5 October was most unpropitious and only six of the starters finished: Gordon Minns, who had been first off twelve minutes in the fateful July 1894 fifty miles race was, in this next road event, first and fastest off six minutes in 2h. 54m. 26s., two minutes three seconds faster than scratch man W. Ward. And this was the first unpaced road race (the term 'time trial' came much later) ever organised — although, thanks to the weather, it was not very successful, the experiment was thought worth repeating.

1895 also saw the appearance on English roads of 'road motor carriages', limited to four miles per hour and required to be preceded by a man carrying a red flag. The 'Motorcar Club' was founded in 1896 and agitated against both the red flag and four miles per hour — emancipation came at the end of the year, the limit initially being raised to fourteen miles per hour, and motorists joined 'scorching' cyclists in suffering persecution from certain police forces. 1896 also saw the establishment of the Daimler Co. the first to make British motor cars.

The North Roaders held two fifties on the road during 1896, the first on the same basis as the 1895 event but for the second, limit men were started first and scratch men last, this, together with company riding, naturally produced faster times. S. J. Prevost, one of the scratch men was first and fastest in 2h. 46m. 57s. in the first, but over ten minutes faster in the second when his 2h. 36m. 6s. made him fastest and second in the handicap — a ride which only gained him a silver medal, the gold going to handicap winner F. Pearse, off eleven minutes, with an actual time of 2h. 4lm. 49s: one entrant for the second fifty was required to produce his N.C.U. licence (having failed to quote its number on his entry form) before being allowed to start. A twelve hours road race, in which 'only tandem or single pacing' was allowed, took place on 19 September, starting at Peterborough, avoiding Huntingdonshire roads but passing through Wisbech four times, presaging future 'twenty-fours'. This was won by A. E. Marsh with 202 miles — his father was a member intermittently between 1891 and 1903 and A. E. brought his schoolboy sons to a club event in 1925, but unfortunately died later in the same year: the two sons joined late in 1933, the younger being lost in the 1939-1945 war and the elder dying subsequently: they are commemorated by the rose bowl 'A. E.' won in the 1896 'twelve' which was returned to the Club by his widow.

The North Roaders still felt the lure of the old road racing game with its excitement of physical competition and companionable rivalry so, having found that the second 'fifty' and the 'twelve' of 1896 caused no trouble with the police, limited pacing was reintroduced in 1897 and 1898 events on the road i.e. at fifty miles, twelve hours and, in 1898, 100 miles. These events were still restricted to members and, in the fifties to riders and pacers on singles: furthermore, after the first fifty of 1897 no pacing was allowed until the first five miles had been covered, the riders thus having passed through Henlow and Clifton villages. Possibly the fifty of 7 August 1897 was the first ever 'veterans' event although the minimum age was but thirty (still we are reputed to live longer now!) — Godfrey White, the winner, achieved the fastest time of the 1897 series in 2h. 24m. 59s. In the twelve hours event, entries from tandem pairs were accepted and pacing by tandems allowed, but in all the events no rider was permitted to be paced by more than two machines at a time. Except for the twelve hours event, in which all started together, competitors were still started at intervals of several minutes.

Although, at the end of 1897, the R.R.A. decided to recognise unpaced records as a separate class, the possibilities of motor pacing were much discussed early in the year and its value was proved when on a windy day Holbein topped 400 miles in twenty four hours for the first time, taking the twelve hours record en route, being paced by a Daimler car for over 200 miles. Brakes on bicycles were, according to a 'Cycling' columnist, becoming acceptable to many riders, but the road racing fraternity scorned them and continued to depend on control through their fixed wheels, even when experimenting with pacing by motorcars and the motor tricycles which had also appeared on the road.

Pacing by singles in the last fifty and by tandems and singles in the 100 miles and twelve hour races was allowed in North Road 1899 events, the twelve hours again having the only group start. But in the first fifty handicap pacing was not allowed, though limit man was started first: he was also first off in the 100 miles — at 3.15 a.m., five minutes earlier than in 1898! The middle fifty was, however, designed to be unpaced, scratch man being started first and intervals of five minutes stipulated. 'Mr. King's 100' was also initiated by the then N.R. President, as an unpaced competition on a Welwyn-Hitchin-Norman Cross and back route, and more unpaced record attempts were made. North Roader F. R. Goodwin, after lowering the London-York and London-Edinburgh records, with motor tricycle pace as far as Newcastle, sounded the knell of paced riding with an attack, on Fenland roads, on his own paced twelve and twenty-four hours records, using a motor car and several motor cycles as pacing vehicles: he pushed the twelve hours record up to 245 miles but desisted before twenty-four hours and was subsequently summonsed and fined in at least eight magistrates courts along his route, his pacers being similarly treated in some — for 'furious' and 'dangerous' riding! The North Road Club pressed the R.R.A. not to recognise motor paced records and this view was accepted at the Association's next A.G.M.

The Club abandoned the promotion of path races when deciding on the programme for 1900 — and did not return to track promotion until over sixty years had passed. The fifty miles road handicaps were all unpaced and, for the first time, start sheets stated the actual time of start for each rider, providing intervals always greater than the difference in handicaps and thus varying between four and nine minutes. The specific ban on company riding did not appear until the third of the fifties, although the new rule (which instructed an overtaken rider to slow to let the other get away and fixed 100 yards as the minimum distance between riders except at the time of passing) had been brought in for the twenty-four hours 'road ride' as the distance events were now called. The 100 miles handicap was designed to be a paced event but was postponed due to lack of support and run in October under rules as for the third 'fifty': the intervals were such that number one (numbers were now allocated but still not used for checking — names had to be called) started at 9.00 a.m. and No. twelve at noon: by ill chance it was a day of high winds and only scratch man W. H. Nutt (long known as 'Gee' because of his appetite) got inside six hours. In the twelve hours road ride all the competitors started together and, while external pacemakers were not allowed, mutual assistance was permitted other than by tandemons to riders of single machines: this was the last club event started as a race. Incidentally, although no ordinaries had been ridden in a North Road event since 1893, a rider in the London B.C. club 100 of June 1900, was so mounted.

In 1901 all North Road events were unpaced and governed by strict regulations against company riding, reinforced with long intervals between starting times: followers on spare machines were forbidden (except for the twenty-four hours ride) and in the circular covering the 100 miles handicap, feeding in villages was forbidden and riders advised to disguise, when riding through villages, that they were in a competition. As if to crown these historical changes a new level in unpaced riding was achieved in the first fifty, when Seymour Cobley, who had won two of the previous year's fifties, beat 'evens' (alias twenty miles per hour) with his time of 2h. 27m. 15s. — the first to achieve this speed in unpaced riding on an out and home course.

The policy adopted in 1901 became the North Raod tradition and for over sixty years the Club promoted only unpaced events (and only on the road) governed by the strict regulations already indicated. The new form of competition avoided any prior publicity — N.R.C.C. regulations, for many years, threatened cancellation of an event should its date or course be noised abroad. Company riding in competition in a limited form continued, particularly in some northern counties, for a number of years: J. M. James having moved north and thus also joined Anfield B.C., collected the Northern R.R.A. 100 miles record, with single pacing, in 1901, with a time of 4h. 43m. 25s., having shown good form in a similarly paced Anfield club event: Yorkshire Road Club long allowed two to ride together when doing 'standard medal' rides. But generally the cycling speed game on the roads of Britain became, for the next forty years, the unpaced 'time trial' (as it came to be known) not only avoiding prior notice but seeking (and obtaining) little subsequent publicity. Competitive road riding became a sport known to very few outside the cycling pastime but nevertheless slowly achieving a popularity never dreamed of by its original sponsors.

CHAPTER III.

The Twenty-Four.

> 'The Harvest Moon brings the months of work and training to its zenith. So . . . there gathered from all parts of the country the participants, their personal assistants, and those dedicated members and friends who are all part of the almost stylised pattern of twenty-four hours, that brings victory to some, disappointment to others, but to all a sense of particip-ation in an athletic contest of no mean order'.

So wrote Arthur Lancaster in his account, in the North Road Gazette, of the 1959 Twenty-four — but his phrases might well have been written about any 'twenty-four'. The bare bones of the leading rides, etc., in all North Road 'twenty-fours' are tabulated at the end of this chapter, but what stories lie behind those results!

The mileage achievable in twenty-four hours, initially related to a calendar day — midnight to midnight — interested a number of riders from the earliest days of cycling and many attempted the feat. Such rides were mostly well authenticated sporting efforts; for example, the first London to Bath and back ride within twenty-four hours — by W. S. Britten in 1878. Others savoured of being mere stunts, such as the two men who rode to and fro between King's Lynn and Wisbech for twenty-four hours; and sometimes considerable doubt arose over the accuracy of the measurement of the course, or whether it had all been cycled — men were proved to have used convenient trains (of which there were then many) to cover some of the distance claimed. Thus, when the National Cyclists' Union's Records Committee accepted as record G.P. Mills' 259 miles in the 1885 Anfield B.C. members' twenty-four hours road race, rides exceeding this had been reported in the press in 1883/4, for riders on 'Facile' front drivers — lever driven, geared up version of the ordinary with a front wheel of only forty-four inches or less in diameter, in comparison with the sixty inches of a tall man's 'ordinary'.

The first North Road C.C. twenty-four hours road race, being the first all day race for amateur riders on any type of machine and for members of various clubs, was, therefore, keenly awaited. Unfortunately the organisation appears to have been open to criticism: both *Cycling Times* and *The Cyclist* commented adversely on the selection of a moonless week-end — and on the lack of facilities for press reporters! The Club could, however, hardly be blamed for the heavy rain of Friday, 3 September 1886, which continued through the night and deterred, among others, a number of Anfielders, gathered at Biggleswade, from coming south to Hatfield railway station approach. Here, at 12.01 a.m. on Saturday conditions were miserable for the twenty-six starters dispatched by Club President A. J. Wilson — ten on safeties, seven on ordinaries, three 'tricyclers' and three tandem tricycle pairs. Darkness and bad road surfaces resulted in many tumbles but Mills, probably by getting clear, was one of the few not to fall. The course followed the already preferred cycling route to Biggleswade — via Hitchin — thence up the Great North Road to Norman Cross, through sleeping Peterborough's quiet streets and across the Fens (a stretch known as 'The Wilderness') to Wisbech, via Sutton Bridge to King's Lynn (104½ miles), by Narborough (odd that Sid Mottram, long term 'twenty-four' organiser, is linked with the Leicestershire Narborough), Swaffham, East Dereham (131 miles) and Hocking to the Gate House one mile from Norwich (146½ miles), returning to Biggleswade for 267¾ miles. Realising that few would race for the honour of greatest distance, provision was made for riders to turn back at nominated intermediate places, according to the final mileage being attempted. In fact, nobody got to Norwich and only three, after turning at Hocking, reached Dereham for breakfast — ordered for twenty-five; in these early years riders were prepared to pause for half an hour for meals such as breakfast and lunch. The three were Mills, Belding and Hill, but back at Swaffham the latter two collided and Mills left them trying to borrow cycles from the local shop: whether or not they succeeded is now uncertain — one report only credited them with the mileage to Swaffham, another gave them 210 miles. Tinsley Waterhouse, a hard-riding Sheffielder and North Roader, turned at Swaffham, getting fewer miles on the bad roads of Norfolk and returning earlier to the drying roads further south as the weather improved. Apprised of this, Mills put in an extra effort to run out time at the Obelisk atop Alconbury Hill on the North Road, while Waterhouse stopped over thirty miles further south at Hitchin, with seven minutes left and, as it turned out, covering two miles less than Mills. The wet roads of the early hours were most trying to the riders of rear driven 'safeties' — the chains were clogged solid with mud.

Changes in regulations and course came in successive years. In 1887 riders going for a place award were required to follow the full course stipulated for their class of machine — the Norwich turn was retained for bicyclists, but tricyclists were to turn at East Dereham. Also in 1887 gold medals were offered for the best mileage both on bicycle and on tricycle and silver medals for the best tandem pair and for mileage of or over 260 for bicyclists, 250 for tandemers, and 230 for tricyclers, and bronze medals for 210, 200 and 180

THE NORTH ROAD 24 HOURS CONTEST

North Road Cycling Club

24 HOURS OPEN RIDE, SATURDAY, 22ND AUG., 1891.

Checking Sheet for Wisbech, 65 miles

Each Competitor must sign his name in the presence of (see below) *and insert the time of his arrival, and any necessary remarks he may wish to make.*

Competitor's Signature.	Time of Arrival.	Remarks. Witnesses
Shorland		
J. E. L. Bates		
L. J. P. Wells	3.45	Tinsley Waterhouse
J. A. Bennett		
J. M. James		
W. Twentyman	3.53	J. S. Scadding
J. D. Walker		
Lancashire	3.55	Tinsley Waterhouse
H. H. Spencer	3.55	do
R. C. Nesbitt	4.13	
F. T. Bidlake	do	
W. F. Ransom	"	J. S. Cuthbley
W. C. Goulding		
W. J. A. Butterfield	4.13	
G. E. Nix		
A. M. Marchant	4.20	Edward G. Worth

N.B.—This sheet to be returned by post on Sunday, 23rd August, to F. T. BIDLAKE, 33?, Essex Road, London, N miles respectively (these were later called standard medals). Also A. J. ('Faed') Wilson offered a silver medal to the first ordinaryist, should greatest distance be done on a safety — or vice versa. The circulars notifying early twenty-fours advertised them as 'under N.C.U. rules' and competitors' instructions required them to sign check sheets at specified points (eighteen of them by 1889) and, between noon and 2.00 p.m. to telegraph 'Club, Biggleswade' stating turning point and expected time of arrival at Biggleswade. Later regulations also indicated that checks would be made at unspecified points, the checkers having 'Club flags — light blue' and check sheets to be signed. Riders were required to wear 'complete road riding costume' and when, in 1887, two competitors appeared with bare knees, there were scandalised complaints and a special warning was issued that the rule against such unseemly costume would be enforced strictly in future North Road events.

Mills went for the tricycle record in the 1887 twenty-four, while Waterhouse changed from his 'ordinary' to a rear driven safety, loaned by Dan Albone, just prior to the start — and had a spill before he had mastered the difference in steering. Also in 1887, presumably linked with Waterhouse, members of the Sharrow C.C. of Sheffield entered, and this club continued to be represented, if intermittently, at least until 1950. So keen were they in 1888 that they sought and were given a concessionary entry fee — clubs entering six or more riders had the fee reduced from 10*s*. to 7*s*. 6*d*. each. And linked with Sharrow's bulk entries is the only known occasion (so far!) on which a woman has started in a North Road event: Mrs. Maughan of the first 1888 Sharrow party did not mention her sex when signing her entry form and we were too polite to reject her when she appeared, beskirted, on her tricycle at Hatfield — Press comment was merely that she might have got further than twenty-five miles had she ridden tandem with her husband.

Club member — and committee man — R. Banner Oakley had made strong efforts to move the start from Hatfield to Hitchin, but only succeeded after the bad weather for the August 1888 twenty-four resulted in the decision to run a second twenty-four in late September — and then only when the respected journalist C. H. Larrette supported the move — and Hitchin Market Square became the starting place.

Oakley also proposed that we memorialise the Prime Minister, then the Marquis of Salisbury, to bring before Parliament a bill to legalise cycle racing on the roads, but the 1888 North Road committee adjourned the proposal sine die. It is doubtful whether any of those then concerned lived to see the issue, in 1960, of Ministry of Transport Regulations governing both cycle road racing and time trialling: the term 'time trials', incidentally, appears in 1888 North Road committee minutes in relation to medal distances. Oakley appears to have been something of a stormy petrel, leaving the Club in 1889 amid angry exchanges and then forming a 'Road and Path Association' to which strong objection was taken by the North Road and similar Clubs.

The northward movement of the start, initiated by Oakley, was resumed in 1891 when the police raised objection to the noise at midnight in Hitchin Market Square — an objection not altogether shared by Hitchin's shop-keepers and hoteliers. The start was moved out of Hertfordshire to beyond Henlow level crossing, then in 1892 onto the Little Paxton(fifty-seventh) milestone and in 1894, the Huntingdon police having banned racing on their county's roads, to Peterborough. These moves, and the increasing mileages being achieved, necessitated finding detours to add to the course, and two of these, in the second 1888 twenty-four, combined with a night (as anticipated by the Spalding Times) so dark 'Erebus was not in it by comparison', vide one report, robbed Holbein of topping the coveted 300 that year. He went off course on a new detour from Girtford to Bedford and took three hours thirty-eight minutes to cover the thirty-eight and a half miles of twisting, unfamiliar roads from Biggleswade to Cambridge and back — both during the Saturday evening. When, many years later, the Biggleswade-Cambridge roads were reintroduced at a late stage, they proved equally unpopular but more recently became acceptable early in the event. Bad weather in early twenty-fours made many competitors reluctant to ride out their time, especially if that would leave them remote from their accommodation at or near headquarters, then Dan Albone's hotel at Biggleswade. So in the first 1888 event Godfrey White stopped with thirty-five minutes to go, Glover and Green left ninety-five minutes unused, and Bidlake stopped at nineteen hours, confident that none of the other tri-cyclists, of whom eleven started (also eleven on ordinaries) would overtake him. And in 1889, when a heavy rainstorm hit the Wisbech area after Holbein had left for Peterborough and the south, a number of riders desisted in the early afternoon but appeared on the result sheet with twenty-four hours totals only five to ten miles greater than their twelve hours mileages.

Phrasing of the 1889 course card reveals Bidlake's secretarial influences — viz. 'over Henlow crossing, then straight until, after bearing R. a bridge with high poplars is crossed, then first left at finger post' — fortunately it was a brilliant moonlit night! Bidlake continued considerably to influence the choice of course for most of the next forty-four years. Detours from Wisbech included one via March, Chatteris and Somersham to Huntingdon and back, while that to Long Sutton went on to Holbeach, instead of back eastward to Lynn, and in later years was extended through Spalding to Deeping and beyond, and the Huntingdon detour was extended to Cambridge; Wisbech to Downham Market was added in 1891. These 'excursions' (another Bidlakism) were initially optional for those riding only for standard medals — by 1891 a safety rider had to cover 300 miles for a silver medal, with equivalent increases for the other types of machine and in bronze medal distances.

In 1889 noon totals were first recorded. Bidlake, whose tricycle bearings had seized up and put him out of the race, got the fault put right and assisted Wilson in this task. This gave Holbein (safety), Langridge (ordinary), Ward and Goulding in an agreed tie on tricycles, the twelve hours records with 175½, 154 and 151 miles respectively. Mills, again in search of tricycle records, started so fast with a bunch of tricyclists that Holbein was the only cyclist with them when he picked up his first pacers at Girtford, on return from Bedford. Mills was most annoyed not to be 'leading the string' and was thus unable 'to get on Holbein's wheel' — he was convinced that he could have stayed with Holbein! But Mills' axle broke at Thorney. For this 1889 twenty-four the Joseph Lucas firm made Wilson a special cycle oil lamp with a side bracket to hold his watch and a light shining on the watch face — easing his time-keeper's task of running out the winner.

The start cards for these early twenty-fours indicate the developments, the rise and decline (for some) in machines and equipment. Thus the Facile and then the 'ordinary' eventually disappeared, the latter by 1892 for the twenty-four — there were but four in 1890 when the pneumatic tyre appeared, temporarily challenged by the cushion, while the cautious stayed on solids. Holbein had cushions fitted to a spring-framed safety — and usually had a team of ten or so, mostly Catford C.C. men, distributed round the course to provide a succession of pacing groups. In 1890, however, Mancunian T. A. Edge challenged all day and sprinted past Holbein in the last minute, but was found to have been turned short inadvertently by his pacer on the detour through the Warden-Southill lanes, back at the end of the course this year. Edge and Spencer (later to become a Bradford Member of Parliament), as well as Holbein, were awarded gold medals, also Bradford C.C. gave Spencer an illuminated address and a gold 'albert' watch chain — while Holbein's and Bidlake's rides appear to be the best ever done on 'cushions'. Second tricyclist and fifth in the race, Will Crosbie, was one of the honorary members elected when our Twenty-four Society was founded in 1949.

The outsanding interest in 1891 was the entry of three of the victorious Englishmen in the first Bordeaux to Paris race in May: these were Mills, Holbein and Bates, plus Twentyman, who failed to reach Paris, and several of their pacers, including Shorland; Holbein had his usual number of pacers out and hoped to reverse the Bordeaux-Paris result — Mills and Shorland preferred to 'take off' at a vantage point and, by sheer pedalling skill and daring, to leave their rivals. Also, in contrast to Holbein's entourage, many competitors had few, if any, personal helpers and managed, in endeavouring to reach their desired mileages, with whatever company riding was afforded by others. The anticipated Holbein-Mills duel was ended at Biggleswade: the bunch had been riding erratically from the start, Spencer skidded (a risk with early pneumatics) and fell, bringing Holbein down, and Anfielder Lloyd rode over them. Holbein and Lloyd needed surgical treatment and Holbein was abed for a week in Albone's Ivel Hotel. Meanwhile Mills, Shorland (now on a rear driver), Bates and Anfielder Bennett battled for twelve hours, passing the record of 190½ miles, Shorland leading with 192½ — Mills retired shortly after noon. Walsh also achieved what remains the 'ordinary' twelve hours record of 175½ miles — his twenty-four hours total is also the best ever. A drizzle set in about 3 p.m. and riders returned to Wisbech plastered with mud — the White Hart 'Boots' swore they left half a hundredweight of it! Lucky riders were washed and sent on in an odd assortment of dry clothes.

The 1891 course totalled 380 miles, but that for 1892 was more ambitious, showing a mileage not reached for many years — 415. Changes in rules from 1892 allowed, after the first check at Lynn, a rider recognized by the checker to call his name instead of stopping to sign the check sheet — a seemingly unfair advantage: also closure of detours on a time basis was introduced, e.g. riders reaching Huntingdon after 7.15 a.m. omitted the extension to Cambridge. At the Huntingdon check (103½ miles) Shorland shouted his name and sprinted away, leaving Bennett and Carlisle (Anfield), Cocker (Sharrow) and Walton (Polytechnic) to stop and sign — and although without pace on most of the Cambridge extension, he was never caught. Shorland's fame and popularity, increased by his first win in the Cuca Cup track twenty-four earlier in 1892, was such that groups of spectators gave Frank a special cheer as he passed, and after finishing on the St. Neots-Cambridge road, he was acclaimed by a crowd gathered in St. Neots Market Square! The unlucky Holbein had broken his arm two days prior to the race.

The field was down to twenty-one in 1893 — from the fifty or more of five years earlier — and the only threat to Shorland was Carlisle (riding as N.R.C.C. this year) but he was dogged with puncture trouble. Bidlake stuck on Shorland's wheel for over 100 miles, including a mad descent of Stangate Hill and, later, a mix-up when a pacing tandem tricycle stopped suddenly, fetching Shorland off, to be ridden over by a spare pacer, and shortening Bidlake's trike! Carlisle was spotted coming up again after the 100 miles point and Shorland went away behind a tandem — to set up a new twelve hours record of 195 miles, as well as a new twenty-four hours record. The finishing order for the first three repeated that in the Cuca Cup twenty-four Race. There were only seven finishers in the North Road twenty-four and sixth was sixty-two year old Atto of Pickwick B.C. — an early racing veteran. Helpers were reported to have used train travel to get from point to point and were depicted, by a 'Cycling' artist, in uneasy sleep in the ordinary compartments.

The plan for the 1894 event was to ride south from Peterborough hoping that, when daylight came, the smaller groups and slower speed, in comparison with the fifty miles races, would not trouble the police. However, a friendly constable revealed that the police would be out in force in Stilton, after spreading tacks across the road at Norman Cross! Bidlake and Wilson thereupon devised a new course, extending the Bourne detour north over the hills, passing that turning place of forty years later — the Windmill Inn at Rippingale — to Sleaford, west to Newark and up the North Road to Retford, where a meal was arranged at the Granby. Detours from Wisbech were also extended — and a Peterborough printer was persuaded to run off the revised course for the thirty-two riders and the helpers. The police vigil on the North Road was rewarded only by the capture of the lone, lampless Biggleswader Odell, sent out to help by Albone. Despite a fine twelve hours record of 211 miles, in training for his third Cuca Cup win, Shorland held to his decision not to ride another twenty-four. Fontaine, after his Edinburgh-London record ride, was expected to win and established a lead at about 100 miles. In addition to Bidlake, North Roaders riding included Pellant, Ernest Gould, Minns, Prevost, Robert Ilsley, Vernon Blake (later becoming notable as a sculptor in France) and Bateman (a Bristolian holding Western twelve and twenty-four hours records) all of whom achieved some cycling fame. There was much studying of the signposts and some riders who got detached went off course — in addition to the usual mechanical trouble casualties. Nevertheless, Bidlake, well served by Shorland, got both twelve hours (194½ miles) and twenty-four hours tricycle records and Fontaine the twenty-four hours bicycle record, Bidlake's being the last of the twelve hours paced tricycle records. Van Hooydonk and Highatt were the first to get a tandem bicycle through a twenty-four and so established record with their 317 miles — both later became North Roaders, as did many another after riding and/or helping in our twenty-four.

Road racing in the counties near London — i.e. in which London clubmen raced — was in abeyance in 1895, banned by both the National Cyclists' Union and the local police forces; further north, at least, the road clubs ignored the N.C.U. ban and, generally, avoided trouble with the police. Hoping to emulate the successes of the Cuca Cup twenty-fours, three London road Clubs planned twenty-four hour races at different tracks. The first — Catford C.C.'s — was cancelled, but the second, by Anerley B.C. at the Putney Track on 21/22 June for unlicensed (by the N.C.U.) riders, was very successful, the early hours being enlivened by a battle between A.A. Chase (N.R.C.C.) and A.E. ('Jenny') Walters (Polytechnic) who, however, dropped out, leaving Fontaine to win with English record of 474 miles. The North Roaders purchased the twenty-four cup — surely now the ugliest as well as the most historical trophy in cycledom! — to increase interest in their event at the new Wood Green Track, in which 'Faed' Wilson had a commercial interest. Unfortunately, construction delays necessitated postponement of our event until but a week prior to the Cuca at Herne Hill, much to the annoyance of promotor Lacy Hillier, who had obtained a new Cuca Cup to replace the cocoa firm's, won outright by Shorland's three wins.A furthe misfortune for the North Road was that a long spell of fine weather broke on Saturday, 20 July and this, combined with a lack of popular riders resulted in poor attendance. We lost £150 on the venture and mileages achieved were well below those in the Anerley and Cuca twenty-fours — but the Cuca, despite better weather, failed to attract the big crowds of previous years.

In the hope of a more successful venture, the 1896 twenty-four was changed to an event for professionals, again at Wood Green, European record holder, Huret of France, and the little Welshman, A. V. Linton (joint winner of the 1896 Bordeaux-Paris race) were engaged but Linton unfortunately fell ill and was unable to ride. Huret objected that our original date was too close to the Paris Bol d'Or twenty-four, so our twenty-four was postponed two weeks and thus clashed with the Cuca! Ominously five North Roaders started in the Cuca and were, presumably, supported by N.R. pacemakers: moreover, if any of his competitors were capable of extending Huret, they were eliminated in an early crash. However Huret rode well for the first half, breaking record from fifty-eight miles to twelve hours (288 miles, twenty-one ahead of Carlisle); by then only four were left in the race and were often all off the track. To provide some entertainment for the few spectators, Chase and Walters were paired to attack paced tandem records for an hour, getting inside record at six miles and pushing the hour figures over thirty miles. Soon after the twenty-four race was resumed Carlisle dropped out, letting a founder, if short term, member of the N.R.C.C. into second place. In contrast, a crowd of 6,000 at Herne Hill cheered North Roader Goodwin to a Cuca win with English record of 477 miles.

Although a fortunately negotiated insurance saved Club funds from more than a nominal loss, members had had enough of such promotions. At the next A.G.M. 'Faed' urged that members be encouraged in private twelve hours and twenty-four hours road rides for standard medals and regulations were appropriately revised. For 1897 a members only twenty-four hours scratch race was planned, with limited pacing by tandems or singles only and the winner was to hold the Cup for a year, the Cup becoming a permanent trophy, instead of being taken by the first to achieve two wins; later, at Bidlake's suggestion, previous winners' names were added to the inscription on the plinth. A special effort, after lack of support nearly caused abandonment, achieved fourteen entries (two tandems) of whom eight (one tandem) started from Henlow level crossing (instead of Norman Cross as first stated) at 10 p.m. on Friday, 17 September. Bidlake appears to have been timekeeper, while Wisbech was again the centre for Fenland detours — but bad weather eliminated all but two and Will Crosbie was voted a special gold medal. In 1898 and 1899 the twenty-four received but two and six entries respectively, both being abandoned and the Cup awarded for the best twelve hours ride of the year.

Coinciding with the waning of the Victorian era and the start of the new century, the 1900 twenty-four was planned as an unpaced event for members on single machines only. And, vide the relevant circular, 'not only will all external pacing be barred, but the competitors will be started separately and prevented by intervals of time or other means, from riding in each other's company'. Sixteen entrants were started at intervals of fifteen minutes from Ickleford, near Hitchin, and at Buckden were sent alternately on different courses, route A being via Huntingdon, Somersham and March to Wisbech, thence via Peterborough to Buckden and back through Peterborough to Wisbech, while route B reversed this. From Wisbech, Fenland detours as in past twenty-fours were used, again alternatively. Thus, the winner, eldest son of the Club's second President 'Boss' King, was able successfully to claim the Road Records Association's first unpaced twenty-four hours record. Incidentally, starting time was 7.00 p.m. on Friday, starting a tradition which lasted, with minor variations, until 1938 — but 1900 was the last occasion the course took riders through the city of Peterborough. Three days before the event a further instruction was issued prohibiting 'the use of motor cycles or motor cars for checkers or witnesses or assistants of any sort' and competitors were to urge motoring friends to avoid the area — all 'owing to the hostile attitude of the authorities towards motors'!

The alternating route system was never repeated but, to avoid company riding, and giving the police cause to suspect racing, riders were started at wide time intervals and, in 1901, in order of expected performance, best first. But 1901 was a bad year (in contrast to 1900 when King did six miles more in his second twelve than the first) and again only two (out of nine entrants) finished: nevertheless, King added eleven miles to his record and had his ride approved by the R.R.A. Later in the year Harry Green, well embarked on his amazing professional record breaking career, pushed the twenty-four hours record up to 394 miles — and ended schemes for combined record attempts with club events. In 1902 the three 'scratch men' — E .A. Cully, A. H. Murray and E. J. Steel — were listed to start at 6.0,

7.0 and 8.0 p.m. respectively, with the remaining six at intervals between. The small entry of four, leading to cancellation in 1903, was blamed on that year's bad weather, limiting training rides. Ten entered in 1904 when, in route changes bringing the mileage to 380 (as in 1891) Stretham appeared as a check point between St. Ives and Cambridge: here A. Inwood (later a long-term secretary) did his first twenty-four job, subsequently swearing it should be raffled for! Through the years there have been many jobs like this, done uncomplainingly — or almost! — such as member (and later C.T.C. Council Chairman) Admiral Hefford doing the check at Whaddon Gap on Saturday afternoon in the 1930s and being there for six hours or so. In the early years of the unpaced series competitors were told to make their own feeding arrangements and,in 1905 for example, that the White Hart at Wisbech would be open all night and the Manchester Arms at St. Ives would 'probably provide whatever is ordered'. In that 1905 twenty-four we suffered one of the very bad days — custard was blown off plates at an outdoor 'feed' at Cambridge! Also punctures were rife and took long to repair — Dr. Wesley took half-an-hour over one of his. So Ward's winning ride was very meritorious but the Cup was awarded to E. H. Grimsdell for 350 miles twenty-four during a successful Edinburgh-London record ride. 1905 also brought the Cross Keys at St. Neots into the twenty-four picture, as the headquarters to which riders ceasing to compete were requested to telegraph - and it remained as twenty-four headquarters or as a venue for club week-ends or meals for some forty years.

1906, the Club's twenty-first year, saw the initiation of the present series of 'Invitation Twenty-four Hours Unpaced Scratch Road Rides' and with it a number of changes. The starting intervals were reduced to two minutes and riders were to check at the nominated points by each calling both his name and the number allocated on the start card; it is, perhaps, stating the obvious to say that check points are so sited as to ensure that the ordained course is covered. On leaving Wisbech for the last time - which, in 1906, was after 243 miles had been covered, riders were permitted to have a single follower, at least 100 yards behind while the competitor was riding. A follower's duties were to assist the competitor in the event of a puncture or mechanical trouble, even to the follower lending his machine to the rider (so, where possible, a follower of similar stature to the rider was selected by their club) or to provide food should the rider suffer hunger and generally to incite the rider to resume should he stop due to fatigue — or ennui! A few years later a rider was allowed two followers — though Bidlake doubted whether this allowed a tandem and a single to join forces for following — but for near two decades 'motor assistance of any kind' was forbidden for the individual competitor.

At the Club A.G.M. when it was agreed that the twenty-four again be

C. HILHOUSE
1906

F.H. WINGRAVE 1909-1910
Taking a drink from Alf Gould in an
ANFIELD '100'

W.A. ELLIS
1927/8/9

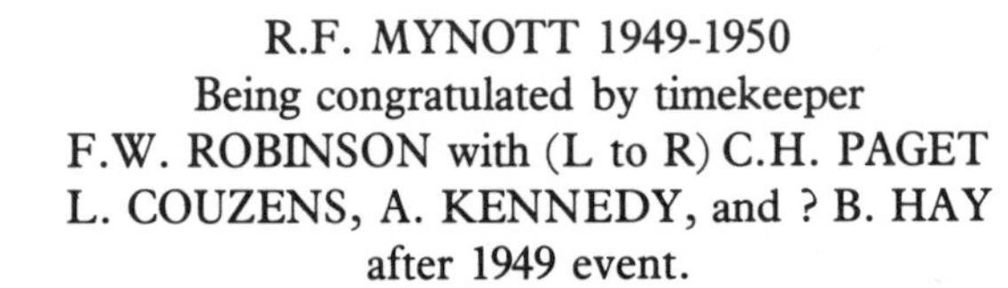

R.F. MYNOTT 1949-1950
Being congratulated by timekeeper
F.W. ROBINSON with (L to R) C.H. PAGET
L. COUZENS, A. KENNEDY, and ? B. HAY
after 1949 event.

made an open event, the committee was told to ensure that only bona-fide amateurs were invited — 'makers' amateurs' having appeared in recent years. Invitations were sent through men's clubs and twenty accepted, the clubs represented being Anerley B.C., Anfield B.C., Bath R.C., Ivy C.C. (Belfast), Midland C. & A.C., North London C.C. (including F. H. Inwood later to become a North Roader and our longest serving captain), Polytechnic C.C., Putney A.C., Unity C.C. and Vegetarian C. & A.C. Thirteen North Roaders entered (and the basis of our twenty-four has been that it is a members' event in which other Clubs' members are invited to participate) but eight of the thirty-three failed to report at 6.30 p.m. on Friday, 31 August, at Biggleswade Bridge. Here Dan Albone was an interested spectator, although he had turned from cycle making to achieve fame in the motor trade, being credited with making the first farm tractor: alas Dan died suddenly within the month. Stomach troubles and punctures soon started to whittle down the field but a torrid sun over the Fens on Saturday finally eliminated all but four! The standard 'racing' costume for road riding had become a black alpaca jacket and black woollen tights, to comply with a 'completely clothed from neck to feet' type of rule, and was hardly the coolest clothing for a hot day — even to folk accustomed to the heavier cycling clothing of those days. Nevertheless, Hilhouse found a hot bath, massage and a change of clothes before finally leaving Wisbech beneficial even though it let Bone (later to become a North Roader) temporarily into the lead. Over fifty North Roaders were out checking and in charge of feeding stations (riders still had to order their food in advance direct to the hotels) and many members of other clubs were also out helping their friends. Little course marshalling was done as riders were expected to familiarise themselves with the course as part of their preparation. But this assembly of members of the North Road and other interested clubs laid the foundations for the great fellowship which has grown in conjunction with the twenty-four hours game. For example, Charles Colbon of Cambridge was out in 1906 as a schoolboy and for successive years, competing (as Oak C.C.) in 1923 and becoming responsible for the detail arrangements in Cambridge until his death in the 1950s, while Sid Capener of Speedwell B.C. claimed, as a youthful Londoner, to have seen our first ever twenty-four and not to have missed one until 1967, when illness in his ninety-second year terminated our annual reunion with this lovable character. And these are but two of our innumerable friends, and equally countless members who, in their turns, have been out for the twenty-four year after year, some including a period as competitors. Back in 1906, and in St. Neots during the evening after the twenty-four, there were so many cyclists in the Cross Keys that a local was heard advising a friend 'Don't go in — it's 'ell in there!'

Thus launched, the Invitation twenty-four has continued except for the intervals of the two World Wars, with varying fortunes in number of riders and weather and in changes of course. The entry rose to forty-two, sent off at minute intervals, in 1912, when 'Dog and Gun' corner at Ely first appeared on the course and floods made conditions difficult, particularly at Mepal, where the river bridge was submerged and at least one rider was reported to have missed the bridge and got into the river. Between the Wars, in 1925, it was decided to limit the number of 'invitations' (by then men were seeking such invitations rather than waiting for them) to fifty, i.e. in addition to the cup holder and members wishing to enter; but when, in 1937, sixty-five members of other clubs desired to ride, as well as ten North Roaders, the earlier decision was waived — by then it was clear that our organisation, greatly aided by willing volunteers from other clubs, could cope with such numbers. But in 1937 a rising southerly wind again played havoc and the faster riders took two and a third hours to cover the thirty-seven miles back through the Fens, where roads tend to be above the level of the fields, to Cambridge.

In 1919 the surface of the North Road was so bad, from wartime neglect, that the miles north of Eaton Socon were omitted from the course but Eaton Socon police interference with some of the twelve riders in our first Memorial fifty miles event in 1920, resulted in the twenty-four start being moved north to that of 1893 — the fifty-seventh milestone at Little Paxton, first detour being up the North Road. In 1922 the start was moved to the first milestone east of St. Neots on the Cambridge road and the course led out directly to the Fens, with an excursion to Godmanchester, on the Via Devana, appearing either on the outward or return journeys. Shortly the course came to be designed to bring riders covering all detours back to Girtford Bridge — the hub for various and varying detours — with 300 miles completed: in 1928 one such detour introduced (or reintroduced) was via the outskirts of Biggleswade and along the Cambridge road to Whaddon Gap — and, as already mentioned, it proved as unpopular on a Saturday afternoon as in 1888 on Saturday evening!

Reverting to 1922, in this year the principal road clubs, primarily those promoting open or invitiation events, joined together at Bidlake's invitation to form the Road Racing Council with the aim of achieving uniformity, and a high degree of responsibility, in the promotion of such events; it issued an agreed set of recommendations to this end. The sport prospered to such an extent, in the changed Britain evolving after the break with the Edwardian world of pre-1914, combined with the hazards of increasing traffic, that it was deemed advisable to change the Council to a controlling body of which all clubs participating in the sport should be members. North Roader Bill Frankum played a notable part in the change and in 1937 the R.R.C.

became the Road Time Trials Council, later having considerable influence on our course. Bidlake was the first Chairman of the R.R.C., a post initially held for one year only, and in 1925 he was invited to chair a meeting called by our coeval, Catford C.C. to consider their proposal to promote an open twenty-four on roads south of London. The modern speed potential of these undulating roads was at once indicated when J. Holdsworth won the first Catford twenty-four — a Saturday/Sunday event in July — with competition record of 408½ miles. Previously competition records had been the rising scores of the winners of North Road events, as Anfield twenty-four winning totals were somewhat lower. Thus Selbach's 1912 winning mileage at last equalled Green's 1901 R.R.A. record and his 1919 score was the first unpaced twenty-four over 400 miles. Holbein and Goodwin had topped 400 with motor pacing and Hunt, between them, with human pacing in R.R.A. records in the late 1890s, while Knipe had achieved the feat with human pacing in the 1902 Anfield club twenty-four. Wessex R.C. entered the field of open twenty-four hours events in 1928 but the totals achieved on their courses, mostly on Hampshire and Dorset roads, initially lagged behind those of Catford and North Road twenty-fours. In the mid 1930s a Yorkshire Vegetarian club initiated a twenty-four but by then Seeley of Calleva R.C. had shelved the record with a phenomenal 444 miles to win the 1935 Catford event.

The 'might-have-been' is naturally a feature of the twenty-four story. If Frank Wingrave had not suffered so many punctures in 1911 (he ran out of spare tubular tyres, by then the racing man's normal equipment giving a light and lively wheel with a quickly replaceable tyre) as to cause him to retire, to become follower to a clubmate for eighty miles, Frank might have scored the three consecutive wins then the hallmark of a twenty-four man. And what would have happened if Selbach had not collided with a local cyclist in the first five miles, damaging his knee at Girtford Bridge in 1913 and retiring after twelve hours; or if Jack Middleton had not managed to go off course in Wisbech and Eric Wilkinson not been knocked out by a rabbit in his front wheel (and he a vegetarian!) while returning from Rippingale in 1935; or Alec Smith (Colne Valley and Vegetarian) with a 438½ win in the Mersey Roads twenty-four (replacing the Anfield) earlier in the year had not been halted by mechancial trouble in 1938? 1938 also saw a slower competitor accidentally peppered with shot from a sportsman's gun early on Saturday as he returned from the Fens and Rohr (who was also a North Roader) achieved a wonderful recovery after much mechanical trouble had limited his half-time mileage to 202. On the mechanical side 1936 was of a different interest - Hall rode fixed wheel, Tullett derailleur gears, while novice Howlett, who led for some eighteen hours, used the normal wide ratio three-speed hub. But reverting to ill luck, surely the hardest case was

Frank Armond's in 1920: he had *started* his racing career in the 1919 twenty-four when he was thirty years old, and despite this, and going off course at Long Sutton, was still lying second on returning to Cambridge - but then his energy evaporated! And in 1922 he was among those who succumbed to a severely cold September night, while in 1923 he was in head-on collision with Century competitor Gibson, both receiving attention at Wisbech from Dr. Kilham Roberts (a North Roader) and a local medico. But in 1920, when holding a lead of thirty-five minutes, a chicken ran into his front wheel as he returned from Peterborough (actually Eye Green) into Wisbech: Frank fell heavily, badly bruising his left thigh and knee and that leg became of decreasing use. Rossiter, much younger but handicapped with a war-damaged right hand, which increased the delays caused by punctures, was now recovering his lost ground, until by Cambridge, with just over an hour to go, Armond's lead was down to two minutes. Armond packed twenty and a quarter miles into his last sixty-eight minutes, but Rossiter got twenty-one and a quarter into sixty-six minutes — indeed hard luck Frank! 1920 also saw Charlie Sewell's only attempt at a twenty-four — he suffered much but wouldn't give in, finishing last with 291¼; Charlie was a great club character, a successful rider at shorter distances and an entertainer at social events — he had the pleasure of seeing first his son and then his two grandsons become successful North Roaders. In a different vein, one of the Sharrow C.C. team in 1921 was A. C. Baynes, later to achieve fame on stage and radio as entertainer 'Stainless Stephen'. He finished ninth in 1921 with 351¾ miles and in later years, if he was appearing at a theatre within reach of the course, he would be out in the small hours, helping — and entertaining the other helpers! In the early 1940s he settled in North London and became a North Roader.

Frank Armond became the Club's second racing secretary in 1925 and in 1926 successfully faced the task of extending our organisation to cover the feeding of all competitors, other than vegetarians — whose club had an excellent organisation catering for their riders' special needs and designed to reduce stops for food to the minimum. Other clubs regularly represented in the twenty-four also developed efficient helping teams, such as Unity C.C. and, later, Century R.C. (which grew out of 'Cycling's' 1911 Century Competition) but even these found it an advantage to make use of the food we ordered at the nominated places. By now the Wisbech hotels were losing interest in us and instead of detours from Wisbech, the course went via Lynn to Long Sutton and Deeping and north to the hilltop Windmill inn at Rippingale, which provided food and turning point — and there were no cuttable detours. Senior members Van Hooydonk and Lloyd ran a 'canteen' service at Spalding while Frank Wingrave performed marvels with a hatful of eggs and a paraffin stove on the Godmanchester detour. In 1927 the Bull

CLIFF SMITH takes '24' Cup for 10th time
CARRIED BY SUMMERLIN AND LOVETT

SID MOTTRAM 24 ORGANISER 1950-1976

at Long Sutton became night headquarters — on the commendation of member Townend — and saw the end of a famous 'scrap' of over eighty miles from north of March, when Rossiter caught Holdsworth and puncture delayed Dougal, closing ten and twenty minutes starting gaps, to Rippingale and back — much of it watched by Bidlake from Price's car, as they rode one on each side of the road and one in the middle. It was strictly illegal, and years earlier 'travelling marshalls' had been introduced as antidote to company riding, but . . . The Rippingale detour became the one on which successive winners moved into a leading position — even in 1927 Ellis moved into fourth place hereabouts.

At Frank Wingrave's instance the 1927 Club A.G.M. approved that motor vehicles be allowed for following on a similar basis as for cyclist followers and in 1928 old racing man, S. F. Edge (of the 1891 Bordeaux-Paris, etc.) reappeared on the North Road scene in charge of Rossiter's motorised helpers. In the following year Rossiter became a professional, successfully to attack Green's End to End record, thus 1928 saw the last of his fine sequence of rides in our twenty-four. In 1930 we saw the first 'Battle of the Browns': E.B. from Wessex, L.W. of Luton and, once or twice, Sid of Century — and a new series of fine rides by a Centurian was initiated when Hall was fifth, behind E. B. Brown, with 406 miles; sixth man, Jackson of Upton Manor C.C. also topped 400. Our 1931 twenty-four was E. B. Brown's third of the year, the others being the Catford (won by Dougal with over 430 miles) and the R.R.A. twenty-four hours record as an extension of Edinburgh—York and Edinburgh-London records. Another multiple twenty-four hours rider, J. Spackman, made his first North Road appearance this year and continued riding in various twenty-fours until he had completed some fifty-six — and now usually appears as a helper at each of the twenty-fours annually promoted. 1938 saw the winners of both Catford and Wessex twenty-fours in our event, and in 1939 the winners of Mersey, Wessex and Yorkshire Vegetarian twenty-fours were on our start card. In 1914 the first World War started a month before the date for our twenty-four and the race was abandoned, in part we feared that a nervous sentry might fire at a rider — but the fervent patriotism roused by that war ensured that many sporting activities ceased and our road game was among these. In 1939 we were unsure whether the second World War would involve Britain before the twenty-four and cancellation was left until the day before the event. In contrast with the first World War the continuance of sporting activities was officially encouraged through the second and we did consider running a twenty-four in mid 1940 to be organised by Frank Marston, but the collapse of France ended that, though we did promote an Open twelve hours later in 1940 and the three subsequent years.

We were ready to resume the Invitation twenty-four in 1945 — the year of Victory in Europe and in Japan — but with what changes! Our Memorial fifty had become a Sunday event in 1927, our Open twelve had also been on Sundays and our resumed twenty-four was, in line with the other immediately pre-war twenty-fours (ours was the first post war twenty-four) a Saturday-Sunday event. It might be appropriate to comment here that the initial objection to Sunday racing was the possible annoyance to the then many churchgoers, but this continued as the policy of the North Road and other clubs because the foremost of other sports were not then played on Sundays. Wartime rationing had ended the 'completely clothed from neck to feet' rule, which had long been made anachronistic by the wide adoption of shorts and stockings (and later ankle socks) by touring and club-riding cyclists: shorts and jacket had thus become accepted for time trialling during the War and continued to be acceptable. Other rationing increased the difficulties of organisation as both petrol (we had become increasingly dependent on motorised helpers) and food were rationed, so the appeals were for ration coupons, as well as attendance on the day. The start was moved to Cross Hall — actually in the Kimbolton road just north of Eaton Socon. Detours west off the North Road had been introduced before the War and were now used in the early stages — the Kimbolton road (but not until 1946) and the Huntingdon-Thrapston road en route to the northern turn at Wansford, moving out into the Fens after returning to Cross Hall — and the avoidance of right turns across traffic, introduced before the War, was continued. Young Cecil Paget, then living at Eaton Socon (George Bullen, living at Hitchin, had been the first provincial 'twenty-four' secretary) was to have organised the 1945 event, but ill health prevented this and Wisbech member, Charles Lynn took over. The Riverside Cafe south of Wisbech replaced (because of the now unwilling licencees) the town's hotels as night headquarters, and 'Fuller's' at Girtford Bridge — named after its original owners and continuing under the Ewings of Polytechnic C.C. as caterers for cyclists — was named as event headquarters. Here after a Sunday of southerly gales, reflected in the leading mileages, founder-member, E. P. Moorhouse, was able to congratulate the winner, Wilkinson, who had previously decided this was to be his last race and has maintained that decision. G. P. Mills, winner of the first North Road twenty-four, fifty-nine years earlier, was still alive and apparently well but unfortunately suddenly took ill and died in November, after our Diamond Jubilee Dinner.

So a new series was started at 2.01 p.m. on Saturday, fifteenth September 1945, when timekeeper F. W. Robinson said 'five, four, three, two, one — go' as he counted the seconds for first man Foot. Bidlake's usual practice was to intone 'Get Ready — Go' but his successors, after the accident leading to his death prevented his being at the 1933 twenty-four, used the count-down method: they were Moxham, Armond,Robinson and, the first non-member to serve us, current timer Wilkinson. In 1946 the starting time was moved to noon — half circle from the original midnight — and so remained until 1972 when 11.01 was adopted. For some twenty of these years Frank Thoday held up nearly every starter and gave him the initial impetus along the course, in fact until the summer Bank Holiday was moved to the end of August and, in 1966, coincided with the harvest moon. After much debate the clash with the famous Bath Road Club's 100 miles event on August Monday was accepted and the week-end proved to have other advantages (e.g. time for riders and helpers to recover and reduced Saturday night traffic) so that, other than for one subsequent Championship, the moon has been deserted in favour of the Bank Holiday week-end.

The journal 'Cycling', in 1930 started an annual 'Best All Rounder' contest, based on riders' fastest times in open events at fifty and 100 miles and greatest distance at twelve hours. the R.T.T.C. became responsible for this contest, dropping the twelve hours during the War for lack of events during those years, and introduced Championships at various distances. The Twenty-four did not attain Championship status until 1948, when we had the honour — and the problems of promoting the first: preliminary difficulties arose over some of the regulations the R.T.T.C. wished to impose and this was only overcome by the firmness and skill of Frankum in negotiation — thus working not only for the North Road C.C. but for the other clubs incorporating subsequent twenty-four hour championships in their events. The Championship went the round of the four promotions: initially the others were Catford, Mersey Roads and Western Time Trials Association, but when the last lapsed Wessex was ready to resume. One accepted regulation entailed every checking and marshalling point being covered by two persons — and in 1948 there were 137 such points on the course. Not directly related to this, in 1948 a 'finishing circuit' was introduced, but only of eleven miles 1,100 yards total, and therefore only usable three times, vide R.T.T.C. regulations, and having a further detour beyond it. Unfortunately, adequate arrangements were not made to ensure that all finishers reached this circuit and a number had to be run out by the traditional method of a follower with watch set to the chief timekeeper's, the point of finish being clearly identified for subsequent assessment of mileage. On the circuit seven assistant timekeepers were stationed at intervals, their watches set to the chief timekeeper's and riders rode until stopped by the timekeeper they reached after their twenty-four hours had elapsed, the total distance being calculated in relation to speed between the preceding timekeepers. In 1948 Basham was the only rider to complete three circuits and was run out on the subsequent stretch by timekeeper Robinson, just short of Seeley's phenomenal 1935 Catford total. Almost as phenomenal wa Keeler's 490 miles in our 1958 event, alas shadowed with an unfortunate mishap: leading the field, on the road as well as in time, he surprised marshalls at Doddington and they failed to persuade him to turn right towards March — he did some five miles which we subsequently measured, before motorised helpers met him returning, identifying this point. As it did not affect the result of the event, we allowed him the known distance off course (this had been done before on the few occasions it had happened) but for official competition record purposes the R.T.T.C. felt unable to follow our example; so for six years the official record remained at Swindon Wheeler White's second 484 miles in 1958, had won the North Road gold medal we had offered for the first to achieve 'evens' (twenty miles per hour) for twenty-four hours. And when Matthews did reach 490 in the 1964 Mersey twenty-four his total was fractionally less than Keeler's. We hoped to get the first 500 in 1968, with a championship field, including 496 milers Carline and Matthews, and a northerly breeze on the Saturday — but the night turned misty and the wind rose from the south on Sunday and robbed us of an honour which went to the Mersey championship in 1969 when Cromack, who had already excelled in all three forms of cycle sport — time trial, road race and track — topped 507 miles. 1951 gave us another form of disappointment: we hoped for a third and record breaking win from Mynott (who had nearly 'achieved the double' in 1949, coming second in our Memorial fifty, and had won spontaneous applause from the crowd at Girtford in 1950 when he was thought to have taken record over 460 miles) but his enthusiasm was completely dissipated in a vain attempt in July on the R.R.A. twenty-four hour record to a schedule for 480 miles; strange that Wingrave, Ellis and Mynott had each, at the apparent zenith of his career, been unfortunate in an attempt on the R.R.A. twenty-four record. Anyhow, Mynott did not enter our 1951 twenty-four — in fact it is doubtful whether he raced again until the mid 1970s when he reappeared on Cambridgeshire roads and rejoined the North Road — but on the day Alan Blackman rode excellently and appeared set for another North Road victory. At about 400 miles, however, when comfortably in the lead and riding as fast as any in the event, suddenly and mysteriously he lost the use of his arms and had to stop. In subsequent years Alan appeared likely to win on a number of occasions but retired for various and not very apparent reasons — nevertheless he still achieved good rides in 1954 and 1959, the latter despite some time off the bicycle, including a sleep on a roadside seat!

Different forms of misfortune dogged Dowie of East Midlands in 1946: having missed his intended train to St. Neots, the nearest he could get by train was Peterborough, whence he persuaded a taximan to take him the twenty-five or so miles to Cross Hall, arriving over thirty minutes late and having to persuade Judge and President England to let him start! Then returning from the north to Brampton cross roads, he turned left in error and after wandering for some time through Huntingdon he saw Cambridge on a signpost and shortly found himself at the turn on the Godmanchester detour — thence he resumed the route of the event but completed the twenty-four as a private trial. Also, Guy of the Vegetarians had the misfortune that year to break his collar bone in a fall from his bicycle.

The entry received for the first post war twenty-four was forty — about twice the 1919 number — but it rose rapidly to seventy-eight for the first Championship and to 107 in 1950 for the first organised by Leicester member, Sid Mottram; fortunately, six withdrew and we only had to refuse one to conform with the R.T.T.C. limit of 100, and by the misfortune of Robinson's death in June, 1950, was also the first twenty-four not timed by a North Roader: Luton Wheeler Eric Wilkinson (the 1945 winner) was invited to take on the task. We had 100 entries again in Championship year 1952, but thereafter interest waned steadily, but suddenly in 1959 the entry went under fifty, below forty in 1962 and down to twenty-two in 1965. The other twenty-fours had similar experiences, each event getting a comparatively good entry in Championship years — possibly Mersey Roads entries have fallen less than in the southern events, indicating greater enthusiasm among northern cyclists? To some extent this mirrors the rise and decline in general interest in cycling, as reflected in the membership of the Cyclists' Touring Club — but hundreds of shorter distance events continue to be listed in the R.T.T.C. handbook — and mostly are well supported.

In 1948 the two Cecil Pagets — father and son, alias 'Mouldy' and 'Mildew' — used our promotion of the first Championship, which was the fiftieth North Road twenty-four, as a lure to bring together many old members, 'Mildew' writing most of the letters. (Incidentally 'Mildew's elder son Richard — alias 'Musty' — joined in 1958 makng the Pagets the first three generations in the Club). Many had not been seen for some time, such as Brock, 'Anti' Brown, Chisman, Cobley, Harry and Frank Cole, Max Crosbie, Mackenzie, Mott, Sangway, Steel and Stancer, while the still active were Armond, Charlie Sewell, Shillito, Haylock and Dunn — most of them with over forty years membership. These, with some of the younger members not yet on duty in the twenty-four, moved from the start to the Cross Keys for an informal lunch. Out of this, in time for the next twenty-four, grew the 'Twenty-four Society' with forty-eight members who engaged to turn out for the twenty-four each year or send a donation of 1*d.* per year of membership towards defraying the cost of the twenty-four. The qualification for membership was to have been riding, racing, record breaking or helping as North Roaders prior to 1910, this limit being advanced annually. In addition to those present in 1948 the original members were Bass, Cheveley, D'Aeth, Fawley, Alf Gould, Hall, Highatt, Lint Ilsley,

Jimmy Inwood, Lempriere, Munro, Nat Smith, Townend, Guy Webb, Frank Wingrave and Woodroffe. Will Crosbie, Bob Ilsley, 'Doowni' Inwood, 'Trossie' James, Judge, Moorhouse and 'Jonah'. Wilson were made Honorary Members. Although not having the necessary years of N.R. membership also enrolled, as a gesture to their long years of service to the sport were Armond, Cessford, Frank Cole, Haylock, Kynaston, Tom Owen, Charlie Sewell and Turvey, while Syd Capener,Speedwell B.C. President and young 'Mildew' were also made Honorary Members.

Cobley was the first secretary and Mouldy Paget the first President — the latter honour held for one year; 'Mildew' became secretary in 1951 but handed over to Armond in 1953, resuming the secretaryship when Armond's turn as President came in 1962. The qualification for membership was relaxed during the late 1950s to fifteen years N.R. membership. Also in the 1950s three ladies were elected to Honorary Membership — Mrs. Armond, Mrs. J. C. Paget and Mrs. Capener; later Mrs. A. B. Smith was also elected. The first 'official' meeting and Dinner was held on the Saturday evenng at the Cross Keys — while the twenty-four was well in progress. Later a succession of venues were tried including, one year, that haunt of the 1890s the White Horse at Eaton Socon — it had become Ye Olde White Horse! It became accepted that wives could be brought to the Dinner and in 1956 it was changed to the Friday evening prior to the twenty-four, making a fine social evening and making helping in the twenty-four simpler. The venue became settled in Bedford about 1958 and attendance grew to the sixties but went over eighty in celebration of Sid Mottram's year as President and twenty-first year as twenty-four Secretary in 1970. Members have been far more generous than the l*d*. per annum and during the years the Society has contributed over £700 to the running of the twenty-four — the twenty-four Cup was renamed the 'Faed' Memorial Trophy in memory of the Club's Founder and first President — on a suggestion made by Frank Armond — the first prize, now of £10 value, increased to £25 for 1974, being Sid Mottram's salute to his twenty-fifth twenty-four, after many years at five guineas, being named the 'Faed' Memorial prize.

Among riders in the 1946 twenty-four was M. Clark of Barnsley, a rider in several pre-war Memorial fifties — he was third in 1934 — and he added another North Road certificate to his collection in 1946, being nineth with 394 miles. Other pre-war Memorial fifty competitors to ride in post war twenty-fours were W. G. Smith (Speedwell B.C.) and G. A. White (Eagle R.C.) White very much with the ambition of collecting another certificate. With a shorter gap in years Arnold (Middleton C.C.) achieved an even higher ambition, winning the Memorial fifty, when a tricycle event, in 1953 and the twenty-four (on a bicycle!) in 1962. At the other end of the scale,

Fred Bause of Clifton C.C. (of York) entered and finished last of sixty-three with 273 miles — in 1950, having completed the 1911 twenty-four as a Unity C.C. man: by 1950 he was riding with an articulated crank on one side to cater for a leg crippled in a road accident — he became a North Roader and usually met us on the York run. In later years another content with a total near 300 — Beech of Comrade C.C. — liked tunes from the 'juke box' with his sit down feed at the Hardwick cafe, which then kept open through the night for us. In contrast, and showing the wide variety of competitor attracted to the time trial game, and to the Twenty-four in particular, the achievements of the leaders rose from four topping 400 for the first time in 1927, fourth being C. Neale who was Wessex R.C. president, to eighteen covering 420 miles or more in 1952, the last of these being the Vegetarian Guy, winner of the Catford but non-finisher in the North Road in 1938. An interesting aspect of the entries in the 1950s was the proportion of North Roaders from the Northern counties — Westmorland, Northumberland, etc. — riding, swelling our numbers to twelve in 1953 and 1954 and represented in the results by tricyclists Green and Noble and by Bidlake award winner White. While Carline, who was second in 1955, later won the twenty-four Championship six times and Cliff Smith, who has since won so many twenty-fours (Catford as well as North Road) first appeared among the leaders in the N.R. twenty-four of 1957, when he was fourth. They were then in their late thirties and have thus achieved notable rides in their forties, as did Burrell and Harding in Championship twenty-fours — at forty a time triallist reaches the official classification of 'Veteran'.

The closure of the Windmill at Rippingale on losing its licence — a fate overtaking many country inns — started in 1957 a succession of major course revisions eventually eliminating Wisbech and the roads from it. Initially course measurement was somewhat empirical and presumed the accurate placing of milestones. When the falseness of this assumption was realised, the assistance of the Ordnance Survey was sought and they supplied us with distances between milestones and other easily identified landmarks. Then, in the late 1920s, a system of course measuring was introduced using a revolution counter for the front wheel of bicycle or tricycle, riding along a chain or tape measured mile, before and after the course measuring session: the first gave revolutions per mile, the second checked against decrease in tyre pressure and the revolutions per mile enabled length of courses to be calculated with greater accuracy; to ensure against change in tyre pressure Luton Wheelers, for a time, used a sorbo-tyred front wheel, making the task even more of a labour! Bidlake started re-measuring North Road courses, and particularly the twenty-four on this basis and the work was continued by Moxham and Maddex in the later

1930s and is reflected in result sheets: these show mileages to the nearest last completed quarter mile until 1934 and then to furlongs until the calculated result from circuit finishes led to decimalisation. After the War others contributed to this work but an outstanding amount of work in both measuring and designing courses was done by Impey, whom we made an Honorary Member in appreciation. Course designing now has to consider car parking aspects as well as actual cycling! The first move in re-design (in which Ted Kings was much concerned) was to bring the start to the Eynesbury area in 1957 and to use the roads between Biggleswade, Baldock and Royston in the early stages — simplified by the by-passing of Girtford and Biggleswade — before going towards Hitchin and from Shefford to Clophill (extensions subsequently amputated) and north along the North Road (A.1 by M.O.T. classification) using westerly detours en route and turning back at Wansford (for a few years after a detour to Oundle) or Norman Cross, to Cross Hall and by St. Neots to Cambridge and the Fens. A complication arose in the early 1960s when St. Neots bridge came near to disintegration and the flow of traffic over the Ouse was controlled by traffic lights: the course was diverted at Little Paxton and went by the Paper Mills to the east end of St. Neots — a useful diversion when the annual carnival and fair blocked St. Neots' streets. As traffic increased the course was re-designed to avoid riders turning in the road other than at the roundabouts built at many junctions — and then brightly illuminated at night by high slung lamps, making light beacons in the Fens, at Stretham and Guyhirn, as well as on the A.l. Re-alignment of the A.1 linked with the by passing of Eaton Socon left the old fifty-seventh milestone on a little used loop of the old Great North Road and, in 1974, it again became the starting point for the twenty-four — and for the Memorial fifty and other events. Concentration of the course was made easier in 1965 when the R.T.T.C. allowed roads used twice on Saturday to be used again on Sunday — a minor effect of the official recognition of cycling sport on the road, which also led to the adoption of colourful shirts and shorts, the shirts embodying distinctive designs and colours for different clubs, and a far cry from the earlier unobtrusive colours. That official recognition, embodied in the 1960 Ministry of Transport Regulations, required organisers of road races (restarted in the early 1940s, despite N.C.U. opposition) to seek prior police approval for each event, while time trial courses had to be notified in advance for the information of the Chief Constable of each county through which the course passes. Reverting to course changes, a finishing circuit was re-introduced in 1952, but of over fifteen miles in length (allowing its unlimited use) and, as far as possible, on little used secondary roads: circuits to the east of Biggleswade and to the west of Girtford and later of Eaton Socon have been used but all contain hills disliked in the last hours of a twenty-four! Every endeavour is made, by judicious cutting of detours to get each finisher on to the circuit and, incidentally, to keep the field compact — in contrast to 1937, for example, when the field of fifty or so took four hours ten minutes to pass through the last Wisbech check. A contributory factor making course concentration more desirable was the waning of cycling clubs along the course, clubs whose members had given much appreciated assistance at towns such as Wisbech, Lynn and Spalding. Thus when the Riverside Cafe at Wisbech was burnt out two weeks after the 1957 twenty-four and was not rebuilt, it was Newark Castle C.C. which filled the gap by erecting a small marquee for a feeding station near Guyhirn Bridge — one of a number of 'mobile' feeding stations suggested by a Blackman — Mottram — J. Sewell sub-committee late in 1957. By then the number of helpers cycling through the shires to and from their various tasks had considerably lessened, replaced by motorised helpers — some of whom, alas, still managed to give offence to local residents. On the whole the police are now quite co-operative, an extreme instance came in our 1968 Championship when Goodfellow's helping car, parked mostly off the road was wrecked by the bad driving of a motorist unconnected with the twenty-four — fortunately without hurt to Mrs. Goodfellow or the other helpers — and a police patrolman coming off duty volunteered to take helpers, food and equipment round the course; despite the delay, for Goodfellow came on the scene after the collision, he finished sixth with 462 miles.

So many memories — of winners in the lead all day, more frequently of changing fortunes throughout the day, of clubmates riding well or suffering and the occasional excitement of a rider pulling off a win in the last few miles. Such was the 1964 Championship when reigning champion Carline was but three miles in the lead (over Smith) with 251 miles at twelve hours and then retired exhausted at 374 miles: Smith and a few others suffered the misfortune of being misdirected by late night revellers near Mepal, probably doing some six miles off course and some, in consequence, retired. But Smith fought back reducing Burrell's earlier lead to seventy-eight seconds when they entered the finishing circuit — Smith thirty-two minutes after Burrell, who increased his lead slightly by the end of the circuit: Smith, however, put in a great effort in the second and third times round the circuit, converting his deficit to a small but sufficient lead and his only Championship - so far. Burrell was the first to win the Championship twice, in our 1956 and 1960 events — though in 1956 he nearly rode instead in the once only Ealing Paragon 24 on roads west of London.

But surely the great attraction of the all day event is that it provides riders of all calibres the opportunity to set out to achieve what is for each of them no mean athletic feat. Also all the work of organisation, service to that organisation and service to the individual rider, which goes into a twenty-four, all honorary and unpaid but much appreciated, are among the finest examples of camaraderie in the world.

PRIZEWINNERS AND THEIR MILEAGES IN NORTH ROAD '24s

Year	First	Second	Third	First Tricyclist	Best Nor (or next b placed m
1866	G.P. Mills N.R.C.C. & Anfield B.C. 227 Ordinary	T. Waterhouse N.R.C.C. 225 Ordinary	B.F. Huntsman N.R.C.C. & Belsize B.C. Ordinary C.W. Brown N.R.C.C. & Finchley T.C. Safety 217	T.R. Marriott N.R.C.C. & Nottingham T.C. 190	J.W. Day E.P. Moc First tanc 207
1887	T. Waterhouse N.R.C.C. 270½ Safety	G.P. Mills N.R.C.C. & Anfield B.C. 264 Tricycle	D. Belding N.R.C.C. 237½ Ordinary	G.P. Mills (2nd place)	
1888 25 Aug.	M.A. Holbein Catford C.C. 266½ Safety	G.R. White N.R.C.C. 254½ Geared Facile	E.E. Glover Bath R.C. H.E. Green (unattached) 234½ Ordinaries	F.T. Bidlake N.R.C.C. 155½ (in 19 hours)	
29 Sept.	M.A. Holbein Catford C.C. 292½ Safety	W. Chater Lea N.R.C.C. 282½ Safety	J.G.H. Browne N.R.C.C. 257½ Safety	W.C. Goulding N.R.C.C. 252	(Best on M. Rae North L 253)
1889	M.A. Holbein N.R.C.C. & Catford C.C. 324 Safety	F.W. Shorland N.R.C.C. 291½ Geared Facile	W.C. Goulding N.R.C.C. 280 Tricycle	W.C. Goulding (3rd place)	260)
1890	M.A. Holbein N.R.C.C. & Catford C.C. 336½ safety (spring frame & cushion tyres)	T.A. Edge N.R.C.C. 333¼ Safety (pneumatic tyres—	H.H. Spencer N.R.C.C. & Bradford C.C. 302 safety (pneumatic tyres)	F.T. Bidlake N.R.C.C. 289 (cushion tyres)	261)
1891	F.W. Shorland N.R.C.C. 326 Safety (pneumatics)	J.F.Walsh Bath R.C. 312 Ordinary (pneumatics)	F.T. Bidlake N.R.C.C. 304 Tricycle (pneumatics)	F.T. Bidlake (3rd place)	J.M. Ja 253 7th Safety (
1892	F.W. Shorland N.R.C.C. 366½	J.A. Bennett Anfield B.C. 352½	J.H. Cocker Sharrow C.C. 346½	F.T. Bidlake N.R.C.C. 207 (stopped after 15 hours)	J.M. Ja 339½ 4th

1892 onwards all prizewinners rode on pneumatic tyres and, except where otherwise stated, on rear driven safeties

7. Shorland R.C.C.	F.T. Bidlake N.R.C.C. 331 Tricycle	H. Hammond Essex Wheelers 325 Front driver	F.T. Bidlake (2nd place)	R.H. Carlisle 308 4th
. Fontaine ytechnic C.C.	E. Buckley Anfield B.C. 358½	F.T. Bidlake N.R.C.C. 356½ Tricycle	F.T. Bidlake (3rd place)	R.J. Ilsley 356 4th
I. Carlisle ield B.C. m 750y	J.P.K. Clark N.R.C.C. 403m 1006y	H.H. Standish London Central C.C. 395m 50y	—	F.R. Cook 372m 1006y 4th
Huret .F.	G.A. Nelson 415	L. Buffell (of France) 350	—	—

(1897 - 1905 were members only events and from 1900 onwards pacing was forbidden)

Gould	W.M. Crosbie 315	—	—	—
ndoned — insufficient entries				
. King Jnr. ½	A.R. Child 322	L. Diespecker 306	—	—
. King Jnr.	H.S. Price 337	—	—	—
. Cully ½	P.S. Murray 342	A. Mackenzie 340	W.W. Robertson 268	—
ndoned — insufficient entries				
E. Ward ½	J.E. Naylor 355	F.W. Wesley 335½	W.W. Robertson 292	—
E. Ward	F.W. Wesley 306	C. Hilhouse 288	E. Bright 224½	—
Hilhouse .C.C. ¼	F.T. Bone Polytechnic C.C. 345½	F. Newell Vegetarian C. & A.C. 335¼	—	—
. Fisher ty C.C. ¼	J.E. Naylor N.R.C.C. 372½	F.T. Bone Polytechnic C.C. 362½	A.G. Markham N.R.C.C. 301½	C. Hilhouse 358½ 4th
I. Briault ty C.C. ½	F.H. Wingrave N.R.C.C. 360½	F.W. Wesley N.R.C.C. 357	E.J. Bass Beaumont C.C. 290	F.T. Bone 355½ 4th
. Wingrave .C.C. ¼	A.G. Keen Unity C.C. 379¼	C.W. Shalford Unity C.C. 377½	E.J. Bass N.R.C.C. 288½	F.W. Wesley 354 6th
. Wingrave .C.C. ¼	R.W. Gillvray Sheffield R.C. 362½	H.H. Agnew North London C.C. 355¼	L.W.B. Martin Bath R.C. 301¼	H. Norman 342 4th

1911	H. Bennett Unity C.C. 386	G. Brown University C.C. 365½	R.W. Gillvray Sheffield R.C. 365	—	H. N 360½ 4th
1912	M.G. Selbach University C.C. 394	H.G. Cook University C.C. 379	F.C. Higgins Polytechnic C.C. 374¾	W.W. Robertson N.R.C.C. 287	F.H 371½ 4th
1913	F.G. Thomas Century R.C. 381½	F.J. Parker Unity C.C. 373¼	C.A. Stevens Polytechnic C.C. 371½	—	H. N 357½ 4th
		1914 - 1918 No "24" during Great War			
1919	M.G. Selbach Unity C.C. 405	F.M. Inwood N.R.C.C. 382	J.G. Shaw Sharrow C.C. 375	A.G. Markham N.R.C.C. 223	F.E. 360 4th
1920	J.W. Rossiter Century R.C. 378¾	F.E. Armond N.R.C.C. 377¾	J. Thomas Northern C.C. 362¾	H. Pryor Anfield B.C. 354½	C.A 291½
1921	C.F. Davey Vegetarian C & A.C. 401½	J.W. Rossiter Century R.C. 392	F.E. Armond N.R.C.C. 383¼	A.E. Burt University C.C. 320¾	F.J. 331
1922	M.G. Selbach Unity C.C. 402	V.J. Viel Unity C.C. 395	J.W. Rossiter Century R.C. 378½	—	F.J. 360½
1923	J.W. Rossiter Century R.C. 402½	H.D. Hall Oak C.C. 383½	F.E. Sanford Highgate C.C. 376¼	A.G. Keen Unity C.C. 310½	F.J. 338½
1924	J.W. Rossiter Century R.C. 377¾	E.C. Pilcher Polytechnic C.C. 373	J.B. Dilley Crescent Wheelers 365¾	F.R. Fisher Essex Roads C.C. 342½	F.J. 330½
1925	J.W. Dougal Marlboro A.C. 394	W.E. Sanford Highgate C.C. 383½	J.W. Rossiter Century R.C. 382½	—	F.W 357
1926	J.W. Rossiter Century R.C. 407½	J.E. Holdsworth Kentish Wheelers 383¼	F.R. Fisher Essex Roads C.C. 381½	—	F.W 379 4th
1927	W.A. Ellis N.R.C.C. 410½	J.W. Dougal Marlboro A.C. 409¾	J.W. Rossiter Century R.C. 405½	—	F.W 395½ 6th
1928	W.A. Ellis N.R.C.C. 413½	J.W. Rossiter Century R.C. 403	T.F. Maddex N.R.C.C. 395¼	F.R. Fisher Essex Roads C.C. 365¼	W.C 354¾
1929	W.A. Ellis N.R.C.C. 406	F. Stott Century R.C. 401½	W.A. Low Kent R.C. 394¾	L.J. Meyers Southgate C.C. 332½	F.W 369½ 6th
1930	W.A. Low Kent R.C. 413¾	R.J.J. Coe University C.C. 405¾	L.W. Brown Luton Wheelers C.C. 405½	E.H. Cooper Highgate C.C. 324	G.H 391½ 8th

E.B. Brown Wessex R.C. 407¾	L.W. Brown Luton Wheelers C.C. 403	R.J.J. Coe University C.C. 399¾	E.H. Cooper Highgate C.C. 327¾	G.H.M. Pitt 399¼ 4th
S.H. Ferris Vegetarian C & A.C. 429¾	L. Hall Century R.C. 413¼	L.W. Brown Luton Wheelers C.C. 406¾	—	G.H.M. Pitt 393½ 7th
S.H. Ferris Vegetarian C & A.C. 431¼	L. Hall Century R.C. 414¼	F.M.E. Parry Unity C.C. 404	—	—
S.H. Ferris Vegetarian C & A.C. 421	L. Hall Century R.C. 400	N.W. Tullett Kentish Wheelers 396¾		G.H.M. Pitt 383¼ 6th
R. Goodman Luton Wheelers C.C. 406⅞	F.N. Robertson Vegetarian C & A.C. 394½	L.S. Davies Viking R.C. 382½	—	G.H.M. Pitt 375⅞ 4th
L. Hall Century R.C. 420¾	N.W. Tullett Kentish Wheelers 416½	W.R.A. Howlett Cambridgeshire R.C. 414¾	A.G. Oxbrow Vegetarian C & A.C. 382⅛	F.H.M. Pitt 386½ 10th
L. Hall Century R.C. 418	A.W. Brumell Vegetarian C & A.C. 413½	F.M.E. Parry Unity C.C. 408⅝	G.S. Smith Southgate CC. 351⅜	G.H.M. Pitt 375¼
L. Hall Century R.C. 422⅛	P.F. Röhr Vegetarian C & A.C. 418⅛	F.N. Robertson Vegetarian C & A.C. 415¼	H.V. Rourke Liverpool Century R.C. 350½	A.B. Marsh 396½ 10th

1939 - 1944 No "24" during War

E.R. Wilkinson Luton Wheelers C.C. 390½	R.J. Haythorne Luton Wheelers C.C. 387⅜	B. Hudson Scala Wheelers 385	J. Spackman Century R.C. 349⅝	A.V. Lancaster 366¾ 8th
R.J. Haythorne Luton Wheelers C.C. 435	G.F. Ely Woolwich C.C. 431⅜	R.E. Finnemore North London C.C. 415⅝	A. Layzell Westerley R.C. 335¾	A.L. Wilkins 393½ 10th
G.H. Basham Wessex R.C. 443½	R. Goodman Luton Wheelers C.C. 432⅝	S.E. Harvey Addiscombe C.C. 431¼	S.W. Parker Ealing Paragon C.C. 368⅞	C.J. Sewell 383⅝

.T.T.C.
Championship)

G.H. Basham Wessex R.C. 454½	S.E. Harvey Addiscombe C.C. 442⅛	E.G. Guy Vegetarian C & A.C. 425⅝	C.E. Green N.R.C.C. 346⅝	E.J. Foot 387⅞
R.F. Mynott N.R.C.C. 447⅛	S.A. Argill Long Eaton C.C. 436⅝	M.C. Pain Luton Wheelers C.C. 431	C.E. Green N.R.C.C. 366⅛	A.L. Wilkins 382⅝
R.F. Mynott N.R.C.C. 459½	R.J. Haythorne Luton Wheelers C.C. 447⅝	E.S. Ellingham Luton Wheelers C.C. 434¼	C.A. Prior Ilford R.C. 408⅝	A.E. Blackman 430½ 5th

1951	A.E. Warden Rapier RC. 442⅜	T.W. Fensom Spalding C.C. 440¼	E.S. Ellingham Luton Wheelers C.C. 435½	W.D. Noble N.R.C.C. 396⅜	A.L. 411⅛
1952	E.J. Mundy Addiscombe C.C. 467m 595y	V. Callanan Norwood Paragon C.C. 459m 94y	G. Andrews Addiscombe C.C. 448m 878y	R.A. Ward Vegetarian C & A.C. 384	E.G. 411m
1953	S. Thompson Rutland C.C. 449¾	T.W. Fensom Spalding C.C. 445⅝	R.W. O'Dell Luton Wheelers C.C. 439	A.S. Fowler N.R.C.C. 392⅛	H.J. 380⅞
1954	S. Thompson Rutland C.C. 456⅝	A.E. Blackman N.R.C.C. 451¾	G. Fouldes Rutland C.C. 447⅜	A.E. Moggridge Shaftesbury C.C. 398	G.E. 429¾ 7th
1955	L. Fensom Holbeach Wheelers 463.047	N. Carline Monkton C.C. 453.693	T.W. Fensom Spalding C.C. 451.546	E.J. Smith Bedfordshire Roads C.C. 384.280	E.W. 408.3
1956	F.A. Burrell Middlesex R.C. 477.702	S. Thompson Rutland C.C. 467.684	J.A. Hanning Vegetarian C & A.C. 463.795	A.C. Stacey Hertfordshire Wheelers 366.347	K.E. 445.2 6th
1957	D.J. Keeler Vegetarian C & A.C. 478.703	J.A. Hanning Vegetarian C & A.C. 460.242	L. Fensom Spalding C.C. 454.263	W.A. Cliff Southgate C.C. 399.170	K.E. 426.9 10th
1958	D.J. Keeler Vegetarian C & A.C. 490.311	L. Fensom Spalding C.C. 471.370	J.A. Hanning Vegetarian C & A.C. 456.217	T.K. Kelly Yorkshire Century R.C. 414.035	J.A. 418.7
1959	C. Smith East Midlands C.C. 464.304	V.A. Stringer Bedfordshire Roads C.C. 451.757	J.A. Westcott Icknield R.C. 448.490	K. Usher Crouch Hill C.C. 423.226	A.E. 445.9 4th
1960	F.A. Burrell Middlesex R.C. 477.702	A.C. Harding Middlesex R.C. 474.728	L. Fensom Spalding C.C. 460.906	J.A. Lovell Kettering A.C.C. 396.365	K.E. 430.1
1961	C. Smith East Midlands C.C. 460.625	D.E. Mills South Ruislip C.C. 438.807	R. Randall Harlequins C.C. 436.210	H.S. Spelling Wren Wh. 395.833	E.W. 403.0
1962	J.F. Arnold Middleton R.C. 462.982	C. Smith East Midlands C.C. 461.429	V.J. Gibbs Luton Wheelers C.C. 438.041	A.C. Jones Hampshire R.C. 372.409	
1963	C. Smith East Midlands C.C. 454.693	E. Tremaine East Midlands C.C. 430.455	V.J. Gibbs Luton Wheelers C.C. 423.510	F.C. Brown Cambridge T & C.C.C. 414.017 (4th place)	A.J. 404.5 9th
1964	C. Smith East Midlands C.C. 473.688	F.A. Burrell Middlesex R.C. 472.774	G.M. Bettis Elite C.C. 463.573	H.S. Spelling Wren Wheelers 389.335	F.J. 423.0
1965	C. Smith East Midlands C.C. 469.343	J.A. Westcott Icknield R.C. 437.642	D.A. Porter Glendene C.C. 424.759	J.A. Lovell Kettering A.C.C. 368.294	F.J. 411.7 7th
1966	G.M. Bettis Elite C.C. 468.919	D.A. Porter Glendene C.C. 434.072	C.W. Hill Leicester Forest C.C. 429.959	H.S. Spelling Wren Wheelers 407.214	A.J. 426.4 5th

C. Smith East Midlands C.C. 481.920	S.A. Argill Beeston R.C. 458.896’	J. Baines Icknield R.C. 454.953	H.S. Spelling Wren Wheelers 399.480	A.J. King 434.443 5th
E.W. Matthews Alrincham C.C. 489.470	N. Carline Morley C.C. 481.518	M. Ward Leicestershire R.C. 479.095	M. Henigham Comet C.C. 410.416	R.W. Usher 435.417
C. Smith East Midlands C.C. 468.500	M.J. Judge Seamans C.C. 455.867	E. Lobley Lea Valley R.C. 428.665	G.T. Jenkins Hampshire R.C. 383.743	D.A. Porter 385.493
C. Smith East Midlands C.C. 459.226	T.A. Bush Bedfordshire Roads C.C. 438.745	C. Bruce Kentish Wheelers 433.716	R. Griffith Crawley Wheelers 368.866	P.S. Ryan 419.139 5th
C. Smith East Midlands C.C. 447.624	I.W.E. Hickman San Fairy Ann C.C. 439.766	R. Sewell N.R.C.C. 433.218	D.E. Keen Lea Valley R.C. 365.907	K.M. Lovett 427.088 5th
G.M. Bettis Bedfordshire Roads C.C. 470.526	W. Clayton Tyne R.C. 467.094	I.W.E. Hickman San Fairy Ann C.C. 464.021	E. Tremaine Leicestershire R.C. 457.895	K.M. Lovett 455.311 7th
G.M. Bettis Bedfordshire Roads C.C. 491.171	L.E. Lowe Speedwell B.C. 435.761	D.E. Mills Hillingdon C.C. 429.958	G.T. Jenkins Hampshire R.C. 416.536	R. Sewell 422.577 4th
C. Smith East Midlands C.C. 451.925	K.M. Lovett N.R.C.C. 448.796	R.W. O’Dell Luton Wheelers C.C. 421.734	—	—
G.L. Hart Luton Wheelers C.C. 452.142	C. Smith East Midlands C.C. 444.003	D. Cruse Maldon & D.C.C. 424.631	J.A. Lovell Kettering A.C.C. 332.837	D.A. Porter 350.422

The Twenty-four was held as an open event except during the years 1897 to 1905 when it was restricted to North Road club members, and pacing was allowed until 1897. In 1895 and 1896 the event was held on Wood Green Track, in 1896 being for professionals. In 1920, 1924, 1928, 1936, and 1945 the competition for the Tricycle Trophy was incorporated and in 1948, 1952, 1956,, 1960, 1964, 1968 and 1972 the event included the R.T.T.C. National Championship.

Since 1934 the Bidlake Memorial Prize has been awarded to the North Roader achieving the greatest distance.

In 1974 in celebration of his 25th N.R. 24, organiser Sid Mottram increased the value of the first prize to £25 out of his special donation to the “24 Fund”.

The "Moxham Prize" for the best North Roader not having previously completed a 24 was initiated in 1937 by S.H. Moxham and continued as a memorial to him.

Winners have been:-

Year		Mileage
1937	H. Paige	361½
1938	E.W. Haldane	374½
1945	A.V. Lancaster	366¾
1946	A.L. Wilkins	393½
1947	W.J. Medgett	382⅞
1949	R.F. Mynott	447⅛
1950	A.E. Blackman	430½
1951	W.B. Noble (tricycle)	396⅝
1953	A.S. Fowler (tricycle)	392⅛
1954	G.E. Edwards	429¾
1958	J.A. White	418.711
1959	A. J. King	390.844
1970	R.D. Cook	389.343
1971	R. Sewell	433.218

In 1948, 1952, 1955/7 1960/9 and 1972/5 there were no qualifying rides.

Event Secretaries (from 1886 to 1894 and 1897 to 1924 the twentyfour organiser was the Club's General Secretary)

1886	E.E. Bernard	1920	A. Inwood
1887	C.W. Newton	1921/3	C. Jay Cole
1888 (both events)	W.F. Allvey	1924	C. Jay Cole and F.E. Armond
		1925/9	F.E. Armond
1889/91	F.T. Bidlake	1930/4	A.B. Smith
1892/3	E. Rivers-Smith	1935	L.C. Cockerill
1894	P. Rivers-Smith	1936	F.E. Armond
1895/6	F. Ormseby Cook	1937	E.J. Foot
1897	W. Ward	1938/9	E.G. Bullen
1900/1	A. Gould	1945/6	C. Lynn
1902	J.H. Wingrave	1947	C.H. Paget, W.C.Frankum and C. Lynn
1903/6	J.E. Naylor		
1907/13	A. Inwood	1948/9	C.H. Paget
1919	A.W. Hellis	1950/76	S.A. Mottram

The award of silver medals to the club team of three aggregating the greatest mileage was introduced in 1930.

1930	N.R.C.C. (Pitt, Robinson, Madeox	1165¾
1931/3	No team finished.	
1934	Unity C.C. (Mence, F. Parry, Davies)	1017½
1935	. . . " . . . (Davies, F. Parry, Mence)	1085⅞
1936	. . . " . . . (Mence, Davies, Davis)	1167½
1937	. . . " . . . (F. Parry; Mence; L. Parry)	1191½
1938	Vegetarian C. & A.C. (Röhr, Robertson, Oxford)	1224
1945	N.R.C.C. (Lancaster, Green (tricycle), Foot)	1030
1946	Luton Wh. C.C. (Haythorne, Ellingham, Pain)	1237
1947	. . " . . (Goodman, Ellingham, Walker)	1283½
1948	. . " . . (Valentine, Haythorne, Goodman)	1252⅞
1949	Century R.C. (Robinson, Budge, Taylor)	1232⅞
1950	N.R.C.C. (Mynott, Blackman, Wilkins)	1299½
1951	Luton Wh. C.C. (Ellingham, Pain, Palmer)	1254⅛
1952	Addiscombe C.C. (Mundy, Andrews, Harvey)	1361⅞
1953	N.R.C.C. (Fowler (tri.), Bridge, Stott (tri.)	1151¼
1954	N.R.C.C. (Blackman, Edwards, Davis)	1304½
1955	Luton Wh. C.C. (Palmer, Haythorne, Forde)	1294.184
1956	Rutland C.C. (Thompson, Coukham, Fouldes)	1365.069
1957	Luton Wh. C.C. (O'Dell, Palmer, Ford)	1292.622
1958	Vegetarian C. & A.C. (Keeler, Hanning, Perryman)	1362.704
1959	N.R.C.C. (Blackman, Haldane, King)	1240.475
1960	Middlesex R.C. (Burrell, Harding, Poole)	1407.236
1961	Harlequins C.C. (R. Randall, L. Randall, Holton)	1234.086
1962	Hampshire R.C. (Davies, Searle, Culverwell)	1137.039
1963	East Midlands C.C. (Smith, E. Tremaine, C. Tremaine)	1295.095
1964	Mid. Shropshire Wh. (Hughes, France, Page)	1296.103
1965	No team finished	
1966	Leicester Forest C.C. (Hill, Buswell, Ellway)	1209.378
1967	N.R.C.C. (King, Summerlin, Davis)	1189.485
1968	Leicestershire R.C. (Ward, Tremaine, Cotteril)	1380.753
1969	Hampshire R.C. (Davies, Taylor, Jenkins)	1188.191
1970	N.R.C.C. (Ryan, Summerlin, Cook)	1209.831
1971	N.R.C.C. (Sewell, Lovett, Hartley)	1269.895
1972	Tyne R.C. (W. Clayton, Robertson, D. Clayton)	1384.898
1973	Fenland Clarion C.C. (Clarke, Airey, Glover)	1138.631
1974	Colchester Rovers C.C. (King, Wadley, Britten)	1090.301
1975	Maldon & D.C.C. (D. Cruse, R.Cruse, Yuill)	1211.849

CHAPTER IV

Other North Road Open Events.

Not least of the aims of the founder of the North Road Cycling Club was the promotion of road events open, by invitation, to members of other clubs and to riders of any type or make of machine. Thus the development of road sport would be taken out of the field of sales promotion and become the responsibility of the men who wished to participate or to see the sport prosper independently of the cycle makers.

However, in those years there was not an anti-advertising clause in the rules governing cycle racing — and the racing rules of the National Cyclists' Union were invoked by the North Road Club to govern the events it promoted in the early years — so press reports normally coupled a rider's name with that of the machine he had ridden.

Since the first events promoted in 1886, except for the years at the end of the nineteenth century, when road sport was in abeyance, and for the period of the first World War, the North Road Club has promoted open events in each year. The 'Twenty-four' story has been outlined in the previous chapter: something of the stories of the other events is recorded in this chapter.

12 Hours.

The Open Twelve Hours event has the shortest history of any of the North Road Open promotions. It was our first contribution to road sport in the Second World War when, in 1940, no other club or association attempted to run an open event at twelve hours. It was largely organised from Eric Foot's air raid shelter in the garden of his North London home, in the midst of the initial efforts of the German air force to bomb Britain into such a state that invasion would appear likely to be successful. The 'Twelve' took place on September 1st when competitors and helpers, particularly from the London area, were weary from air raid disturbed nights. Nevertheless few, if any, mishaps affected the organisation, and gaps — due to enforced absence — being covered before the riders reached the point involved. Foot was also responsible for our 1941 Open 'Twelve', again managing to get together sufficient materials for food and drinks, helpers to dispense these, as well as marshals and checkers round the course. The furthermost points from headquarters — 'Fullers' at Girtford Bridge — were milestone 'Thrapston 2' on the road from Huntingdon, Wansford on the North Road and Cambridge, where Colbon and his clubmates rendered similar service, if for a shorter period, to that given in the twenty-fours. In 1941 100 riders were listed on the start card, an increase of forty-two on the previous year.

Cecil Paget Junior became responsible for our two open events in 1942, organising them from his home in Eaton Socon. He was impressed by an innovation in twelve-hours finishing arrangements tried in a Manchester Time Trials Association event in 1941; instead of each competitor having a following rider over the final miles, with the duty of stopping the competitor on the completion of his twelve hours, a circuit of roads of about twelve miles became the course from about 200 miles: timekeepers with synchronised watches were placed at intervals of two miles and competitors continued until stopped by a timekeeper after completing the twelve hours stint: mileage was calculated on the basis of speed between timekeepers. So in 1942 Cecil went to the Manchester event to see how the scheme worked and to discuss it with local officials — one in particular, T.M. Barlow, was very helpful and thirty years later (in his eighties) was still giving the time trials game devoted service as National Competitions and Records Secretary of the Road Time Trials Council. Liking what he saw and heard Cecil Paget persuaded the Club and then the North London District Council of the R.T.T.C. to adopt the system for our 1943 Open Twelve and a circuit was devised linking the Girtford — Bedford and Shefford — Girtford roads. In 1942 sixty entries were received, for 1943 there were two less but a Tricycle Association event was run in conjunction with the North Road Open and had twelve riders.

W.R. Kitching of Yorkshire provided the excitement in the first three of these twelve hours events. In 1940 he disappeared mysteriously in the last hour, when comfortably in the lead: eventually it was found that he had been 'swept up' by an Army car crossing the Shefford — Girtford road by the 'Warden Lane'! Fortunately Kitching was not seriously hurt and his mileage to the collision spot gave him sixth place behind J. Ivory, Comet C.C., whose 233½ miles was two and one eighth better than Eld of Leicester Forest C.C. and another two more than Densley of Redmon C.C. In 1941 Kitching, again when comfortably in the lead, became depressed or distressed and stopped. However, after twenty-five minutes he recovered, resumed and won with one and one eighth miles less than the 1940 winner — who was fifth in 1941, behind Doody (Leamington C.C.) 228⅛, Baker (Addiscombe C.C.) 227⅛ and R. Finnemore (North London C.C.) 224⅞ — the last later proving himself a good twenty-four man but before the opportunity came for that he was one of three non—starters in 1942, having been sent overseas on official service a few days prior to the twelve. In 1942 Kitching was closely pressed for many hours by Griffin of Verulam C.C. but their final mileages were 233¾ and 229⅞, Baker again being third with ¼ mile more than in 1941. This year the R.T.T.C. District Council ruled that leading riders should be 'run out' by tandem pairs — so timekeeper Robinson, steered by the author on Frank Armond's tandem, followed Griffin and Kitching, in turn, over their final miles. This ruling was, of course, linked to the lack of petrol for motor vehicles at this period.

Kitching joined the North Road Club after the 1942 twelve but in 1943 he fell under the spell of the revival of massed start road racing and the British League of Racing Cyclists formed to govern this sport — a body 'outlawed' by the existing cycle sport governing authorities — so Kitching made himself ineligible for R.T.T.C. time trials and also resigned from the Club — he has recently rejoined, without, we imagine, envisaging a return to competitive cycling! Thus he was not in our 1943 twelve which was won by J.E. Witcomb of Twickenham C.C., his 229⅞ miles being four and five eighths better than D.R. Jackson of Altrincham Ravens: two Oak C.C. men were next — R. Filsell, 223⅜ and G. Griffin 222. E.R. Wilkinson (Luton Wh.), who was to win the first post war twenty-four, was sixth in this twelve. The tricycle event was won with 202¼ miles by Mullner of South Western R.C. — one C.E. Green of Yorkshire Century was fifth tricyclist with 187¾ miles; later — despite his home being in the Lake District — he became a North Roader and focal point for a growth of N.R. membership in the northern counties.

In 1944 the date of the Open Twelve was 20 July, with Paget as secretary again, but prior to that date the Germans launched their flying bomb attack on London. Many women and children were evacuated to Bedfordshire and filled the accomodation in Biggleswade, Sandy, etc. normally available for riders and helpers — and the food Mrs. Ewing of 'Fullers' at Girtford would have saved for the Twelve went to the evacuees. So the Twelve was cancelled — and for 1945 the Club's programme of Open promotions envisaged revivals of the Memorial Fifty miles and the Twenty-four.

Team medals were awarded each year to the three riders aggregating the highest mileage for their club: the winning clubs were — 1940 Wyndham R.C., 1941 Addiscombe C.C. (despite Kitching's ride Yorkshire R.C. were five and a quarter miles in arrears), 1942 Oak C.C. and 1943 Altrincham Ravens. Best North Roaders in the four years were — 1940 C.J. Sewell, twenty-fifth with 201⅞; 1941 and 1942 L.E. Copping, twelfth each year with 216⅝ and 214½. In 1943 Copping broke a crank when lying third and lost much time — his tandem partner J.M. Sloper came fifteenth with 206⅜ miles.

With, eventually, some fifty-five of our members serving in the Armed

Forces, others on Civil Defence duties and yet others whose work caused their evacuation from the London area, it was no mean achievement to have promoted these wartime twelve hours events. We are indebted to the many members of other clubs (including T.M. Barlow in 1943!) whose assistance made the four events possible.

100 miles.

Going back to 1886, the second open event promoted by the North Roaders was at 100 miles on August 28 and, again, the first event at the distance open to riders of any type of machine. The course started at the forty-seventh milestone from London on the Hitchin — Bedford road, ran south to Henlow, thence through Biggleswade and north along the North Road to the eighty-eighth milestone and back to the forty-sixth near Biggleswade: this remained the basis for courses for successive 100's, variations — which also came into twenty-four courses many years later — were a detour from Cross Hall through Kimbolton in the 1889 'hundred' and a double use of the Norman Cross, Kate's Cabin, Peterborough, Norman Cross triangle in the 100 of 1888.

For the early 100's gold medals were offered to the first on bicycle and the first on tricycle and, in 1886, the first tandem pair: subsequently the tandem award was reduced to silver medals and a minimum number of riders on each type of machine was stipulated. Medals were also offered to all within specified times and in 1886 the bicycle silver standard was fixed at 6h. 39m. 5s., that being the fastest 100 so far achieved: tandemons had to be inside 6h. 45m. and tricyclists 7h. 35m. Bronze medals were offered for 7.30, 7.45 and 8.30 respectively. These times were relaxed in 1887 to 6.45, 7.15 and 7.45 for silvers and the bronze tandem figures to eight hours. But in both these years the winner — E. Hale, Gainsboro' C.C. and Ripley C.C., and holder of the record — failed to reach the silver standard, doing 7h. 3m. 44s. in 1886 and 6h. 46m. 7s. in 1887, on both occasions riding a 'Premier Safety'— vide press reports and subsequent advertisements. In 1886 Adams and Astbury, on a tandem tricycle, were second in 7h. 20m. 5s. and G. Smith, on a 'Rover' safety third in 7h. 30m. 6s., followed by Anfielder A. Fletcher on an Albone safety and R. McCormack on an ordinary in 7h. 47m. 24s. and 7h. 49m. 11s. — these two, due to the lack of a marshal — or a signpost at the fork atop Alconbury, kept left in error and returned through Huntingdon — a somewhat hillier route: S. Lee appears to have been the best tricyclist in 8h. 29m. 48s. There was some criticism of the checking arrangements, which entailed the signing of cards at half a dozen points Dan Albone complained about the behaviour of some riders in

Biggleswade after the race — only the ebullience of youthful athletes, but still annoying.

A tandem tricycle pair — North Roaders C.W. Brown and G.R. White on a 'Marlboro' Club'— were second in 1887, taking 7h. 6m. 50s., while G.P. Mills was fastest tricyclist in 7h. 46m. 33s. It was reported that Brown and White did not stop for food until seventy miles — and that Hale tucked into the food for twelve minutes at Norman Cross! H. Crooke's 7h. 9m. 59s. on an ordinary was record, as were Mills' and the Brown—White figures — S.F. Edge, on a safety beat Crooke by two yards in the sprint for the line. Edge — then an Anerley B.C. man — was first in 1888, when the entry rose to fifty-four (of whom forty-six started) his 6h. 33m. 11s. being the second best 100 miles time so far, while Godfrey White achieved a double record, riding through non-stop and in ordinary record time of 6h. 48m. 14s. — third in the race. Chater Lea, also then a North Roader, was second in 6h. 41m. 55s. on a safety while North Roader R. Tingey was the best tricyclist in 7h. 21m. 21s., beating Goulding (also N.R.) by eighty-two seconds. White's achievement was aided by a change in checking arrangements — cards being issued to the riders at the start to be handed to the checkers en route.

The 1889 '100' attracted sixty-seven entries but seventeen of these, regarded as being from undesirable riders, were politely declined and thirteen of the remainder did not start, in part due to the bad weather — maybe this also resulted in the bicycle riders not really trying. The tricycling bunch having been started first, the tandemons, the ordinaryists and safety riders following at intervals of five minutes: on this occasion tricyclists Goulding and Crosbie were never caught and were seventh and eighth in 7h. 9m. 55s. and 57s. Three seconds covered the first three — P.C. Wilson (Bath R.C.) and Hale being beaten in the final sprint by Edge — 6h. 55m. 7s. A.F. Ilsley was best North Road bicyclist — fifth in 7h. 5m. 23s., two seconds better than clubmate J.G.H. Browne: best on ordinary was Geddes of Catford C.C. — ninth in 7h. 11m. 31s.

As often on our 100 day, 1890's was one of strong southerly wind and as the first forty-five miles were northerly seven men beat the fifty miles record, P.C. Wilson being a yard ahead of E. Dangerfield (both Bath R.C.) and Wilson's 2h. 32m.35s. was hall-marked by the Road Records Association. Dangerfield, who started the journal *Cycling* the following year, won the 100 in 6h. 10m. 47s. (G.P. Mills was one of his pacers) nearly eighteen minutes ahead of A.F. Ilsley, whose elder brother R.J. was the best ordinary rider in 7h. 26m. 30s. and fifth in the race, sixth and best tricyclist being Bidlake in 7h. 35m. 27s., gaining three minutes on W. Ward in the last one and a half miles. The Bath Roaders promoted their first Open 100 — on a North Road course — in 1891 and it was won by

'Bath Road' Smith, sprinting Edge, forty-nine seconds inside six hours — but not record: Bath Roaders Walsh and Nesbitt, however, took the ordinary record in an agreed tie in 6h. 19m. 6s. but the course was found to be short. Walsh won the North Road 100, on his ordinary, some three weeks later in 6h. 22m. 15s. from Edge (now Surrey B.C.) whose 6h. 27m. 37s. was two seconds better than Anfielder R.H. Carlisle: J. Rowley sprinted ahead of fellow North Roaders W. Butterfield and W. Crosbie for the tricycle gold medal — this on a very hot day when, despite vinegar on the head and flap-backed headgear, many retired. Tandemons were not among the leaders that year but the Ilsley brothers changed this in 1892 when their 6h. 10m. 37s., having chosen the right moment to get away, was nearly twenty-seven minutes better than Edge's time, Flanders (N.R.) being third in 6h. 43m. 37s. — there were only twenty entries of whom seventeen were started by Bidlake, deputising for A.J. Wilson.

A sealed handicap for North Roaders was introduced in 1893 and helped to increase the entry to near fifty again, but overnight rain soaked the roads making for heavy going and a number of notabilities did not start; others found the North Roaders 'Club Cottage' at Eaton Socon difficult to pass! However with the roads improving four North Roaders sprinted for the finish, W.O. Kirby getting in first in 5h. 56m. 13s., Pellant, Earl and Briggs being seven to twelve seconds slower — and only nine others finished.

The 1894 100 date was August 25 but after the fateful July Club Fifty it was first postponed and after the experience with the twenty-four, the 100 was abandoned. And, with the twenty-four and various club events, the 1895 100 was run on the track — the Catford track being used for the 100 — and was won by Bath-Roader Frost, who got inside British record at fifty-four miles, his 3h. 55m. 47s. being nearly ten minutes inside the 100 record within four minutes of world record. North Roaders F.R. Goodwin and A.F. Ilsley were second and third some ten minutes slower: only 1000 or so spectators saw the start but the crowd increased as the race proceeded.

And that was the last North Road Open 100 until 1912, by which time most main roads had been given tar bound waterproof surfaces — though Alconbury Hill, for example, remained but waterbound and increasingly rough for another decade. By 1912, to counter the spread of the 'maker's amateur' type of rider, who had concerned the Club in 1906 when the twenty-four became an open event again, a number of clubs, including North Road, North London and Unity had introduced an 'anti-advertising' clause to event entry forms, the wording being attributed to Bidlake. In 1912, however, the Bath Road Club had not introduced this clause and the Anfielders only a modified version which resulted in certain riders of dubious amateur status being in their Whit Monday 100. The North

Roaders who had entered, withdrew and for a similar reason invitations for the Olympic road race were declined. The 1912 club 100 was moved to August Bank Holiday and invitations issued to other clubs subscribing to the anti-advertising clause: these were Crouch Hill and North London (but they had already arranged an inter-club event), Century, Kingsdale, Leicestershire, Northampton Institute, and Unity: with eight North Roaders this gave a field of thirty-five, but it was yet again a bad day for the North Road courses — south-westerly gales, heavy showers and a 9 a.m. start gave time for the wind to strengthen! There were three non-starters and fifteen were eliminated by punctures and/or the weather, including North Roaders Frank Wingrave and Jack Webb, both on scratch with Bennett of Unity who was fastest in 5h. 34m. 52s. — ten minutes eighteen seconds faster than North Road violinist Lempriere, the only other inside five hours fifty minutes.

The anti-advertising clause was fully adopted by all clubs promoting open events in 1913 and provisional arrangements again to promote the North Road 100 as an invitation event on August Bank Holiday were abandoned. But early in 1914, after discussion of the idea at the A.G.M., the Committee decided to restart the Open 100 as an invitation handicap event, incorporating the club 100, invitations to other clubs' members being limited to those not slower than five hours forty minutes — hoping that this limit might later be reduced to five hours thirty minutes: and a permanent trophy was to be purchased, to be held by the fastest rider — a fund being opened for this purpose. The first of this envisaged series was on Saturday, 4 July 1914 — not a very good day — with forty-one on the start card, but the Unity men stood down to attend the funeral of their President — Edmund Payne, the actor. H.H. Gayler, Polytechnic C.C. was fastest in 4h. 58m. 25s., having been fastest in the Anfield's Whitmonday 100 and the first inside five hours in the unpaced series of that event — as Kensal Rise C.C. he had been seventh in our twenty-four a few years earlier. H.W. Henry (North London) was second — 5h. 0m. 5s. — and W.A. George (Etna) third in 5h. 3m. 42s: only fourteen completed the 100 and but one of these a North Roader — Norman in 5h. 19m. 41s. When the first war-time North Road Dinner was held Gayler was already in the forces and unable to collect the shapely gilt cup — a replica of one owned by the then future King George VI — and, alas, Gayler was killed during the War: afterwards his club initiated an Open twelve Hours event in Gayler's memory.

It was seven years before the new cup was again up for competition, Century R.C. being then invited to send six men to compete in our 1921 '100', when the North Road entry was also, by chance, six. Yet another hard day resulted in only two Centurions and four North Roaders finishing, Rossiter taking the cup with his 5h. 29m. 38s. — a second short of three minutes faster than F.G. Thomas, now a North Roader. After a further five years the invitation 100 was resumed but only received twenty entries including six North Roaders: only fourteen started and one of these dropped out to minimise Harbour's misfortune in puncturing — Durst of Marlboro A.C. swopped bicycles with the Bath Roader who achieved an excellent 4h. 47m. 55s. Vegetarian Stan Baron was second in 5h. 4m. 56s. followed by Unity's young Densley — 5h. 7m. 13s. and their veteran Keen — 5h. 12m. 21s. Baron was then assistant editor of *Cycling* but later became 'open air' columnist of the *News Chronicle* and, in the 1940s achieved fame as a war correspondent. Punctures were rife and I suffered one due to a misunderstanding with a helper handing up a drink in a 'stone ginger beer' bottle, then the normal container: the bottle fragmented on hitting the road and a splinter stuck in my back tyre — I was fifth in 5h. 17m. 8s. Some years later metal bottles were made which riders carried in cages on their bicycles: such bottles were then used for handing up drinks, later being replaced by plastic bottles.

In 1927 the 100 was moved from June to a late September Saturday and attracted forty-three visitors and six members. The course was similar to that for the paced events except that the start was near Biggleswade and after the short run to Girtford, sharp left and south by Shefford to near Hitchin, then north for forty-five miles to Water Newton, back to Norman Cross, a short leg towards Peterborough before returning along the North Road to finish north of 'Muck Junction' on the Cambridge to Oxford railway north of Sandy. A similar entry was received in 1928 and a few more in 1929, topping fifty. This year organiser Frank Armond had particular difficulty in getting sufficient helpers out on the Saturday morning — most people still worked at least five and a half days in the week and had to make special requests to be away from work. After deep debate the 1930 '100' was changed to a Sunday event and the entry rose to the maximum permitted 100 — probably this was also related to the start of the *Cycling* Best All Rounder competition (for the best average speed over fifty and 100 miles and twelve hours) — despite which there were twenty-two non-starters, including such notables as Marshall, J.J. Salt and Bloodworth. About this time Bidlake evolved a theory that, as a team was not complete until its slowest member had finished, the medals should be awarded to the team with the best placed third man rather than to the team aggregating the fastest time — and this system was applied to the 1931 '100': the 'Bidlake system' was not widely adopted but a few clubs still apply it today, over forty years later. Bidlake was otherwise engaged in 1931 (he timed but a few of this series of 100's) and Anfield President W.P. Cook timed for us — and was 'supported' by the fast Anfield team of the time — Orrell, Pitchford and Salt. In 1933 it was decided to move from the late September/early

October date to July but when the Road Racing Council's calendar of events appeared it was found that by some mischance we clashed with another event on a North Road course — the Luton Wheelers twelve hours. We moved to the equivalent of an early Whitsunday — 21 May — while the Lutonians intimated a willingness to change if we felt unable to do so. Our entry dropped to forty but included most of the best 100 milers and we had the unusual distinction of providing an occasion on which the great Norwood Paragon rider, Frank Southall, was beaten.

In 1934 we got 3 June and the entry increased to seventy. In response to the expressed views of the police — in recent years they had assisted us in controlling crowds at finishes — we moved the finish of both the 100 and the Memorial fifty off the main road by turning competitors left in Tempsford, along the Everton Lane, beautifully tree-lined and sheltered. The entry dropped to fifty-one in 1935 and towards the end of the year the Committee decided to discontinue the Invitation 100, using the money so saved to help with the finances of the Club's Gazette.

The Vegetarians dominated a number of these events, particularly 1927/8/9when C. Marshall took the cup each year with times of 5h. 1m. 10s., 4h. 50m. 18s. and 5h. 1m. 21s., the first and last being on days of southerly gales. Even when we got a northerly in 1928 it was strong enough to make the forty-five miles from Hitchin to Water Newton a hard slog. In 1927 P.C. Corke (Belle Vue) was second in 5h. 5m. 47s. and North Roaders Jack Middleton and Bill Ellis third and fourth — 5h. 6m. 9s. and 5h. 9m. 28s. — with fifth man nearly five minutes slower, and this but two weeks after Ellis had scored his first win in the Twenty-four. 1928 saw a great battle between Marshall, his clubmate Cave (who had won the Bath Road 100 seven weeks earlier) and Middleton until Jack punctured at twenty-five miles. Thereafter, although twenty minutes apart on the road Marshall and Cave remained within seconds of each other in elapsed time and alternating in the lead, Marshall pushing a high (for those years) fixed gear of eighty-seven while Cave persuaded an eighty-one along and finished thirty-two seconds slower. Middleton was third fifty-seven seconds outside five hours and J.J. Salt (then Liverpool Century) fourth in 5h. 3m. 18s. North Roader Bullen did a notable first 100 of 5h. 8m. 57s., forty-eight seconds faster than Ellis — despite which A.J. Brumell's 5h. 11m. 2s. gave the Vegetarians the better aggregate and the team medals. In 1929 there were many punctures to add to the difficulties, Marshall being among the victims but soon recovered the lead. Cave, on the other hand, was depressed by his punctures and slowed to near five hours twelve minutes — behind W. Holland (Midland C. & A.C.), Harris (Glendene), Brooke (Gomersal) and Doubleday (Catford). Tenth fastest A.W. Brumell (brother of A.J.) gave the Vegetarians the team medals again — on aggregate.

Marshall failing to start and Frost (Allondon R.C.) being elimiated by punctures in 1930 ended an anticipated battle between these two and Southall won, although slowed by the gale to 4h. 55m. 4s., second being A.W. Brumell in 5h. 1m. 19s. then Doubleday — 5h. 3m. 21s., A.W. Saunders (Marlboro A.C.) — 5h. 6m. 20s. and Lauterwasser (Finsbury Park) — 5h. 7m. 4s. R.R.A. President to be, A.H. Glass achieved a fine tricycle ride, despite some eleven minutes delay with punctures and mechanical trouble, doing 5h. 21m. 18s. to take the gold medal offered in this 100 for the fastest tricyclist — a reversion to the practice in the original events. Entries on either type of single machine were now acceptable but not from tandem pairs. Marshall again failed to start in 1931 when, unusually, we had a good day but there was a crop of punctures, winner C. Holland (M.C. & A.C. and younger brother of W.) finishing on a borrowed fully laden clubman's machine but retaining the lead taken at about half way — 4h. 43m. 15s. to 4h. 44m. 55s. by W. Marsh (University C.C. and younger brother of the Dave who won the first Memorial Fifty) while Cave was third in 4h. 46m. 46s. and F. Turner (Cheshire R.C. — and in the Memorial Fifty earlier in the year) fourth — 4h. 49m. 5s. fellow northerner Pitchford was the best Anfielder — sixth in 4h. 52m. 39s., while S.H. Ferris (later to achieve fame in our twenty-four) was the fastest third team man — twelfth in 4h. 55m. 26s., twenty-eight seconds behind A.W. Brumell, giving the Vegetarians the team medals: Salt was the third Anfielder, after leading to nearly half way, sixteenth in 4h. 56m. 58s. Non-starters and punctures eliminated a number of leading 100 milers in 1932, including Southall, who was leading at fifty miles, and a new North Roader, W. Harrison. C. Holland only took the lead after seventy miles yet his time was 4h. 45m. 15s. to A.W. Brumell's 4h. 51m. 1s. and 4h. 52m. 0s. by P.T. Stallard of Wolverhampton Wheelers, who, a decade later, became a leader in the re-introduction of massed start racing on British roads. The hardness of the day is proved by only six getting inside five hours, the last of them being W. Marsh: ten seconds outside was Jack Middleton, now in the M.C. & A.C. with his brothers, Coventry being their home. Despite these two M.C. & A.C. rides the Upton Manor club took the team medals, their fastest third man being fifteenth to Sid Middleton's nineteenth place.

In 1933 Saunders won in 4h. 40m. 43s. to Southall's 4h. 41m. 6s., Lipscombe (Ingleside) being third in 4h. 42m. 25s. and Harrison gave North Road fourth place with his personal best 4h. 44m. 5s., fourteen seconds better than twenty-four hours winner Ferris, closely followed by three other Vegetarians — Phillips, Brumell and Cave, ensuring the team medals again under either system. Ninth in 4h. 54m. 49s. was Seeley of the Calleva and of the then amazing 444 miles in the Catford twenty-four: Sixteenth man did exactly five hours — and I brought club tricycle record down to 5h. 22m. 1s. — the weather was kind this year. It reverted to make the 1934 '100' the usual tough ride and fastest time slipped back to 4h. 49m. 58s. by Southall's clubmate and tandem partner S.M. Butler, H.J. Wheatley (Kent R.C.) doing 4h. 51m. 4s. with Jack Middleton four minutes slower after stops to pump up a sagging tyre: he was followed by Ferris — 4h. 56m. 15s. and Dougherty (Rugby R.C.C. and Memorial Fifty winner) — 4h. 56m. 34s. H. Jackson of Wolverhampton was the only other inside five hours and Norwood Paragon won the team medals — we had reverted to aggregate times but they would have won on the Bidlake System. Despite another bad day E.J. Capell (Allondon — and Best All Rounder to be) brought our event record down to 4h. 38m. 10s. in 1935, also in 1935 K.H. Mosedale (Calleva and to be the first inside four and a half hours — a Bath Road 100 win) was second in 4h. 40m. 2s. Another Allondon man, later a North Roader, D.G. McCarthy was third in 4h. 46m. 42s. — seven seconds faster than Seeley, while Eric Wilkinson, winner of our 1945 twenty-four and its timekeeper since 1950 was sixth, his 4h. 50m. 11s. being nearly two minutes slower than Nash of Cheltenham. Three others were inside five hours — Vegetarian Shillibeer, Jack and Sid Middleton while Vahey was third man of the Calleva team, giving them the medals in this last of our Open 100's.

However, two years later we invited our local coevals, the Kingsdale, North London and Unity clubs to join us in an Inter Club 100 which achieved a field of fifty. Unity supplied twenty of the riders and, by a considerable margin, the winning team of four led by C.W. Hiller, taking the Invitation Cup with 4h. 43m. 24s., and his clubmates being second, fourth and sixth. North London team was second and, despite all their riders being outside five hours, Kingsdale third while I was fastest North Roader — 4h. 59m. 36s. after puncturing. Kingsdale and North London each had eight riders — the Kingsdalers postponing their Club Twelve hours event to participate — and fourteen North Roaders entered. A similar event was held in mid-August 1938, when the North Road team, possibly helped by Unity leader Clark puncturing, was victorious. Alf Marsh, whose father and grandfather had been North Roaders, took both the Invitation and Club 100 Cups in 4h. 57m. 36s., by eight seconds from Les Couzens, Clark being third in 4h. 59m. 14s: Marsh was seven minutes down at thirty-nine miles but reduced his deficit to two minutes at seventy miles. Fateful 1939 saw this inter club event on August 20, two weeks before Britain entered the Second World War. Early in the year North London had told us they would be unable to field a team — to their and our regret. Unity won the team medals again but Ron Hawkins kept the Invitation Cup in North Road hands with 4h. 58m. 59s. — the only rider inside five hours. Alf Marsh, fifth in 5h. 12m. 6s., may not have recovered completely from his 407⅛ miles for second place in the Yorkshire Vegetarian twenty-four three weeks earlier and the last open twenty-four until 1945.

In 1940 we were completely routed in an interclub 100 with Finsbury Park C.C., their A. Edrupt winning in 4h. 53m. 46s., Spary being best North Roader, fifth in 5h. 9m. 40s: the teams had been reduced to three men and only eleven started. They did it again in 1941, only by a larger margin, their L. Murphy being fastest in 4h. 52m. 17s. while best North Roader was McCarthy, fourth, fifty-nine seconds outside five hours (a week earlier he had done 4h. 45m. in the Bath Road 100). The weather was filthy — wet and very windy — but of the sixteen entries (ten North Roaders) there were only two non-starters, our Sid Mottram being one, but five failed to finish — despite (or possibly because) the notorious (in twenty-fours) Biggleswade — Cambridge road being substituted for the North Road. A similar event was planned for 1942 but neither club could find sufficient 100 milers and an inter-club Fifty was substituted. The effects of call-up to the Forces had made it difficult to muster sufficient competitors or helpers for the individual clubs to run events so subsequently we combined with the Finsbury Park to overcome the difficulties without regarding the events as inter-club competitions.

As a result of a discussion initiated at the A.G.M. in January 1944, at the first subsequent committee meeting it was decided to offer our Invitation 100 Cup to the Road Time Trials Council for annual award to the winner of the National Twelve Hours championship being inaugurated that year, together with Championships at twenty-five, fifty and 100 miles: the twenty-four Hours Championship was not started until 1948. The offer was accepted and the cup, purchased in 1914 with members' donations, undoubtedly has a place of honour which would please those members.

An epilogue to the 100 story came in 1964 when Edmund Dangerfield's son Roland, on ending his link with '*Cycling*' returned to us, via a current staffman at our Annual Dinner, the gold medal awarded to his father for his win in the 1890 North Road 100 and presented to him at the 1890 Annual Dinner.

Hardriders' Twenty-Five Miles.

In the 1930s a new 'pipe opener' event was added to the time trial calendar — a February twenty-five miles ride on a hilly course in Surrey. In 1939 our coevals, Kingsdale C.C. brought this type of event to the country North of London, devising a course approximately twenty-five miles long (it was part of the spirit of these events to be light heartedly unconcerned, to a mile or so, about the distance) over the very hilly lanes between Potters Bar and

Hertford. The Kingsdalers were unable to continue running the event through the war years and Oak C.C. kept it going from 1941 to 1946, Kingsdale resuming responsibility in 1947. From 1950 to 1953 North Roaders had a number of successes initially led by Geoff Edwards who was third in 1950 and 1952 and second in 1951 and 1953 when Alan Blackman won the event in 1h. 13m. 38s: we were second in the team race in 1950 and won the team medals in the succeeding three years. But Kingsdale C.C. were, by then, having a difficult time and had to withdraw before the 1955 event, when North Road took on the organisation to keep the event going while other clubs considered the problem. Norion C.C. accepted responsibility from 1956 to 1958 but was unable to continue so the North Road took the event as a permanent addition to its annual programme. The original course was modified in 1950 and at some time subsequently was measured and found to be twenty-six and a half miles long. In addition to the 'sporting nature' of the course, the late February date brings the risk of bad weather, snow (giving point to the area being called Little Switzerland) making for slippery roads and anti-skid gritting adding puncture risks. In 1963 the amount of snow on these Hertfordshire hills necessitated cutting out one loop and the resulting shorter course was reflected in the winner's time — it is, incidentally, a scratch event, not imcorporating a handicap (other than the course and conditions!). When the event was started the lanes used carried very little traffic, particularly in the winter months. But as ownership of motor vehicles increased and all year round personal motoring became common, traffic hazards developed. After the 1967 event the course was revised to reduce the hazards and adjusted to an exact twenty-five miles. Organising secretary for the North Road series of these events have been Alan Fowler and Geof Edwards. Geof was also, for the initial four years (1967 onwards) co-ordinator for the G.H. Stancer Memorial Committee promotion of a National Ten Miles Championship for schoolboys, with regional heats from which the leaders go to a national final event.

In 1965, after consultation with other members of the erstwhile Thistle C.C., North Roader A.C. (Bert) Swan, on behalf of his Thistle clubmates, presented us with a fine perpetual trophy for the Hardriders' Twenty-Five, asking that it be called The Thistle Trophy.

Winners of the North Road Hardriders' Twenty-Five are:-

1955	R.W. Gosman, Barnet C.C.	1.19.37
1956	A.J. Howling, Castille R.C.	1.12.49
1960	T. Moore, Zeus R.C.	1. 8.53.
1961	J.Bumpas, Finsbury Park C.C.	1.12.14

1962	D.E. Meakins, Welwyn Wh.	1.12.35
1963	T. Nimmo, Letchworth Velo	1. 5.58
1964	S.O. Lovatt, Century R.C.	1.10.58
1965	B.P.McKeown, Welwyn Wh.	1. 9.19
1966	B.P. McKeown, Welwyn Wh.	1. 8.15
1967	B.Lapworth, C.C. Islington	1.10.28
1968	J. Winstanley, Finsbury Park C.C.	1. 8.33
1969	J. Winstanley, Finsbury Park C.C.	1. 9.57
1970	C. Kearley, Whitewebbs C.C.	1. 7. 4
1971	J. McMillan, West London Coureurs	1. 5.56
1972	J. McMillan, West London Coureurs	1. 5.33
1973	R. Cary, Whitewebbs C.C.	1. 9. 8
1974	D. Sheehy, Hainault R.C.	1. 9.39
1975	D. Poulter, Highgate C.C.	1.11.58

Fifty Miles.

Although, as described in Chapter II, the first open events promoted by the North Road Club was at fifty miles, in the ensuing years the Club's committee considered that sufficient (or even too many!) open events at fifty miles were being promoted on North Road courses and did not include an open or invitation fifty in the North Road Club programme for many years. Moreover the fifty miles races for club members were soon receiving entries of such size and quality as to make these events as interesting as many open events.

And after time trialling had replaced racing as our road sport the North Roaders were content to promote, initially, just the Invitation Twenty-four Hours. However in 1913 we ran an open Novices Fifty, in an endeavour to recruit members — our definition of a novice was a man not a member of a cycling club (other that the national Cyclists' Touring Club) — and we received ninety-five entries. The event was run on roads between Henlow and Buckden on a Saturday afternoon: entrants were advised to carry lamps! A similar event was offered in May 1914, attracting fifty-six entries and a third in June 1919, but this only gathered fifteen entries — possibly put off by the distance, but the principal road clubs, following the tradition established in paced racing, did not run events at less that fifty miles. While these events may have recruited some men to the sport and to other clubs, who did not cavill at being at the finishes with sweet words and application forms, very few joined the North Road Club — this may well have been the fault of the North Roaders. But ex-secretary Johnnie Naylor did interest one of the 1919 novices — Charles Cessford, — who has been a faithful and appreciated member ever since.

After the first World War, memorials to the men who died in it were erected in almost every village — on green or churchyard sites — and town and were established by many sporting and social bodies, cycling making its national memorial an obelisk at Meriden, one of the villages credited with being the centre of England. The North Roaders also wished to remember their eight clubmates who had died during the War and through 1919 in the club Gazette and at club gatherings the nature of such a memorial was keenly debated. Some strongly favoured a stone memorial beside 'our road', but Bidlake — by then established as our third President — argued that this could be costly, possibly presumptuous, and would be difficult to obtain permission for erection. He favoured an annual scratch fifty miles event limited to the best twelve men of each year, with a valuable cup to be held by the winner, this was coupled with Sangway's suggestion of a private Club plaque for display on Club occasions. The Committee adopted Bidlake's proposals as did the A.G.M. in 1920 — after a most interesting debate — and both an attractive cup and a silver model of Hadley Highstone were purchased, the latter with a plaque on its ebony base, carrying the names of our fallen — eight for 1914 — 1919, a further four being added after the 1939 — 1945 war. This model (the original is beside the North Road north of Barnet) stands in front of the chairman at North Road Annual Dinners. It is, perhaps, ironic that when the cycling world wished to remember Bidlake after his death in 1933, part of his memorial is a small walled garden in the junction between the road from Shefford and what was the North Road (it is now replaced by a dual carriageway east of the old road).

But the Memorial Fifty, inaugurated on Saturday, 10 July 1920, proved to be a fine series of events, rapidly building up a great reputation, and becoming one to which men aspired to be invited; some were decidedly annoyed not to be invited in a year during which their achievements, in their own opinion, merited that honour. In 1920 other clubs were invited to submit the names of members considered eligible, with supporting evidence and the twelve were selected from these. Thereafter, a number of North Road officials each kept a careful record of notable road rides, particularly at fifty miles, and on the evidence thus accumulated the best twelve, in the Committee's view, were chosen and invited. The choosing of the first half dozen was normally easy: thereafter selection became increasingly difficult as the number of places still to be filled lessened.

Maybe Bidlake was moved to suggest fifty miles because that was the distance of the first North Road open event: whether or not this was so, there was a reminder of the early history of road riding when a police officer in Eaton Socon stopped some of the riders in the first Memorial Fifty and held some so long for questioning and taking names and addresses that four

1931 MEMORIAL '50'

1st F.W. SOUTHALL

2nd F.G. FROST

3rd F.T. BROWN

4th G.W. JENKINS

retired from the race. That this interference should occur in an event limited to twelve and with intervals of three minutes in starting times was strange even though there had, just previously, been some unfortunate incidents thereabouts in Sunday morning events. Two Memorial Fifty riders were fined at the local magistrate's court, offering no defence on the advice of the North Road Club, which paid the fines. There were still comparatively few motor vehicles on the roads and their speed was much less — they were officially subject to a twenty miles per hour speed limit — so that cycling at just over twenty miles per hour appeared to be fast travel. For a couple of years, until the officious policeman was moved, courses were redesigned, as far as possible, to avoid Eaton Socon and when this road was used riders were advised to avoid the appearance of fast riding: riders used the tops of their dropped handlebars and some carried pipes in their pockets and pretended to smoke as they rode through the village!

In the early years the net spread wide and current winners in the Twenty-four Selbach and Rossiter were among the best twelve for the Memorial Fifty, but as the sport rapidly increased in popularity and men rode faster an element of specialisation developed and those who concentrated on the shorter distances dominated our selections. Through the years the majority of riders only received an invitation in one year — how transitory is high performance in some! But others dominated the cycling sporting scene for many years and none more than F.W. Southall of Norwood Paragon C.C. who, between 1925 and 1933 (after which he became a professional) was invited to ride in the Memorial Fifty on eight occasions. Spanning a slightly longer period — 1936-1946 — the Second World War reduced the number of invitations to E. Larkin (Monkton C.C. and Hemsworth Wh.) to five. Also invited on five occasions were D. Marsh (Shaftesbury C.C. then University C.C.) 1920-1924; F. Stott (Century R.C.) 1921-1924, 1926; L.J. Ross (East Liverpool Wheelers) 1931-1935; J.W. Brooke (Gomersal Open Road Club) received invitations in 1926 and from 1928 to 1932; and F.A. Lipscombe (Ingleside C.C. then Century R.C.) seven between 1930 and 1937. Recipients of four invitations were F. Greenwood (Midland C. & A.C.) 1921-2, 1924-5; A. Wilson (Hull Thursday C.C. then Yorkshire R.C.) 1922-1925; S.A. Artaud (Essex Roads C.C. then N.R.C.C.) 1923-4, 1926-7; W.B. Temme (Glendene C.C.) 1925-1928; F.G. Frost (Allondon R.C.) 1928 and 1930-1932; C. Holland (Midland C. & A.C.) 1930, 1932, 1934, 1935; H. James (Glamorgan R.C. then Vegetarian C. & A.C.) 1933-36; B.W. Bentley (Walton C. & A.C. - a Liverpool club) 1933-1935, and 1937, and E.V. Mills (Addiscombe C.C.) 1935-1938. Seventeen men were invited three times, ranging from L. Meredith (Bath R.C.) 1920, 1922, 1923 to G.H. Fleming (Belle Vue C.C.) 1937, 1938 and 1946 when he contributed to the ending of this outstanding series by being one of ten who either refused or ignored our invitation. Until 1938 this 'Fifty' was unique in memorial events, tantamount to a fifty miles championship: invitations extended to Scotland in 1924, and to Ireland in 1930. It also survived the initiation, by *'Cycling'* of the *'Best All Rounder'* competition in 1930, for which the limited field made it ineligible — although, for example, in 1935 C. Holland preferred to ride in an open twelve hours event hoping to improve his position in the 'B.A.R.'.

It is interesting to note the clubs represented through the years and three are outstanding for the long period they have had members on the start card and all three were represented in the first of the series in 1920; while not continuously represented thereafter Bath R.C. still had a member in the twelve in 1945, Century R.C. in 1937 and Midland C. & A.C. in 1936, the last on twelve occasions and three of the men, in different years were the brothers Walter, Charles and Alfred Holland! On one other occasion a pair of brothers — the Burrells of Upton Manor C.C. — were in the Fifty of 1929. Rarely, in any one year, did a club get more than one member invited but in 1921 both Century R.C. and Shaftesbury C.C. had three each, Century R.C. repeating this in 1922 and Monkton C.C. did it in 1936 when there were two other riders from that south west corner of Yorkshire.

Among the reasons for the demise of the event must be the break in the series during the Second World War, the introduction, by the Road Time Trials Council, in 1944 of a fifty miles National Championship but with a field leaving it eligible for the Best All Rounder competition, now taken over by the R.T.T.C. and arousing even greater interest. And, of course, the changing outlook of riders on their sport and pastime.

The winners of this series of Memorial Fifties were: 1920 and 1921 D. Marsh, Shaftesbury C.C., 2h. 22m. 52s. and 2h. 18m. 22s; 1922-1924 A. Wilson, Hull Thursday C.C. (then Yorkshire R.C.), 2h.18m.10s., 2h. 17m. 48s. and 2h. 19m. 5s; 1925 and 1926 W.B. Temme, Glendene C.C., 2h. 11m. 43s. and 2h. 12m. 16s; 1925 and 1931 F.W. Southall, Norwood Paragon C.C., 2h. 6m. 40s. and 2h. 8m. 5s; 1928 J. Lauterwasser, Finsbury Park C.C., 2h. 10m. 15s; 1929 and 1930 G.W. Jenkins, Hastings & St. Leonards C. & A.C., 2h. 11m. 9s. and 2h. 11m. 57s; 1932 and 1935 F.A. Lipscombe, Ingleside C.C. (then Century R.C.), 2h. 10m. 36s. and 2h. 7m. 42s; 1933 L.J. Ross, East Liverpool Wheelers, 2h. 7m. 20s; 1934 R. Dougherty, Rugby R.C.C., 2h. 13m. 55s; 1936 E.V. Mills, Addiscombe C.C., 2h. 6m. 58s; 1937 and 1938, H. Earnshaw, Monkton C.C., 2h. 9m. 18s. and 2h. 6m. 43s; 1945 R.J. Maitland, Solihull C.C., 2h. 4m. 21s. and 1946 A.E.G. Derbyshire, Calleva R.C., 2h. 6m. 5s.

For the first six years the event started near Shefford and the course included secondary road detours off the North Road. In 1926 a near absolute out and home course, all on the North Road, was used and in 1927 the event was moved from Saturday afternoon to early Sunday morning — which had become the time and day for the majority of road time trials. The event had a mid July date until 1933 when July became considered too early to select the best twelve fifty milers and a late September or early October date was adopted. This, however, had its disadvantages — with the ever increasing number of events offered and the number of times competitors rode, some had had enough by this late date and, for the still active there were clashes with late qualifying events for the B.A.R. The 1927 and 1928 events were particularly notable for North Roaders — their clubmates Stan Artaud and Jack Middleton were among the twelve in 1927 finishing third and sixth and Jack again in 1928 when he was seventh. And there was, of course, the growing pride in bringing such notable riders into competition with each other year by year.

During the Second World War we endeavoured to contribute to the continuing road sport by promoting an Open Fifty Miles Handicap event, as well as that at twelve hours. We succeeded in July 1941 and June 1942, getting fifty-nine entries — twelve from North Roaders — in 1941 when Eric Foot had great difficulty in getting sufficient help and stood down himself to fill a gap. Fastest time was 2h. 15m. 13s. by T.A. Hart, Rickmansworth C.C., North Roader McCarthy being third and the handicap was won by Holmes of Luton Wheelers with a net time of 2h. 6m. 11s. In 1942 young Cecil Paget was more fortunate with the amount of help proffered but received six fewer entries: fastest time was 2h. 11m. 9s. by P.D. South, Wisbech Wheelers, Copping being the best North Roader — sixth fastest but leading the N.R. team (McCarthy and Sloper being the others) to the team medals — after being second to Kent R.C. in 1941: Holmes again won the handicap. Another Open Fifty was planned for 1943 — first for June and then for the Sunday prior to August Bank Holiday but nothing came of it and no such event was planned for 1944.

After the failure of the 1946 Memorial Fifty the North Road committee decided to convert it to an Open Tricycle event, in part because of the long interest of the club in tricycling and because of a theory that the tricycling community retained the old time enthusiasm. Unfortunately, as we later found, no minimum limit was placed on the athletic ability of the entrants to this only open fifty miles event for tricyclists and North Roaders were soon reacting against the slowness of some competitors. Also annoying was the general behaviour and peculiar costumes of some of the tricycling 'characters' accepting the possibly too easily proffered invitations, so in 1955 somewhat stringent standards were introduced — in preference to an individual assessment of men's likely behaviour or performance. This resulted in vehement protests both from the Tricycle Association and from individual tricyclists, but the entry of twenty-eight — some thirty less than the preceding years — was of the quality felt appropriate to our Memorial Fifty. And the event still provided a socially excellent August Bank Holiday weekend — it having been moved to August Sunday after becoming a tricycle event. Support decreased slightly in 1956 and some, at least, of the Tricycle Association officials remained strongly antipathetic to the restriction on entries — but it appears to be a coincidence that the Tricycle Trophy, whose allocation had been passed to the Association by the Trophy trustees, has not since been allocated to the North Road Twenty-Four Hours. At the Club's A.G.M. early in 1957 a resolution was passed to convert the Memorial Fifty back to a bicycle event, but as an open scratch event restricted only by R.T.T.C. regulations: the resolution was to take effect in 1958 to enable a new date to be obtained. The last of the Tricycle Memorial Fifties — the last tricycle event (so far) to be promoted by other than the Tricycle Association — was on August Sunday, 1957 and one of the two North Roaders riding was Edmund Green, who had been nominated as T.A. president by G.H. Stancer when G.H.S. wanted to retire from that office, mournful but, we hope, understanding. A series of fine rides were achieved by the winners of the Tricycle events. These events brought together the cream of the tricycling athletes as well as the peculiar folk tricycling also attracts — and I have ridden a tricycle since 1930, collecting a couple of Memorial Fifty certificates. The winners were:- 1947 F.G. Whetman, Wembley Wheelers (and he, like Turner in the 1921 Memorial, was but one-armed!) 2h. 26m. 53s; 1948 K.J.Brooker, Luton Wheelers, 2h. 23m. 9s; 1949 F.N. Whateley, Rapier C.C., 2h. 24m. 58s; 1950 to 1952 and 1954 A. Crimes, Crewe Wheelers, 2h. 18m. 50s; 2h. 15m. 41s., 2h. 16m. 30s. and 2h. 17m. 23s; 1953 F.J. Arnold, Middleton C.C., 2h. 13m. 20s; 1955 and 1956 M.J. Dunn, Catford C.C., 2h. 14m. 35s. and 2h. 19m. 29s; 1957 G. Clayton, Spartan Wheelers, 2h. 15m. 19s.

Before moving on to the next Memorial Fifty in 1948, the North Road personified by Reg Bridge, organised the R.T.T.C. Championship Fifty on a North Road course — it was won by R. Firth, Altrincham Ravens C.C., 2h. 6m. 17s. by four seconds from K.H. Joy, Medway Wheelers, and a further four seconds from the winner of our 1946 Memorial Fifty, A.E. Derbyshire.

The new series of Memorial Fifties opened on 20 July 1958 — a day of heavy rain, lightning and thunder — on the London-Newmarket road north of the thirty-second milestone (from London), with a leg to Cambridge, a course long popular with clubs from eastern London which had been used for some years for Saturday afternoon N.R. club events — it was nearer to London than the North Road course now considered suitable. Despite the weather — which may explain the twenty-one non-starters from the field of eighty-three (a disappointing entry) — twenty-five riders did personal bests including North Roader George Wingfield, bringing club record inside two hours, while first and second fastest men B. Wiltcher (Zeus R.C.) and J.A. Finch (Ross Wheelers) improved on course record with 1h. 56m. 8s. and 1h. 56m. 34s. And E.G. Kings' organisation made us proud and set a standard which has been maintained by his successors H. J. Bridge, P.S. Bury, R.A.C. Risley, R.D. Cook and R. Sewell. Wiltcher won again in 1959 with 1h. 56m. 17s. — proving that a man preferring to race in company can 'go it alone'. Then for our seventy-fifth anniversary year it was decided to make the 1960 event an International Fifty, linked with the well established Isle of Man Cycling Week of racing and fun. This entailed a considerable amount of work for Ted Kings and cost the club some £230, but it was an outstanding event in the history of British time trialling. There were riders from Belgium, France and Holland, teams being nominated to represent these three and England, Scotland and Wales. R.G.A. Jowers (Clarence Wheelers) won and led the English team to victory in 1h. 56m. 49s. — thirty-one seconds faster than R.F. Colden (Camberley Wheelers) who was not in the English team! A Scot A.H. Dickson (Ivy C.C.) was fourth in 1h. 59m. 48s. with a Belgian, R. Deconinck, fifth, eleven seconds slower and Dutchman G. Wesselling sixth in 2h. 0m. 11s. followed by D.J. Hughes (Acme Wheelers) for Wales with 2h. 0m. 23s. G. Ian (Nottinghamshire Wheelers) was third fastest, second counter in the England team but led his club to victory for the fastest club team medals. Fastest Frenchman was R. Beaux — tenth in 2h. 0m. 40s. Only the R.T.T.C. has subsequently promoted an International fifty miles in Britain and then, so far, only on two occasions.

After that the ensuing events were, initially, something of an anti-climax: and a succession of poor days, weatherwise, slowed the winning time in those years to outside two hours. And, for a time, the entry lapsed from over the maximum permitted 120 the International gained. In 1961 Harold Bridge (Reg's son) took over from Ted Kings, while Ted became principal timekeeper (times are also taken at twelve and a half, twenty-five and thirty seven and a half miles) in place of our old friend, of twenty-four hours fame, J.W. Rossiter: and when the prize arrangements were changed, in 1968, to substitute three handicap prizes for the fourth and fifth fastest time awards, Ted Kings also became handicapper for the event. And the winners since the International have been: 1961 D. Bonner, Old Portlians C.C., 1h. 57m. 20s; 1963/4 P. Ryan, Sans Souci C.C. then Edgware R.C., 2h. 0m. 8s. and 1h. 58m. 26s; 1965/7 A. Bridges, Mercury C.C., 2h 0m 2s., 2h. 0m. 47s. and 2h. 0m. 10s; 1968 T. Ewing, Wembley Phoenix C.C., 1h. 55m. 50s; 1969/71 R.W. Buchan, Norwood Paragon C.C., 1h 56m. 14s., 1h. 58m. 51s., and 1h 56m. 31s., 1972 G. Donnington, South Eastern R.C. 2h. 0m. 18s; 1973 C.R. Miller, Rockingham Forest Wheelers, 1h. 54m. 26s;

1974 A.E. Metcalfe, Hartlepool C.C., 1h. 52m. 20s; 1975 D. Benson, Rockingham Forest Wheelers 1h. 59m. 52s.

In 1974 the Memorial Fifty was preceded by an open tandem event which attracted the entry of nine pairs of whom M. Savage and R. Stirling, Glade C.C. were fastest in 1h. 43m. 49s., rough surfacing of a stretch of the course — now back on the North Road — caused many punctures. The experiment was repeated in 1975 but only one pair survived puncture and other troubles — North Roaders David and Roger Sewell finished in 1h. 53m. 48s.

North Roaders have managed to be among the first twelve, who, if not prizewinners, were awarded a certificate — a practice retained after the demise of the original form of the event: and our best finishers have won one of the two sets of team medals offered. Prominent among our riders is George Wingfield who, in 1960 was the first North Roader to be among the best twelve in the Best All Rounder competition, and was among the first twelve in our fifty on six occasions between 1958 and 1969. He led our team to take the bronze medals for the second team four times and to first team silver medals once and he was in the second team, led by Ken Lovett, in 1962: John Palmer led our team to another set of bronze medals in 1965, while Jim Ewers led us to the 'silvers' in 1970 and the 'bronzes' in 1971 and 1972; it was Tony Hartley who led our team to second place and in most of these years Ken Lovett was in the team.

Thus we may continue to be proud of the North Road Memorial Fifty — even if some, at least, among us sigh for its eminence between the Wars.

CHAPTER V.

North Roaders in other Clubs' Open Events and the Road Record Scene.

(a) *Notable rides in other Clubs' Opens.*

The Anfield Bicycle Club showed great interest in the North Road C.C. from its foundation and through the years we have shared a number of members, most notably, of course, G.P. Mills. And over many years an annual feature of the N.R. programme was Shrewsbury for Whitsun to support our representatives in the Anfield 100. Before the start for the event had been moved from near Liverpool we went there in force in 1891 when among some useful rides Bidlake and W. Crosbie broke the Northern R.R.A. tandem bicycle records for fifty and 100 miles — unusual to read of a Bidlake ride on two rather than three wheels but he was back on his favourite mount in 1895 when he broke the Northern R.R.A. 100 miles tricycle record in 6h. 16m. 27s. A series of fastest times was started by Goodwin near the end of the paced series when he did the fastest time of the paced series in 1898 — 5h. 1m. 31s. Partly by the ill luck of Anfielder Knipe puncturing North Roader Nutt opened the unpaced series in 1900 by being fastest and handicap winner. Nutt was fastest again in 1902, T.G. King, Jnr. and Jones being second and third. Cobley was fastest in 1901 and second in 1903 — when Jones was third again. Frank Wingrave's fine series started in 1904 when he was not only fastest but scored event record — he repeated this in 1905 and 1907 — when his time was 5h. 17m. 44s. — and he was second in 1906. Jack Middleton brought N.R. time down to 5h. 2m. 31s. in 1928 and if I hadn't slipped back that year we would have won the team medals then being offered — I was seventh in 5h. 6m. 19s. in 1930 and three years later Harrison was similarly placed with our first inside five hours ride — by just over five minutes. In 1954 Davis went round in 4h. 40m. 27s. but then Blackman scored our best ride in recent years when he was fourth in 1956 in 4h. 29m. 34s. and he did a useful 4h. 38m. 52s. in 1960 — something for others to aim to beat. Another Anfield link was through their twenty-four hours event won by Pitt in 1932 and he was second and third in the next two events.

Frank Wingrave also achieved fastest time in the early unpaced Bath Road 100s — in 1905 and 1906 — his 5h. 9m. 58s. in 1906 being despite of a series of punctures entailing six changes of machine. Prior to those rides we had been in the top ten in the paced events between 1890 and 1893, Bob Ilsley being the best — third in 1892. His brother Arthur was second in the 1895 track event and fourth in 1896 in 3h. 58m. 52s., while Pepper and E. Gould were second and third in 1897. After 1906 we were regularly represented and some good rides were done but we didn't reach high places, perhaps the best being Wingfield's seventh place in 1960 — 4h. 13m. 55s. — and two years later, when it was also the R.T.T.C. Championship, he led our team to third place.

The first reference to team medals in our records is in 1911 when W.J. Webb was fastest in the Kingsdale Fifty and we won the team race — Lempriere and C. Jay Cole being the others. The next year Lempriere, Webb and Wingrave were invited by the N.C.U. to ride in an Olympic selection event but the club was doubtful of the amateur status of other listed possibles and declined the invitation. In 1928 Jack Middleton did put a North Road name in the Olympic Road Race — he finished twenty-fifth — but in the late 1920s he and Artaud provided the club with many fastest times and led various members to win the team medals — later in his time with us we saw the unusual combination of Jack with his brothers Sid and Reg winning the team medals. Among events which fell to us in this period were, at fifty miles, Manchester Wheelers, Peterborough, Cheltenham, North London and Oxford City. Jack was also a good 100 miler, outstanding at this distance were his Speedwell wins in 1927 and 1929 while he won three Midland C. & A.C. twelve hours in succession.

They were briefly followed by Harrison and Pollard who scored second and fourth and with Risley took the team medals in the 1932 Shaftesbury fifty miles, Harrison also being second in the Vegetarian Fifty and the Polytechnic 'Gayler' twelve hours. A decade later Copping was doing useful rides but fourth in the 1943 Oxford City Fifty was about the best placing he achieved. At the end of the 1940s a group of youngsters came into the Club among whom were some first rate time triallists — Alan Blackman, Ken Davis, Geoff Edwards and Alan Kennedy were perhaps the best of these and all have also proved themselves excellent club officials. Most successful of these was Blackman who scored many second fastest times in the innumerable twenty-five miles events then and now available, but in 1951 Withers came briefly into the club and in that year and the following two years he scored many fastest times, leading us to team victories. Oddly enough his most outstanding achievement was to beat competition record in a Rosebank Thirty, but subsequently so did three others! However we did hold team competition record after the event was completed. Withers rarely rode events longer than thirty miles but he did score places in three fifty miles events and his second in the 1952 Belle Vue Fifty brought club record inside two hours — 1h. 59m. 33s. After many second places Blackman scored a fastest time in the 1954 Unity Fifty and he achieved some notable 100 miles rides, in particular being second in the 1952 Westerley 100 and fastest in the 1955 Kentish Wheelers 100 while his ride in the 1957 South Ruislip event brought club record to 4h. 15m. 56s. He also did a course record ride of 250 miles in the South Western R.C. twelve hours and his twenty-four hours rides have been mentioned in Chapter III.

In 1955 a new star came to the club and signalled his arrival by winning a Century R.C. Novices twenty-five in 1h. 5m: later in the year, in a Becontree Wheelers twenty-five, when another new member to play a notable part in the club, Lovett was nine seconds inside the hour, Wingfield knocked over five minutes off his initial win to be but five seconds outside the hour. From these beginnings Wingfield, in particular, went on to many victories at twenty-five, fifty and 100 miles and led teams to victory. In 1959 he seemed to be the 'eternal second' but this place in the Westerley R.C. 100 gave club record — 4h. 9m. 54s. and with Hayden and Edwards first team, the same two backing Wingfield in the Middlesex R.C. twelve hours, his 251 miles giving him third place. 1960 gave him at least three wins at fifty miles with 1h. 58m. 30s. in the Marlboro and at least two 100 miles wins with 4h. 10m. 46s. in the South Ruislip and these with 257.57 miles in the Middlesex R.C. twelve hours gave him twelfth place in the British Best All Rounder contest — the first North Roader to get into the first twelve. In 1961 he improved his fifty time to 1h. 56m. 19s. to win the Glade event and improved his twelve hours marginally in the Broad Oak to 257.92 (with Thompson and Hayden we won the team medals) while his best 100 was 4h. 13m. 29s. (second in Westerley) but he missed the accolade of being in the first twelve in the 'B.A.R.' when the course for the Glade Fifty was belatedly found to be marginally short and he slipped back to seventeenth: in consolation he was invited by the R.T.T.C. to the Champions Dinner.

In 1962 a new name appeared in the supporters to Wingfield in team wins — David Sewell, whose father Jack and grandfather Charlie were both time triallists and great North Roaders in every sense — though perhaps his first team medal was gained with Hayden and Lovett in the Marlboro Fifty. By 1963 David was earning team medals at 100 miles and twelve hours. David's younger brother Roger entered competition in 1964 when he was second in the Westerley R.C. Novices twenty-five, but he was not, at that stage, a frequent performer. A different notable second place that year was Ken Lovett's 246 miles in the Luton twelve hours. In 1965 John Palmer strengthened our team — leading on occasion — in hill climbs and at events up to 100 miles: he was fastest in the Marlboro A.C. Fifty and East Surrey R.C. Twenty-five. He continued to win places in the first three and lead teams now including Welsh and Hall in 1966 and until July 1967 — alas four days after being eleventh in our Memorial Fifty he was killed in an accident while cycling home from work — one of the sad occasions in clubdom.

The brothers Ken and Richard Usher joined us in 1968 — Ken with many fine achievements both on two and three wheels to his credit — specially at the longer distances. They gave us our first places in other clubs' twenty-four hours events since the pre-war efforts of Pitt and Alf Marsh. Ken was second (to that prolific N.R. winner, C. Smith) and Richard third in the 1968 Catford twenty-four with mileages of 452 and 442 but Ken had an accident injuring a foot and in 1969 could only help Richard take second place in the Wessex twenty-four. In 1971 Ken did a series of fine tricycle 100s bringing club record down to 4h. 47m. 42s. and a good tricycle twelve hours — but alas they didn't produce the hoped for twenty-four. In the 1969-1971 years Ryan was taking the North Road name into the top places, winning the 1969 Shaftesbury Fifty — then his original club was revived and he became a second claim North Roader. In these and subsequent years Parsons, both the Sewell brothers, Wingfield (staging a 'come-back'), M. Harvey, Ewers and Cook were all concerned in team wins. Hartley, having moved south from Yorkshire and joined us became a team leader in 1972. The Sewells paired up on a tandem scoring two wins at thirty miles in 1973 and being well placed in other events in one of which they reduced club record to 1h. 1m. 42s. By 1975 David and Roger were doing well at fifty miles and after being second fastest in the Archer R.C. event in June, in September they won the Severn R.C. tandem fifty and achieved club record — 1h. 51m. 7s.

While these successes are very pleasing many older cyclists wonder whether the detrimental effect on the social life of many clubs resulting from members supporting so many of the plethora of open events now promoted is a desirable feature of the current cycling world.

(b) *Road Records.*

Initially the N.C.U. was, through its Record Committee, equally prepared, on appropriate evidence, to hall-mark as best on record both rides in road races and individual attempts on records. And North Roaders showed an early partiality to record breaking, our founder A.J. Wilson riding a tandem tricycle with C.E. Liles of Ripley C.C. (and of the 'Major Liles Memorial Trophy' of the Tricycle Association) collected the relevant fifty miles record in our first open event, as recounted in Chapter II. Also in that chapter the amazing 1886 achievements of G.P. Mills are described.

Record achievements in 1887 — and subsequent years — in North Road twenty-four hours and early 100 miles events have been chronicled in Chapters III and IV — inlcuding the modern twenty-four hours competition records, now under the aegis of the Road Time Trials Council. Also in 1887, prior to our 100 miles race, C.W. Brown had reduced the 100 miles tricycle record and, later in the year, Mills and Tingey pushed the tandem tricycle twenty-four hours mileage to near 300.

Chapter II also recounted the formation of the Road Records Association in 1888, when the records recognised were but at fifty and 100 miles, twenty-four hours and over the Land's End to John O'Groats route: the N.C.U. passed its books for these to the new Association. The R.R.A. at once added the 'half-day' — twelve hours — record to the list and later brought in a succession of place to place and the 1000 miles records. The place to place records gave a special aura to record breaking, a romantic interest leading devotees to relate weather conditions to specific records — to such a south-westerly means a good day for Land's End to London or a northly for Edinburgh to London, etc. As they came in, these place to place records were there and back over the shorter routes from London and one way (the rider choosing direction) for towns farther apart. The total number of records now recognised by the R.R.A. (i.e. other than those recognised by the Women's R.R.A. and regional associations) is eighteen. In the early years North Roaders anticipated the introduction of some routes and one distance, T.A. Edge extending his 1892 'End to End' ride to cover 1000 miles in five days, eleven hours, thirty-eight minutes: four years later he rode 1000 miles, on a route independent of the 'End to End', in four days, nine hours, nineteen minutes and the R.R.A. added the distance in 1897 but it was ten years before a successful, and unpaced ride was achieved — sixteen minutes faster than Edge's. In 1888 A.M.H. Solomon rode from London to York in twenty-two and three quarter hours (and was, apparently, only the second to achieve the feat) and ten years later E.J. Steel did an unpaced London to Portsmouth and back ride in 9h. 3m. 33s: in both cases these routes were added to the R.R.A. list the following year. At the other end of the historical time scale we have managed to start the lists of two of the three records introduced since the second World War. Thus, incited by Harry England and Frank Armond and encouraged by organiser Ernie Haldane, follower Frank Marston and many helpers en route, I established the first Pembroke — London record, riding my tricycle over the route in 1947 — aided by a wind which turned round overnight. And in 1959 Geoff Edwards captured the first Cardiff-London record — and the first North Road bicycle record for thirty years — riding via Gloucester with the wind and across it from there with rain adding to the discomfort so that it was a feat to get three minutes inside the set lowest standard.

Other than for the 1000 miles and the recently introduced twenty-five miles records North Roaders appear among the successful riders for every record recognised by the R.R.A. Early in the Club's history it was decided that a member breaking a national road record should be entitled to wear a gold club badge in place of his silver badge and near 120 members have achieved that honour. Many only collected one record to gain the coveted 'yellow label': others, either because of the period in which they were riding or of the lure of record riding, broke many. None was more prolific than 'Monty' Holbein — who was also in Catford C.C. and recruited many pacers from that club — with over thirty records to his credit — on bicycle, tricycle and both types of tandem. He was the first to top 300 miles and later, with motor pace, 400 miles in twenty-four hours and might have achieved many more records had he not touched a wheel of the pacing motor tricycle, fallen and been run over by a tandem, which broke his leg — this in an 1897 attempt to improve the twenty-four hours mileage: a fall during convalescence resulted in another break and he gave up cycling, on medical advice, to become a notable long distance swimmer. Our nearest modern equivalent is Ted Tweddell of Carlisle who has written his name fourteen times in the R.R.A. book, mostly on tandem tricycle with different partners both before and after joining the North Road — the York-Edinburgh record saw him first on solo tricycle in 1929, then on tandem tricycle in 1931 and with a new partner again in 1956 — a remarkable span of sporting activity!

Each year until 1904 (except for 1900) over half the records approved were by North Roaders, our best year being 1889 when we collected fifteen out of seventeen records. As more clubs with road racing interests were formed and their members increased participation in road sport there was, naturally, a decline in North Road predominance, but the lure of earning the right to wear a gold badge remains.

And what stories there are behind the bald lists of records — sufficient on the End to End bicycle rides to fill a book by Alan J. Ray! The prime achievement of Shorland's Brighton and back was that he beat Selby's famous coach record, the result of the skilled driving and smart changing of fine teams of horses: the beating of Selby's time soon became a cycling ambition and had been done by a team of cyclists riding in relay — Shorland was, in 1890, still riding the lever driven Geared Facile. In 1891 J.M. James (alias 'Jim Jams') rode to York with the first of the Club runs to York — a sociable twenty-one hours stint — and rode back five days later, surely with some of his run companions as pace-makers, to regain the record. In the same year Mills suffered from an excess of zeal — to put it kindly — by a helper and collapsed four miles short of John O'Groats from an overdose of cocaine which put him to sleep for several hours! But he still got inside five days for the first time — inside four and a half days in fact.

Picture Bidlake, making his second 1892 attack on the London-York tricycle figures, starting with the Shorland-Holbein tandem tricycle, riding close to their back axle and thus taking advantage of their pacing teams — and still being with them at York!

1893 and 1894 saw a number of records which, although listed in the paced series, were in fact unpaced. In the case of the Begbie/King tandem tricycle fifty, their pacing teams turned out on the wrong day! The Child/ Earl tandem bicycle fifty was not only unpaced but they fell at forty-seven and a half miles and Earl broke his collar bone. Definitely paced were Chase's three fifty miles records of 1894, the second being in the famous North Road Club Fifty in which occurred the accident giving the Huntingdon police the opportunity to ban road racing — vide Chapter II. His 1898 Fifty record was the first unpaced record to be recognised by the R.R.A. Also ridden in an 1894 club event, prior to the fateful fifty, was W.W. Robertson's tricycle twelve hours.

Chase's 1897 100 miles record of 4h. 16m. 35s. was on an 'out and home' course in a thick white fog which made pace taking too risky so that it was mostly unpaced. A different sort of risk then and until, some thirty years later, when timekeepers were allowed to follow in motor vehicles, was linked with trains: straight-away set distance records routes and starting times had to be related to train services — and, even then, trains sometimes failed to arrive on time: thus Robey/J.H. Wingrave missed the fifty miles tandem bicycle record in 1898.

For excitement Ernest Gould's second 1899 attempt on London-York must rank high: he was riding a free wheel with but one brake — and that brake failed after a few miles! He just equalled his previous ride of twelve hours six minutes — with the skilful use of a foot on the front tyre when braking was desirable! A different form of excitement in 1899 covered Fred Goodwin's motor-paced attempt on the twelve hours and twenty-four hours records, using a Fenland course. He was stopped by successive village policemen and charged with furious and dangerous riding — he gave up after twenty hours having taken the twelve hours figures just over twenty miles per hour, and, allegedly, he lost count of the number of summonses he had to answer and fines to pay — and some of his pacers were also fined. And in consequence the R.R.A. banned motor pacing on subsequent attempts: human pacing was not ended officially until 1933 but, except in one instance, no paced record was approved after the last years of the nineteenth century.

Linked with the dearth of road racing only five clubs remained affiliated to the R.R.A. in 1900 but eleven records were hall-marked, three being by North Roaders and, in particular, the club twenty-four was so organised as to enable President 'Boss' King's son to claim the first twenty-four hours unpaced record.

Particularly demonstrating the continuing improvement in speed marking the passing years was the Murray brothers London-York ride of 1901 — thirty-eight minutes faster than the last paced record on this route. And the Grimsdell/Bryer tandem fifty record of 1903 was but 110 seconds slower than twenty-five miles per hour — it was eleven years before this record was broken and two hours beaten. Twenty-four years after Grimsdell and Bryer, Middleton/Artaud made it a North Road record again taking five minutes off the Stott's four years old record and setting a time which stood for seven years: and it was the only time they rode tandem together — Stan Artaud averred that he just shut his eyes down Hitchin Hill!

1904 was a particularly interesting year for North Road record breaking, ending in September when 'Grimmy' (as Grimsdell was long known) carelessly announced that he'd got next Saturday off, was going for twelve and twenty-four hours standard medals and, while he was at it, might as well go for London-Edinburgh record! Not only did he go, and have quite a lot of mechanical trouble which included his front wheel collapsing — and being rebuilt while he rode on, using his spare machine — but a fortnight later found he had pushed a gear of ninety-one inches instead of seventy-eight! He was followed, mostly by North Roaders, practically all the way but while that wheel was being dealt with he was alone and reached Newcastle and the High Level toll bridge. The only money in Grimmy's pockets was a golden sovereign and the toll was one penny: the toll keeper would neither change the pound nor let the rider go free so Grimmy started begging 'Give me a penny for my toll please — I have to get to Edinburgh tonight, sir'. Eventually a sportsman came to the rescue and wished him luck — and Grimmy really had to reach Edinburgh before midnight as his ride would not have been accepted as record, under the rules then in force, had he ridden any distance on Sunday. He finished forty-two minutes before midnight and over three hours inside record as well as improving on a ride by a Bath Roader disallowed on a technicality. Dr. Wesley's End to End success early in the year was also notable for the aid given by North Road followers over much of the route — the previous year, before joining the N.R., he had attempted this record but finished well outside time, whereas in 1904 his problem was that he got well ahead of schedule and thus missed some of his helpers. Railways proved very valuable, enabling helpers to rest while leap-frogging ahead of the rider and, in one instance, his spare bicycle was sent on from Edinburgh to Dalwhinnie and a telegram sent to the house at which he was to eat — by amazing coincidence at Dalwhinnie Wesley found one of the front fork blades of the machine he had been riding was broken!

Between the Wesley and Grimsdell rides, on August Bank Holiday — starting two hours after Sunday ended — North Roaders staged a mass attack on Portsmouth and back records. Max Crosbie was first off, at two a.m., on tricycle, from Ripley: Walter Ward started at 3 a.m. on solo while Robert and Frank Wingrave went off at 2.45 a.m. on a tandem allegedly looking more like a track racer than for road use! Ward nearly caught them dealing with bottom bracket trouble before they reached Hyde Park Corner and later in the ride they had to change over when the strain of steering the brute became too much for Robert. Years later Frank told me that at Butser Hill Robert vaulted off, ran up pushing with one hand on the saddle and jumped on again at the top! All were successful and, despite their problems, the Wingrave's record stood for twenty-one years.

Earlier in the year 'Grimmy' and Bright got together to collect the first Liverpool-London tandem record. But Cobley was less fortunate — for once, says rumour, Bidlake advice proved unsound — for a last minute course change resulted in the R.R.A. not accepting Cobley's 100 miles tricycle ride. To fit in with his office commitments Cobley started at 6.55 p.m. on a Friday from the top of Hitchin Hill, south to Stevenage, North to Newark and back four miles to where Bidlake (having trained from Hitchin) waited. Cobley knocked near nine minutes off record then with follower Max Crosbie, Bidlake and Bright rode back to Grantham where, with police aid, they knocked up the Angel at 2 a.m. to get beds. Cobley and Crosbie crept out to catch an early train back to London and their offices — leaving Bright to borrow money from the local C.T.C. Consul to pay the hotel bill!

The Wingraves demonstrated their ability again in 1907, taking eighty-two minutes off an Anfield pair's London-York record — and forty-nine minutes off H. Green's single figures which was a notable feat: their time stood for nineteen years and was then only improved by thirteen minutes. Eight years later — twenty-seven after the Wingraves' ride — our Spary/Loten pair took a further forty-five minutes off London-York and then seventy minutes off Liverpool-London partly aided by using the Mersey Tunnel to give a better route. They also attempted Bath and back but their tandem mysteriously collapsed and, regrettably, their record chasing ended.

1910 marked the slow start of a revival of interest in the tandem tricycle when Leake and Stancer collected the Brighton and back on the double three-wheeler: Stancer later, amongst many notable services to cycling became in turn secretary (twice) and President of the R.R.A. Theirs was the last N.R. record for ten years when Armond brought Land's End - London under twenty hours — a fifty-four minutes improvement — and the Inwood brothers took fifteen minutes off the Bath and back tandem bicycle figures, to the delight of their father 'Doowni' who had resumed his long service as club secretary. Two Franks — Armond and Thomas — got together to push the twenty-four hours tandem bicycle figures up to just short of 400 — later remeasuring of the roads, initially for our twenty-four hours course, showed that they must have topped 400. In 1923 Thomas had a lucky escape when his tricycle frame broke early on a Land's End-London attempt— he was fortunate to find a repairer at Penzance able to replace the fractured tube, enabling Thomas to restart twenty-four hours after his scheduled time — on July 31 — and take nearly three hours off record. Both Armond and Thomas, riding single gears, took the longer less hilly route joining the Bath Road west of Marlborough: later, with the use of variable gears for racing becoming popular, more direct routes via Amesbury were followed — North Roaders so doing were Copping/Sloper on tandem bicycle, Wilkins on tricycle and Tweddell/Stott on Tandem Trike. Wilkins got well ahead of his schedule and missed some of his helpers, but his later attempts to bring the Pembroke-London trike record back to the N.R. failed to get appropriate conditions. And the record story is frequently punctuated with incidents of attempts put off or failed by adverse weather — particularly, of course, by wind in the wrong quarter or, more rarely, non-existent. Ken Davis described this last condition as 'like riding through porridge' in his vain attempt on the London–Edinburgh in the 1960s. The previous day would have been perfect!

Reverting to Frank Thomas, in 1925 Cockerill persuaded Frank to help in the celebration of Cockerill's twenty-first birthday by going for Edinburgh-London on my tandem bicycle — after some initial difficulty in meshing their differing pedalling styles. A successful birthday outing it proved and their record stood for five years—I think it was a different tandem that Frank Marston and I used to recapture that record in 1936 to gain the 100th and 101st gold badges.

There was a mild state of activity in the 1950s, Tweddell being the most frequent record breaker, initially, in this period, he rode with Stott of Newcastle-on-Tyne and later with Sandham of Maryport modernising tandem tricycle records — as did Fowler/Cook on London-York. Blackman, Brennan and Green improved tricycle records — 100 miles, Liverpool-Edinburgh and Edinburgh-York, Brennan briefly (and by only thirty-six seconds) recapturing the 100 miles in 1961. Racing men in general and ours in particular nowadays seem to be too busy competing in open events, now available in their hundreds, to leave time for the special effort entailed in attempting records — despite the attraction of writing one's name for ever on the Record Association's book of fame.

Records made by North Roaders.

('n.m.' — non-members on tandem: except for three 1885 records, those accomplished prior to membership are not listed), (mp — motor paced).

Fifty Miles.

Ordinary 1888 A. Pellant 3h. 14m. 13s. and 3h. 14m. 7s. and G.R. White 2h. 57m. 47s.
1890 R.J. Ilsley 2h. 56m. 46s. and H.J. Howard 2h. 49m. 17s. (best on solid tyres) *1891* R.J. Ilsley 2h. 46m. 20s. and S.C. Houghton 2h. 45m. 55s.

Bicycle 1886 G.P. Mills 2h. 47m. 36s. *1889/90* M.A. Holbein 2h. 43m. 32s., 2h. 40m. 38s. and 2h. 38m. 57s. *1890/1* R.L. Ede 2h. 38m. 3s. and 2h. 24m. 44s. 1893 A. Pellant 2h. 21m. 46s. *1894/5* A.A. Chase 2h. 19m. 2s., 2h. 16m. 3s., 2h. 7m. 15s. and 2h. 0m. 5s. and *unpaced* 2h. 7m. 8s.

Tandem Bicycle 1888 D. Albone/R. Tingey 2h. 59m. 39s. and D. Albone/E. Glover (n.m.) 2h. 52m. 3s. *1890* J.G.H. Browne/W.M. Crosbie 2h. 42m. 3s. *1892* R.J. Ilsley/W.W. Robertson 2h. 21m. 11s. *1893* A.R. Child/A.O. Earl 2h. 10m. 58s.

Unpaced 1898 A.A. and F.W. Chase 2h. 2m. 25s. *1903* E.H. Grimsdell/C. Bryer 2h. 1m. 50s. *1929* J.K. Middleton/S.A. Artaud 1h. 46m. 12s.

Tricycle 1888 R. Tingey 3h. 2m. 44s. and G.P. Mills 2h. 53m. 25s. *1889* W.C. Goulding 2h. 50m. 5s. *1891* S.D. Begbie 2h. 35m. 17s. *1894* F.T. Bidlake 2h. 22m. 55s.

Unpaced 1900 J. van Hooydonk 2h. 35m. 10s.

Tandem Tricycle 1886 C.E. Liles (n.m.)/A.J. Wilson 3h. 16m. 58s. and G.P. Mills/A.J. Wilson 2h. 46m. 3s. *1891* S.D. Begbie/H. Arnold 2h. 36m. 45s. and 2h. 19m. 9s. *1894* S.D. Begbie/T.G. King, Jnr. 2h. 16m. 50s.

Unpaced 1922 A.J.H. Gott (n.m.)/F.C.W. Dainton 2h. 20m. 40s. *1943* L.E. Copping/J.M. Sloper 1h. 52m. 41s.

100 miles.

Ordinary 1888 G.R. White 6h. 48m. 14s.

Bicycle 1888 and 1890 M.A. Holbein 6h. 20m. 26s. and 5h. 54m. 2s. and T.A. Edge 5h. 27m. 38s. *1894 and 1897* A.A. Chase 4h. 39m. 28s. and 4h. 16m. 35s.

Tandem Bicycle 1889 M.A. Holbein/P.C. Wilson (n.m.) 7h. 24m. 10s. *1890* J.G.H. Browne/W.M. Crosbie 6h. 25m. 39s. *1892* F. Lowe (n.m.) J.M. James 5h. 53m. 7s. *1893* S.D. Begbie/W.W. Robertson 5h. 41m.20s. A. Brown/M.A. Holbein 5h. 36m. 12s. and A.R. Child/A.

McM. Todd 5h. 16m. 24s. *1894* F.R. Cook/A.E. Marsh 4h. 54m. 13s. *1895* J.W. Stocks (n.m.)/M.A. Holbein 4h. 46m. 18s.

Unpaced 1898 W.D. Robey/J.H. Wingrave 4h. 56m. 18s. and A.F. and L.G. Ilsley 4h. 45m. 1s. *1902* E.H. Grimsdell/E.A. Cully 4h. 41m. 2s. and A.F. and R.J. Ilsley 4h. 36m. 29s.

Tricycle 1887 C.W. Brown 7h 54m. 10s. and G.P. Mills 7h. 46m. 33s. and in *1888* 6h. 58m. 54s. *1889* F.T. Bidlake 6h. 55m. 58s. *1890* G.R. White 6h. 40m. 22s. and T.A. Edge 6h. 10m. 8s. *1892* M.A. Holbein 5h. 54m. 46s. *1895* F.T. Bidlake 5h. 15m. 57s.

Unpaced 1903 A.G. Markham 5h. 57m. 22s. *1954* A.E. Blackman 4h. 34m. 20s. *1961* G.M. Brennan 4h. 31m. 16s.

Tandem Tricycle 1887 C.W. Brown/G.R. White 7h 6m. 50s. *1890* S.D. Begbie/P.E. Driver 6h. 50m. 16s. (best on solids) and H.R. Pope/W.W. Arnold (n.m.) 6h. 30m. 19s.

Unpaced 1925 C.A. and E.M. Sewell 4h. 59m. 0s. *1943* L.E. Copping/J.M. Sloper 4h. 13m. 57s.

Twelve Hours

Ordinary 1889 G.T. Langridge 154 miles

Bicycle 1889†90 M.A. Holbein 175½ and 177½ *1891 to 1894* F.W. Shorland 192½, 194½, 195 and 211 *1894* A.A. Chase 213 *1895 and 1897* M.A. Holbein 217½ and 219 (motor paced) *1897* E. Gould 226½ *1899* F.R. Goodwin 245 (m.p.)

Unpaced 1898 A.F. Ilsley 187 and E. Gould 191 and *1899* 201½

Tandem Bicycle 1889 P.C. Wilson (n.m.)/M.A. Holbein 163 *1892* H. Arnold/J.P.K. Clark 179 *1893* A. Brown/M.A. Holbein 200 *1894* F. Busvine/A. Smythe (n.m.) 204½ *1895* J.W. Stocks (n.m.)/M.A. Holbein 221 *1897* A.E.Walters (n.m.) M.A. Holbein 230

Unpaced 1900 H. Charles/D.K. Hall 210½ *1901* E.H. Grimsdell/E.A. Cully 219½ *1909* E.H. Grimsdell/M.R. Mott 221

Tricycle 1888 G.P. Mills 147 *1889* W. Ward and W.C. Goulding (tie) 151 *1890* A.F. Ilsley 159½ and G.R. White 164 *1891/2* M.A. Holbein 174½ and 183½ *1894* W.W. Robertson 184½, E.J. Steel 190½ and F.T. Bidlake 194½

Unpaced 1901 R.S. Cobley 177½

Tandem Tricycle 1890 J. Rowley/H.H. Arnold 164 *1891* J.J. McCarthy/A.J. Wilson 164½ *1892* A. Brown/M.A. Holbein 177½ *1893* F.T. Bidlake/ M.A. Holbein 181½

Unpaced 1951 E. Tweddell/J.W. Stott 242½

Twenty-Four Hours.

Ordinary 1885 G.P. Mills (as Anfield B.C.) 259

Bicycle 1886 G.P. Mills 295 *1889/92* M.A. Holbein 324, 336½ and 359 *1892/3* F.W. Shorland 360½ and 370 *1895/7* M.A. Holbein 397 and 403½ (m.p.) *1898* F.R. Goodwin 428 (m.p.)
Unpaced 1900/1 T.G. King Jnr. 346½ and 357.
Tandem Bicycle 1895 G.P. Mills/T.A. Edge 377 and J.A. Bennett (n.m.)/ M.A. Holbein 397½
Unpaced 1921 F.G. Thomas/F.E. Armond 399
Tricycle 1885 C.H.R. Gosset (before joining) 231¾ *1887* G.P. Mills 264 *1889* W.C Goulding 280 *1890* F.T. Bidlake 289 *1891/2* M.A. Holbein 311½ and 337 *1894* F.T. Bidlake 356½
Unpaced 1908 F.W. Wesley 326
Tandem Tricycle 1887 C.W. Brown/W.C. Goulding 259 and G.P. Mills/R. Tingey 298½ *1893* F.T. Bidlake/M.A. Holbein 333
Unpaced 1926 F.G. Thomas/M. Dunn 347¾ *1952* E. Tweddell/J.W. Stott 412½

London-York

Bicycle 1890 J.M. James 16h. 52m. 0s. and T.A. Edge 14h. 33m. 0s. *1891* J.M. James 14h. 22m. 0s. *1892* F.W. Shorland 12h. 10m. 0s. *1899* F.R. Goodwin 10h. 16m. 0s. (m.p.)
Tandem Bicycle 1895 G.P. Mills/T.A. Edge 12h. 33m. 0s.
Unpaced 1901 A.H. and P.S. Murray 10h. 59m. 0s. *1907* R.A. and F.H. Wingrave 9h. 30m. 0s. *1934* G.B. Spary/J.M. Loten 8h. 32m. 0s.
Tricycle 1889 H.R. Pope 2lh. 4m. 0s. and F.T. Bidlake 18h. 28m. 0s. (best on solids) *1891* W.J.A. Butterfield 18h. 9m. 0s. *1892* F.T. Bidlake 15h. 28m. 0s. and 13h. 19m. 0s.
Tandem Tricycle 1892 T.R. Marriott/F.W. Briggs 15h. 20m. 0s. and F.W. Shorland/M.A. Holbein 13h. 19m. 0s.
Unpaced 1951 E. Tweddell/J.W. Stott 9h. 49m. 0s. *1953* A.S. Fowler/R.D. Cook 9h. 9m. 0s.

York-Edinburgh (all unpaced)

Bicycle 1905 C. Hilhouse 12h. 35m. 0s.
Tandem Bicycle 1936 A.B. Smith/F.E. Marston 8h. 47m. 0s.
Tricycle 1905 F.W. Wesley 14h. 27m. 0s. *1936* A.B. Marsh 11h. 18m. 0s. *1953* C.E. Green 10h. 28m. 0s.
Tandem Tricycle 1956 E. Tweddell/C. Sandham 9h. 38m. 0s.

London — Liverpool

Bicycle 1892 T.A. Edge 14h. 34m. 0s. *1895* E.J. Steel 12h. 29m. 0s.
Unpaced 1929 J.K. Middleton 10h. 43m. 0s.
Tandem Bicycle (unpaced) 1904 E.H. Grimsdell/E. Bright 12h. 25m. 0s.

1909 P.W.B. Fawley/L.V. Peirse 10h. 50m. 0s. *1934* G.B. Spary/J.M. Loten 8h. 38m. 0s.
Tricycle (unpaced) 1907 F.W. Wesley 14h. 48m. 0s.

Liverpool — Edinburgh (all unpaced)

Bicycle 1906 A. Mackenzie 14h. 2m. 0s.
Tricycle 1906 F.W. Wesley 15h. 33m. 0s. *1958* G.M. Tait (now Brennan) 10h. 54m. 0s.

London — Edinburgh

Bicycle 1889 F.W. Shorland 44h. 49m. 0s. *1894* G.P. Mills 29h. 28m. 0s. *1899* F.R. Goodwin 25h. 26m. 0s. (part motor paced)
Unpaced 1903 F. Wright 31h. 48m. 0s. *1904/5* E.H. Grimsdell 28h. 3m. 0s.and 26h. 10m. 0s. *1928* W.A. Ellis 21h. 53m. 0s.
Tandem Bicycle (unpaced) 1905 E. Bright/P.H. Miles 27h. 54m. 0s. *1925* F.G. Thomas/L.C. Cockerill 23h. 18m. 0s. *1936* A.B. Smith/F.E. Marston 20h. 18m. 0s.
Tricycle (unpaced) 1905 F.W. Wesley 32h. 42m. 0s. *1939* T.F. Maddex 25h. 17m. 0s.
Tandem Tricycle (unpaced) 1956 E. Tweddell/C. Sandham 21h. 16m. 0s.

Land's End — John O'Groats.

Ordinary 1886 G.P. Mills 5 days 1 hour 45 mins.
Bicycle 1891 G.P. Mills 4 days 11 hours 17 mins. *1892* T.A. Edge 4 days 0 hours 40 mins. *1894* G.P. Mills 3 days 5 hours 49 mins.
Unpaced 1904 F.W. Wesley 4 days 7 hours 25 mins.
Tandem Bicycle 1895 G.P. Mills/T.A. Edge 3 days 4 hours 46 mins.
Tricycle 1885 T.R. Marriott (before joining) 6 days 15 hours 22 mins. *1886 and 1893* G.P. Mills 5 days 10 hours 0 mins. and 3 days 16 hours 57 mins.

Land's End — London (all unpaced)

Bicycle 1902-3 J.E. Naylor 25h. 25m. 32s. and 22h. 7m. 18s. *1920* F.E. Armond 19h. 46m. 0s.
Tandem Bicycle 1947 L.E. Copping/J.M. Sloper 15h. 4m. 0s.
Tricycle 1923 F.G. Thomas 22h. 2m. 0s. *1948* A.L. Wilkins 17h. 44m. 0s.
Tandem Tricycle 1951 E. Tweddell/J.W. Stott 16h. 21m. 0s.

London — Bath and back.

Bicycle 1894 C.G. Wridgway 12h. 55m. 14s.
Tandem Bicycle (unpaced) 1903 E.H. Grimsdell/J.C. Paget 12h. 0m. 4s. *1920* F.M. and E.G. Inwood 11h. 43m. 35s.

Tricycle (unpaced) 1903 W.W. Robertson 16h. 16m. 38s.
Tandem Tricycle (unpaced) 1953 E. Tweddell/J.W. Stott 10h. 34m. 55s.

London — Brighton and back.

Bicycle 1890 F.W. Shorland 7h. 19m. 0s. *1894* C.G. Wridgway 5h. 35m. 32s. *1895* A.A. Chase 5h. 34m. 58s. *1896* C.G. Wridgway 5h. 22m. 33s.

Unpaced 1898 E.J. Steel 6h. 23m. 55s.
Tandem Bicycle (unpaced) 1906 J.C. Paget/M.R. Mott 5h. 9m. 20s.
Tricycle 1890 E.P. Moorhouse 8h. 9m. 24s. *1893* W. W. Robertson 7h. 24m. 2s.

Unpaced 1903 H.S. Price 6h. 53m. 5s. *1938* L.H. Couzens 5h. 20m. 57s.
Tandem Tricycle (unpaced) 1910 L.S. Leake/G.H. Stancer 5h. 59m. 51s. *1935* L.H. Couzens/W.G. Allen 5h. 6m. 52s. *1948* R.A. Petrie/R.F. Mynott 4h. 48m. 57s.

London — Portsmouth and back (all unpaced).

Bicycle 1904 W.E. Ward 7h. 50m. 37s.
Tandem Bicycle 1904 R.A. and F.H. Wingrave 7h. 13m. 10s.
Tricycle 1904 M.A. Crosbie 9h. 26m. 47s. *1938* L.H. Couzens 7h. 40m. 38s.
Tandem Tricycle 1948 L.H. Couzens/P.S. Bury 6h. 59m. 15s.

London — Pembroke (all unpaced)

Tricycle 1947 A.B. Smith 14h. 0m. 0s.
Tandem Tricycle 1951 E. Tweddell/J.W. Stott 12h. 58m. 0s.

London — Cardiff (unpaced)

Bicycle 1959 G.E. Edwards 7h. 27m. 0s.

CHAPTER VI.

Other Competitive Activities.

Track (or Path) Racing.

Although from the earliest days of competitive cycling there were those who specialised in riding on the track and others who competed only on the road, there were also some happy to participate in any form of cycling sport. So, vide the end of Chapter I, a number of North Road founder members also helped to form the Racing Cyclists' Club and of them 'Faed' Wilson, proving his versatility, at an 1886 Easter meeting in Dublin, won both the one mile and two miles races from scratch.

In 1887, in the month prior to the twenty-four hours road ride, Langridge and Albone were winning prizes in handicap races at Eastbourne and Biggleswade. The annual sports at Biggleswade naturally attracted support, (successful support on the grass circuit marked out), from North Roaders in the ensuing years. Earlier in the year G.P. Mills, in contrast with his long distance road rides, won a one mile handicap at Derby.

A year or two later an increasing interest in track riding had developed: thus in 1889 founder member Moorhouse broke tricycle records from twenty-six to thirty miles and fifty-one to fifty-five miles at Paddington track, where Bidlake and Goulding broke tandem tricycle records. A number of North Roaders joined the Stanley C.C. (taking its name after the famous explorer of Africa) for its path racing and in 1890 Arthur Ilsley, Tubbs and White took the first three places in the one mile tricycle race while in the ten mile bicycle event the order of finish was Bob Ilsley, Arthur Ilsley, White and Bidlake. For Arthur Ilsley, in particular, this was the start of six years successful track activity, winning prizes at Biggleswade and with Rowley winning a tandem race and breaking records from nine to sixteen miles in an hours paced race — in which, nevertheless, they were beaten by a solo rider by twenty yards. Twice in the period he beat the half, three quarter and one mile tricycle records at Herne Hill, where, with elder brother Bob, he also took World record for the flying quarter mile and English records for one mile and six to twenty-five miles in 1893 and won a five miles tandem race in 1894. With the end of road racing Arthur won the first club fifty at St. Albans track, in 1895 Faed Wilson had run a fifty there in place of the fourth Club fifty but, in contrast with the number in the road

FRANK W. SHORLAND

fifties, only received nine entries — young T.G. King won, and the first club fifty at the new Wood Green track — when Arthur recorded 2h. 5m. 22s. Between these rides he won a ten miles tricycle race at an open meeting organised by North London C.C., setting new records from six miles and won the N.C.U. ten miles tricycle championship — held at Manchester. In 1896 he was second in the Bath Road 100 held at Herne Hill, won the Club Fifty in 1h. 56m. 24s. at Wood Green where he also won a joint Stanley-N.R. six hours race with the amateur record of 151 miles seventy yards — T.G. King, Jnr. being second after leading for five hours. He also rode in the third Cuca 'twenty-four' in 1894 and was the last of the five finishers, covering 406m 1008y — when many good men were among the thirteen non-finishers.

Back in 1891 Holbein had essayed to be the first to cover 400 miles on a bicycle, riding on Herne Hill track with ample pacing but November was rather late in the year for such an attempt and although the gearcase fitted to his bicycle — a new idea — may have saved his chain from the rain, it was most uncomfortable for Holbein and his pacers and he was nearly forty miles short of his target at the end, covering 361m. 1446y. But the ride roused a great deal of interest and led to G. Lacy Hillier for the London County C. & A.C. to consider promoting a twenty-four hours race and Root & Company, the Cuca cocoa makers, to offer a 100 guineas cup for such a race. The plans came to fruition on Friday/Saturday, 22/23 July 1892 at Herne Hill when nine men started at 8 p.m. — not many but including such notable riders as Bates, Bidlake, S.F. Edge, Holbein and Shorland. The last after doing good rides on the Facile changed to a safety in recent years but for this Cuca twenty-four he reverted to a front diver — a geared up Crypto and a product of the Boothroyds responsible for the Facile. Prior to the Cuca Shorland had been second to the famous Zimmermann in the N.C.U. Fifty miles championship at Paddington and fourth to North Road winner Ede in the twenty-five miles championship. Bates led for the first hour of the Cuca but then Shorland went into the lead and gradually wore down the opposition. Bidlake collected tricycle records up to 200 miles before he retired: the other retirements left J.M. James in second place and when Shorland was having a bad time gained quite a number of laps — but Shorland's normal good riding was demonstrated by *'Cycling's'* artist depicting Shorland riding with his hands behind him talking to 'Faed' Wilson by the deaf and dumb finger language! Shorland and 'Jim Jams' both achieved the feat of 400 miles in the day for the first time, Shorland's 413m. 1215y. was a short lived world record, while James' total was 407m. 185y.

The 1893 Cuca, again in July, had eighteen entrants of whom the greatest challenger to Shorland was thought to be the 'little Welshman' Arthur

Linton and indeed they had a great battle for 100 miles — for which Shorland paid later but Linton retired at 115 miles. This and other retirements brought Bidlake, doing a fantastic ride on his tricycle, into second place behind Shorland — on a safety again. Both established world records at twelve hours of 233m. 1840y. and 220m. 1100y. They went on, despite Shorland having a bad period between 340 and 400 miles, to establish world records for twenty-four hours of 426m. 440y. and 410m. 1110y. — the latter still standing as record and on that day being over 12 miles better than third man Hammond of Essex Wheelers. Four others rode out the twenty-four hours.

The 1894 Cuca raised enormous interest with the prospect of Shorland making the cup his own with a third win. At the instance of bicycle riders tricycles were banned and many thus thought Bidlake would provide the greatest challenge — but the Cuca came only a week after that fateful collision in the North Road club fifty, Bidlake was still aching and bruised, and retired at 200 miles in the eleventh hour; instead the greatest challenge came from Fontaine of Polytechnic C.C. In the early hours Shorland established a lead of four laps, despite which some light hearted banter was reported, viz. Fontaine 'I've got my eye on that cup, Frank' — Shorland 'Yes, but you won't get your hands on it!' A great battle ensued with Fontaine trying to regain the lost laps but he eventually retired exhausted in the seventeenth hour. Shorland, although not unaffectd by the battle, went on to establish new world's records. The crowd of 25,000 were particularly pleased when record holder Huret of France took the front of a pacing tandem during the last hour. Shorland covered 460m. 1296y. to make the first Cuca Cup his own — to the enthusiastic cheers of the crowd at Herne Hill — and to ride his last race. There were also enthusiastic crowds outside the Gamage store in High Holborn: keen cyclist A.W. Gamage, a member of the Finsbury Park C.C., arranged a service of messengers to bring hourly mileages from Herne Hill for display in his windows: six policemen, a sergeant and an inspector were kept busy moving the crowds and Gamage was threatened with prosecution for causing a disturbance! Petersen of Coventry was second with 431 miles — four more than Chapple of Chelsea. North Roaders Clark and Arthur Ilsley were the only other finishers and, for the first time, all covered more than 400 miles.

A second Cuca Cup was offered and Lacy Hillier continued to promote a Cuca Twenty-four. No North Roaders rode in the 1895 Cuca, vide Chapter III, it being only a week away from the North Road Twenty-four at Wood Green but when we made our twenty-four a professional event in 1896 six North Roaders entered for the Cuca twenty-four at Herne Hill on the same day. And in the last hours of both events telegrams were sent from Wood Green to Herne Hill advising Huret's progress but initially failing to rouse

Fred Goodwin from the doldrums he was then suffering. However he was well in the lead and did revive in the last hour to give another North Road win and amateur record with 476m. 1702y. Another North Roader A.E. Pepper was third with 425m. 330y.

Not least of the problems for organisers of paced races, particularly over long distances, was arranging an adequate supply of pacers — on solo and multicycle machines — a body of men who rode many miles at high speed and got scant public praise for their efforts. The N.C.U. enacted rules covering pacers — status and use: Goodwin was under a cloud and lost his licence for two months because he had unwittingly accepted pace from a 'trade tandem' — i.e. a tandem and riders sponsored by a firm in the cycle trade. Lacy Hillier found the N.C.U. rules difficult to meet and so no Cuca twenty-four was organised in 1897, towards the year's end his Club — London County C. & A.C. — was suspended for non-compliance with these rules in a 100 miles race early in the year and was disbanded in 1898.

With the ending of paced racing on the road in 1894 the North Road Club gave serious consideration to building, alone or in conjunction with a club of like standing, a race track in North London. And in particular negotiations were started with Mr. Tufnell to acquire or lease part of his Park on which to erect a track — a scheme not favoured by the cricket club already using part of the Park. Such searches were, however, abandoned when it was found that a new track was being built in Wood Green by a company one of whose directors was 'Faed' Wilson. The speed potentiality of the cement surface of the new track was demonstrated by Arthur Ilsley in successive club fifties and when he organised the Club Twelve hours at Wood Green J.P.K. Clark and Fred Goodwin broke tandem record with their winning 262m. 1100y: T.G. King, Jnr. was second nearly four miles behind with Bob Ilsley third, and the youngest Ilsley, Lint, was sixth. There were few spectators present and the cycling press was commenting on the financial problems for clubs running track meetings.

At the end of 1895 came news of a North Road success in India — ex-secretary E. Rivers-Smith winning the one mile scratch race at a sports meeting in Bombay. Other successes came at home in 1896 with Goodwin and Prevost collecting tandem records from seven and ten miles in mid-May at a North Londn C.C. meeting, while in the North Road Fifty in which Arthur Ilsley got inside two hours, W.W. Robertson broke English tricycle records from twenty-six to thirty-seven miles — when a bursting tyre stopped him. In the London County C. & A.C. Century Cup race — which started the pacing dispute with the N.C.U. — Goodwin was second in 3h. 54m. 34s. to Palmer, beating Frost who, however, won the Anerley 100 a week later, Goodwin again being second. In 1897 Goodwin won a Middlesex County May meeting ten miles scratch race, with a new North

Roader, Ernest Gould, one of three in the same lap. Goodwin also won the Century Cup in 3h. 55m. 22⅖s., hard pressed by Pepper in the early stages, and a fifty mile scratch race at a Middlesex County Queen's Jubilee meeting at Wood Green in lh. 55m. 54⅖s. Then came his dispute with the N.C.U. and as a result he was unable to ride in the Bath Road 100 miles at Crystal Palace. Frost won his club's event, North Roaders Pepper and E. Gould being second and third, while Pepper was third in the Anerley 100. Gould delighted his clubmates by beating a large field to win the 100 kilometres world championship, this year held at Glasgow: he also won the N.R.-Stanley six hours race at Wood Green with 140m. 200y., Lint Ilsley being second and Van Hooydonk third. In 1898 Gould knocked forty seconds off A.E. Walters' 100 miles record, riding at Crystal Palace and using a weird 'Elliptic Chainless' bicycle: en route he was inside record from ninety-two miles onward and from 145 to 160 kilometres, the 100 miles taking 3h. 24m. 34s.

Towards the end of 1897 another Clark — R.P. — made successive attacks, at Wood Green, on tricycle records from one mile to fifty miles, reducing the mile to 2m. 10⅕s., increasing the hour figures to 25m. 1085y. and taking 2h. 16m. 54⅖s. for the fifty miles: in November he completed his sequence of records up to 102 miles. In October Hitchcock and Earl broke tandem records, also at Wood Green, from fifteen to twenty-seven miles, doing 27m. 1000y. in the hour.

In November 1897 the N.C.U. at last gave teeth to its anti-road racing policy by ruling that 'No licensed rider may take part in any race or paced record attempt on the road'. At a Special General Meeting on November 25 the Club decided to secede from the N.C.U. and to continue its present policy. Despite this North Roader W. Ward was elected secretary/treasurer of the N.C.U. London Centre for 1898 and the 1898 fifty miles race at St. Albans track was planned 'subject to a permit being obtained from N.C.U.'. However the circular announcing this event advised that as holders of N.C.U. licenses would probably have them revoked and thus be professionalised the race would be for unlicensed riders: licensed members wishing to ride as pacemakers should return their licenses. A.E. Marsh won the club fifty and H.A. Wingrave — the first of the five brothers to score — won a club 100 at St. Albans — their times were 2h. 4m. 32s. and 4h. 37m. 33⅕s. respectively — Wingrave also taking a one hour's race with 25m. 1510y.

Three North Road club races were planned for 1899 using the St. Albans track, but the May fifty miles got so small an entry that it was abandoned. The 100 miles race in June received eleven entries including both J.H. and R.A. Wingrave and was won by Pepper in 4h. 10m. 10s., Butler being second and Jack Wingrave third. The one hour race in August only had seven entries, Butler winning with 25m. 550y. in, vide the result sheet, 'unfavourable weather'. And this was the last North Road track promotion for some sixty years during which the North Road became completely a road club.

In mid-August F.O. Cooke won the Stanley C.C. six hours race at Wood Green — where, for lack of cycling interest, the track had been the venue for a Buffalo Bill show. At the year's end Wood Green track was closed and the site sold for housing development — and the Stanley C.C. ended its path racing activities. And this summary of North Roaders' path racing achievements omits a number such as Ede and Shorland being voted, by *Cycling's* readers, as eighth and eleventh of the twelve Best Path Racers of 1892, while in Litchfield's 1894 twelve hours race at Putney track young Steel improved by nearly three miles on Bidlake's 1893 tricycle record — Steel covered 223m. 1085y. And, perhaps, one should comment that path racing, even at its best, failed to exercise the attraction that the competitive camaradie of the paced road game provided.

One North Roader, Arthur Chase, continued competing on tracks, initially in England but soon achieving great fame in Europe. After a number of outstanding road rides subsequent to joining the North Road in time for the fateful third 1894 club fifty miles he proved his versatility by winning the half and one mile scratch races at Biggleswade sports. Later, in the 'Anchor' twelve hours at Herne Hill , Chase had a race long duel with A.E. Walters of Polytechnic C.C., who won with world record of 258m. 120y, Chase being two laps in arrears, while in October he broke the High Beech track records from one mile to one hour. In June 1896, Chase, now a professional, was in one of the famous 'Simpson Lever' chain matches: his opponent, Huret, was riding the Simpson chain and won the match — but this was regarded as a tribute to the Simpson pacing teams rather than to the alleged merits of the chain. This seems to be borne out by Chase's subsequent successes, winning a ten miles professional race and then going to Copenhagen to win his first world championship — the 100 kilometres (from J.W. Stocks) — and was afterwards presented to the King of Denmark. In September he easily won a fifty miles match against Wridgway at Wood Green. In 1897, at Glasgow, Stocks beat Chase in the 100 kilometres professional world championship and in the first stage of the Catford Gold Vase competition, the six hours race, Chase was inside world record at 100 kilometres but subsequently did not finish. Later, in successive fifty miles matches in Paris he beat T. Linton and Bonhours, breaking the sixty kilometres record in the last.

In 1899, at the Friedenau track in Berlin, he won an international 75 kilometres race beating a good field from Austria, France and Germany and at the same track in October he again won the 100 kilometres world championship, in 1h. 55m. 2⅕s. Walters being second and Bonhours third.

In 1900 Arthur Chase had a brilliant season — so much so that at its end the Club presented him with a special gold medal. In July, at Crystal Palace and paced by a motor tandem steered by his brother, F.W. (with whom a few years earlier he had broken tandem records) Arthur broke records up to twenty-two miles when the tandem chain broke. Next day he broke the standing start paced one mile and raised the British hour record to 37m. 196y. In September, in Paris, he won a fifty miles match against two leading Frenchmen raising the world hour record to 38m. 469y. and a week later, in Berlin, won a 100 kilometres race improving the German hour and 100 kilometre records — the latter to 1h. 47m. 14⅕s.

In 1901 his successes were restricted to paced record attempts at Crystal Palace, starting in September with the flying start one mile. By the year's end he held every British professional path record from one to 100 miles, including the one hour (38m. 40y.) and three hours (108m. 1026y.). He was at the opening meeting of the new Buffalo track in Paris in 1902, winning a motor paced fifty kilometres match against Bonhours and De. Guichard in 52m. 55s. In July at Crystal Palace he beat his own flying start mile and further reduced it at Canning Town in August — to 1m. 20⅘s. Back at Crystal Palace in late October paced by brother F.W. on a motor cycle he broke records from four to forty-two miles, covering 41m. 1325y. in the hour — quite a feat for a four and a half horsepower motor cycle as well! This, however was the end of his competitive cycling career — a career of outstanding merit: thereafter the brothers concentrated on the production and promotion of their B.A.T. motorcycles on which F.W. had already been breaking records — he covered 44m. 210y. in an hour in 1902. By 1905 they had become Chase Motors Limited marketing Chase motorcycles. Arthur remained a North Roader until 1911 though participating little, if at all, in club life.

Other than for training for road riding — Frank Wingrave was a devotee of this — no North Roader rode on the track until 1924 when Charlie Sewell, with his brother Ted, riding as Belle Vue C.C. men at a joint Belle Vue — Rodney C.C. evening meeting at Herne Hill, established a standing start one hour tandem record. Initially announced as 27m. 32y. the yards were later changed to 880: the record withstood successive attacks until 1926 when F.W. Southall and Watkins added three quarters of a mile. Ted Sewell did not join the N.R. until later in 1924 but the Sewell family, particularly Charlie, his son Jack and, more recently, his grandsons David and Roger have played so large a part in North Road life from the 1920s that we may be excused for an interest in the tandem record.

Another secondary interest came in 1935 when our member Len Copping was one of the quartet which won the North Middlesex and Herts. C.A.

4000 metre team pursuit championship for the Metropolitan Police C.C. It was another two years before another North Roader as such competed on the track — in August 1937 Les Couzens won the Tricycle Association track championship (a pursuit event) and also broke the flying start mile record reducing Bath Roader Harbour's recent record to 2m. 21⅗s. In 1933 road racing, but unpaced, had been reintroduced to Britain at the Brooklands motor racing circuit and attracted to this form of racing and path racing in 1935 Eric Povey became a member of Marlboro A.C. to pursue these aspects of our sport. And John Rhind spent a fortnight's holiday at the training headquarters of the Velo Club Levallois near Paris — the French having a high reputation in road racing, a major sport in Europe.

A further result of these changes in outlook — and in British cycling sport — and possibly anticipating that an agreement would be reached between the newly established Road Time Trials Council and the National Cyclists' Union — was that, at the Club A.G.M. in January, 1938, it was decided to re-affiliate to the N.C.U. There was, allegedly, a desire among young members to participate in the types of racing controlled by the N.C.U., but none did so in 1938 or 1939 when the threat of war may have taken possible participants into the Armed Services. A further complication developed during the war, in part due to the closed circuits used for massed start races being taken over for military purposes: a number of racing cyclists defied authority — both of N.C.U. and of police — and re-started group racing, albeit without a covey of pacers as fifty years earlier, on the lightly trafficked wartime roads. They formed the British League of Racing Cyclists to control their sport.

At the end of 1948 Geoff Edwards, then 'Captain for Open Events', wrote in our Gazette explaining the unofficial ten mile events, told us that some of the current young racing men planned to compete in both individual and team pursuit championships in 1949: he reported a time of 5m. 25s. in a trial run over 4000 metres. In 1949 Alan Kennedy got to Round four and Edwards reached Round three in the London Centre Pursuit Championship: in the Team Pursuit Championship our team — Blackman, Dean, Edwards and Kennedy — got through to the semi-finals of the London Centre and to eighth finals of the National Championships: they took third place in the London Centre by doing 5m. 9⅖s. to beat the Marlboro A.C. team.

At a Marlboro A.C. meeting, at which the team had a ride over, Edwards, riding as a second claim member, won the Marlboro five miles Point to Point race — cheered on by some twenty North Roaders.

They competed again in 1950 in London Centre, National and North Middlesex and Herts. Pursuit Championships and the Club joined the

Paddington Track League — but the participants were, and remain, modest about their achievements.

In 1951 our team again reached the semi-finals of the London Centre Championship, scoring a time of 5m. 5⅕ s. — their fastest but ⅕ second slower than Willesden C.C., and then lost third place to Belle Vue C.C. In 1952 the Kentish Wheelers put us out in Round three — unlucky Mark Withers had crashed during Olympic Selection trials at a Brighton meeting on the evening prior to our meeting with Kentish Wheelers. But the problems of travelling from Enfield, where most of the team members lived, into Central London for the Paddington or Herne Hill tracks, assembling and disassembling bikes, etc. palled: marriage had its effect also and Bert Swan found that he hadn't a team to train and encourage.

In 1955 Ken Lovett competed on the grass track at Enfield Stadium at the Enfield-Gladbach (linked in one of the town twinning schemes) meeting and was second in the Sprint and in the Points race. In the return match, in Germany, in 1956 he won 'The Devil' despite translation difficulties over which was the last lap. The interchange continued in 1957 but the cycling matches were at Paddington and here Ken won the 1000 metres standing start time trial but was disappointed in his 1m. 17s. until he learned that the German he beat by 2m. 9s. had done 1m. 15.8s. at Dortmund. And for this ride he was awarded the Harris Memorial Trophy for the outstanding performance at the Enfield-Gladbach meeting.

Other than Lovett's no track riding was done for a decade — until September 1962, when, under the influence of Jack Sewell, we combined with South Ruislip C.C. in the promotion of an inter-club Sunday afternoon meeting at the Gosling Stadium at Welwyn Garden City. Apart from Ken Lovett, Jack Sewell's elder son David was the only one with recent track experience — as second claim South Ruislip and these two and George Wingfield were the winners in North Road events — but the meeting also proved a notable social success, members wives providing refreshments. In subsequent years, and with Hillingdon C.C. when that absorbed South Ruislip, at least one meeting was promoted annually, usually preceded by an interclub twenty-five miles road time trial. In 1965 Geoff Edwards, paying a chance visit to Gosling Stadium, found Geoff Welch competing at a track league meeting and later enquiries revealed that Geoff Hall and Michael Harvey were also competing in such events, modestly not telling the club and thus depriving themselves of encouraging support.

In 1968 a club track championship was introduced as a John Palmer Memorial — John having been killed in a road accident in 1967 — using a cup from Charlie Sewell's prizes, offered by Jack, his father having died in 1966. It seems appropriate that the first champion, after a close fought trio of contests, should be David Sewell.

Meetings were planned for May and September in 1970 but, a great shock, Jack Sewell died in March. David took over the organisation and lost the Championship to Lingwood at the May meeting — it was fortunate that it took place then because the September meeting was rained off. David won again in 1971 but the 1972 meeting was also rained off and this has, so far and unfortunately, discouraged promotion of further meetings.

10 Miles Events.

Back in 1888, when opposition to road racing grew to the stage causing the N.C.U. to ban the road racing of the time and of paced record attempts on the roads, the North Road C.C. considered the problem at its Annual General Meeting. Experience of ten miles events organised in 1886 led the Club, at its A.G.M., to rule that it should not promote any further events at distances less than fifty miles. Despite this, in September 1888 two events over ten miles courses between St. Albans and the top of Digswell Hill were promoted for members only — the results cannot be traced but it is known that there was some police interference, to the indignation of those concerned! Nevertheless the policy of regarding fifty miles as the minimum distance for events was confirmed and persisted after road racing had been replaced by time trialling until 1923. Then, with the persuasion of the offer of a Cup by Bedford member Dr. Kilham Roberts twenty-five miles time trials for members were inaugurated in September, 1923 — in 1922 the same donor had presented a Cup for the 300 miles Barnet to Doncaster and back ride.

In view of our long concern, shared by the majority of the leading clubs, not to arouse police hostility by the promotion of short distance (and, therefore, more obvious) events, it is amusing to find that the first modern North Roader to compete in ten miles events was policeman Len Copping! And these were events organised by the Metropolitan Police C.C., and in one case at least, an inter-event with another police club, the riders were started at half-minute intervals instead of the accepted minimm of one minute; this event was in 1937 — the term 'modern' being comparative!

Not until our track riding of 1949 and the early 1950s did ten miles events reappear in North Road life and then but as unofficial trials indulged in as timed training spins on close to London courses on the Barnet bypass — to polish the speed of the contestants. By 1959 Peter Bury was reporting on a series of Wednesday evening ten miles events timed by Ted Kings: in 1958 Ted had been much involved in the redesign of the twenty-four hours course and had started his career as a R.T.T.C. official, culminating, in 1965 with his appointment as its National Secretary. So our club evening amusements had, by Ted's association with them, become respectable!

And in 1960 came official recognition, by the issue of Ministry of

Transport Regulations, of the time trials game, followed slowly by participants changing their attitudes to their sport. So, by 1963, the N.R. delegates persuaded the R.T.T.C. London North District Council to forward to National Council the proposal that all competitors in open events should carry numbers. Also in 1963 Club Captain Reg Risley drew attention to the membership span covered by the eight participants in a July mid-week ten — ranging from the mid 1930s to the current time. But at its A.G.M. the North London D.C. agreed to ban evening tens on the Barnet bypass because of the ever increasing traffic. However a Christmas morning ten was tried and, despite cold and wet, five competed, two being on trikes, and Mike Harvey was fastest in 27m. 52s. This frolic was repeated on many subsequent Christmas mornings.

But the G.H. Stancer Memorial Committee, operating a fund launched after Stancer's death, in 1962, led a great change in attitudes to 10 mile events when in 1966 it instituted a Schoolboys' ten miles Championship: heats were run throughout the country and the leading riders in the heats were brought together in a Final. And the Memorial Committee asked North Roader Geoff Edwards to be co-ordinating Secretary for this Championship. The R.T.T.C. was intimately involved, the area heats being organised by the District Councils and Yorkshire D.C. promoted the first final — for Stancer was born and grew up in Yorkshire, moving to London in 1904 and joining the North Road. A journalist, he became editor of *'Cycling'* and consequently founder and first President of the Century R.C. which grew out of *'Cycling's'* Century Competition in 1911: in the mid 1920s he became Secretary of the Cyclists' Touring Club and remained such until his retirement when he became C.T.C. President — after another North Roader, Admiral Hefford, had held that office as a bridge from Ducal to Commoner presidents. G.H.S. was also, in turn, secretary and president of the R.R.A. — which has yet to add ten miles to its record books!

In 1968, sponsored by Ted Kings, the North Road ran an open ten miles for Schoolboys and Juniors and this event was repeated in subsequent years, extending the entry to cover other groups until, in 1971, the field included Boys, Juniors, Seniors and Veterans. But, after reporting the results of the 1971 event, organiser Peter Bury expressed the view that there were, by then, so many open tens that it was doubtful, in view of its three other open promotions, whether the Club should continue to expend the effort involved— and the Committee agreed.

In 1972 Tony Hartley achieved a time of 22m. 20s. in a ten miles event — the fastest so far achieved by a North Roader.

Modern 'Massed Start' Road Racing.

As had already been mentioned, when the Second World War closed the venues for road racing on closed circuits — the areas being taken over for various military purposes — which had been in use for races since 1933, a number of ardent riders refused to accept the resultant suspension of road racing. They organised massed start races on public roads — on which motor traffic had been considerably reduced in wartime conditions — and, as the N.C.U. took strong exception to this road racing, the British League of Racing Cyclists was formed to control the sport and otherwise cater for the needs of the competitors. The North Road C.C. was one of the many clubs supporting the N.C.U. policy, as it was propounded in 1942.

Thus, in support of this policy, the first experience of North Roaders, as such, in modern road racing was on the roads in Finsbury Park in May 1949. This was in a North Middlesex and Hertfordshire Association event over twenty-eight laps of the by no means level circuit — approximately thirty-eight miles; Derek Edwards was our best in ninth place, Alan Blackman and Kennedy being fifteenth and sixteenth, after being involved in a 'pile-up', and these three took second team place: Geoff Edwards took the prize for the greatest number of lap points, despite mechanical trouble in the eighteenth lap and a vain pursuit thereafter. At the end of July Alan Kennedy won the N.M. & H.A. Championship over fifty miles on a circuit near Matching Green in Essex where, in August Geoff Edwards was sixth in the N.C.U. London Centre fifty miles race and his brother Derek equal fifth in an Eastern Counties Junior twenty-five miles. Back in Finsbury Park early in September, over forty-four laps — sixty-two miles — Geoff Edwards was second in the N.C.U. London Centre Championship, Alan Blackman was fourth and they collected a number of 'prime' awards en route. Later in the month, on the Matching Green circuit in a N.M. & H.A. Junior event at twenty-one miles Geoff Harness was third, Derek Edwards fifth with Alan Swain 'on his wheel': in the senior race, at fifty miles Alan Blackman was second and Derek ('Dixie') Dean third with Geoff Edwards within inches.

Early in 1950 John Rhind suggested, in view of members interest, that we promote a 100 kilometre massed start, 'on a closed circuit of course' — but the idea was not pursued.

In 1952 the road racing enthusiasts within the N.C.U. persuaded that body to sanction races on public roads, to the extent of a monthly event in each N.C.U. Centre, limited to forty starters in each, and one National event with sixty riders. But our erstwhile road and track racing enthusiasts had lost interest, concentrating — successfully — on time trialling.

A new generation took up the road racing game in 1955, when, in July, our junior team won in a twenty-three miles race at the Stapleford Tawney circuit (on another erstwhile R.A.F. aerodrome), Ken Lovett being second, Mike Ennis fifth and George Wingfield sixth in an event promoted by Dixie Wheelers. In August Ennis was equal fifth in the N.C.U. Junior Championship — forty-two miles at Church Lawford ex R.A.F. station. Maybe our new massed start men's activities were not adequately reported — at the Club A.G.M. in February 1956 a proposal that the Club affiliate to the B.L.R.C. was only defeated by five votes — 17-22. The same motion lost by only one vote in 1957 but succeeded in 1958 whereupon a poll of the Club was demanded — and resulted in a tie! President Harry England gave his casting vote in favour, supporting the A.G.M. decision. But before action to affiliate could be taken the N.C.U. and B.L.R.C. had amalgamated as the British Cycling Federation.

In 1960 both road racing and time trialling received official recognition by way of Ministry of Transport Regulations, road racing having to receive advance police approval in all respects but only course details, date and time have to be notified in advance in the case of time trials. It was under these regulaions that, after nearly seventy years, the North Road C.C. re-entered road race promotion when, on 7 April 1963, Michael Hill organised an Open Road Race for Juniors. In line with the current practise — so vastly different from that of the Club's early years — a circuit of some ten miles of hilly by-roads was traversed anti-clockwise the necessary number of times. This race was won by A.G. Couch, Twickenham C.C., North Roaders Geoff Hall and David Kings (son of Ted) being second and fourth. Later in the year our youngsters rode in Junior and Schoolboy races on the Crystal Palace circuit, performing well but not getting placed. In 1964 the race was won, with a margin of forty-six seconds, by J. Stammers, Wren Wheelers, the only North Roader being outclassed. In mid April George Wingfield rode in the three events of the 'Enfield Week-end' and finished eighth on the overall score but, on 2 May, after working hard at the front over many laps of a sixty-five miles race, he was tailed off in the last lap — but perhaps George's efforts helped David Sewell to take fourth place.

The 1965 A.G.M. appointed Michael Harvey to the new post of Road Racing Secretary, he having already persuaded four other clubs to join with us in forming a road racing league. Michael Hill, however, continued organising the Open Junior Road Race, but only fifteen started, on 11 April: Howard of Whitewebbs C.C. won, second man being at one second and then a gap of two minutes — no North Roader started. However Geoff Hall and Welsh, David Sewell, George Wingfield and Ken Lovett rode in other events early in the season but only Welsh gained a place. In August Michael Harvey was criticising our riders for lack of team spirit in their riding but reported that Roger Sewell had taken second place in the B.C.F.

North London Junior Championship. Welsh was third in the first Combine race and sixth in the second in which Roger and David Sewell were third and fifth and John Blackman (no relation of Alan) fourth. Later John was designated captain of our road racing team, having increased his road racing experience during a recent period in Australia. David Sewell won the third Combine event from Roger, Geoff Hall being fourth.

Early in 1966 John Blackman accumulated sufficient points from placings to be promoted to first Category and the North Roaders provided first team in the first Combine event. Our Open Road Race was changed to cater for second and third Category riders — and received 200 entries — forty were accepted for the race and ten as reserves — in accordance with B.C.F. regulations. After using courses near Essendon and Much Hadham the 1966 event was run on four circuits of a course near Puckeridge and totalled approximately forty-two miles. This race was won by D. Sparks, Wren Wheelers, in 1h. 45m. 17s., David Sewell, in tenth place, being best North Roader. Between April and August John Blackman, George Wingfield, Peter Lancaster and Geoff Hall were placed fifth, sixth and/or seventh in various Open Road Races while in the Verulam C.C. promoted Combine event David Sewell was second and was supported by members in fourth, fifth, sixth and ninth places. Michael Harvey surveyed the year with satisfaction — we finished with two first category riders and four in the second category.

In 1967 our Open Road Race was expanded to two events — a fifty miles for Categories one, two and three and a thirty miles for thirds and Juniors — both over a ten miles circuit near Barkway on 16 April, the events starting at 10.30 a.m. and 1.30 p.m. The thirty miles was won by R. Sweeting, Westerley R.C. by three lengths from T. Ewing, Wembley Phoenix — who, in 1968, won our Memorial Fifty. The fifty miles was won by A. Gowland, Polytechnic C.C., three others being in the same second: Gowland later, as a professional, was in the winning team in the 1972 'Skol' six days on the special track erected at the Wembley Stadium. The organisation of our road races was taken over, at short notice, by Adrian Soane. North Roaders failed to score either in our Open or in other events and despite our Michael's efforts the Combine broke up.

Symptomatic of this change, at the 1968 A.G.M. the posts of Road Racing and Massed Start Secretaries were merged with Michael Harvey in the office. Our Open Road Races — thirty miles for Juniors in the morning, fifty miles for Seniors in the afternoon — took place on 12 May and were jointly organised by Roy Cook and Eric Povey. The Junior race was won by G. Owen, Harp R.C. in 1h. 19m. 0s. and the Senior by M. Dobson, Highgate C.C. in 2h. 6m. 35s. — both events being 'oversubscribed' with entries.

At the end of July, in the Club's name, Michael Harvey promoted the B.C.F. North London Junior and Senior Championships over a course south-east of Hatfield — four laps plus (forty-five miles) for Juniors, and seventy miles for Seniors. B. Searle, Whitewebbs C.C. became Junior Champion and J. Winstanley, Finsbury Park C.C. the Senior Champion, his time of 2h. 53m. 27s. being over two minutes faster than second man: Winstanley's ability on a hilly course has also been proved in the North Road Hardriders' twenty-five. No North Road names appeared in the Championship fields and although David Sewell later in the year won a Priory Wheelers road race interest had so waned that in 1969 the post of Massed Start Secretary lapsed and, despite their apparent popularity the promotion of our Open Road Races also lapsed.

Michael Harvey continues as one of our representatives to the B.C.F. and serves on the committee of the North London Division. And in 1975 — near the end of July — he promoted two North Road Open Road Races on the new 'Temple Mills' road circuit specially constructed in the Lea Valley Regional Park and coming into use this year. One, over one lap of the twelve miles circuit, was for schoolboys and girls and was won by Gareth Smith of V.C. Braintree. The other race was a one and a half hour handicap event won by one of the scratch men, M. Baker of Harp R.C. who had also collected a number of the 'prime' prizes offered on the day by Frank Armond, Bill Frankum and Ron Hayden.

NORTH ROAD CYCLING CLUB 1895

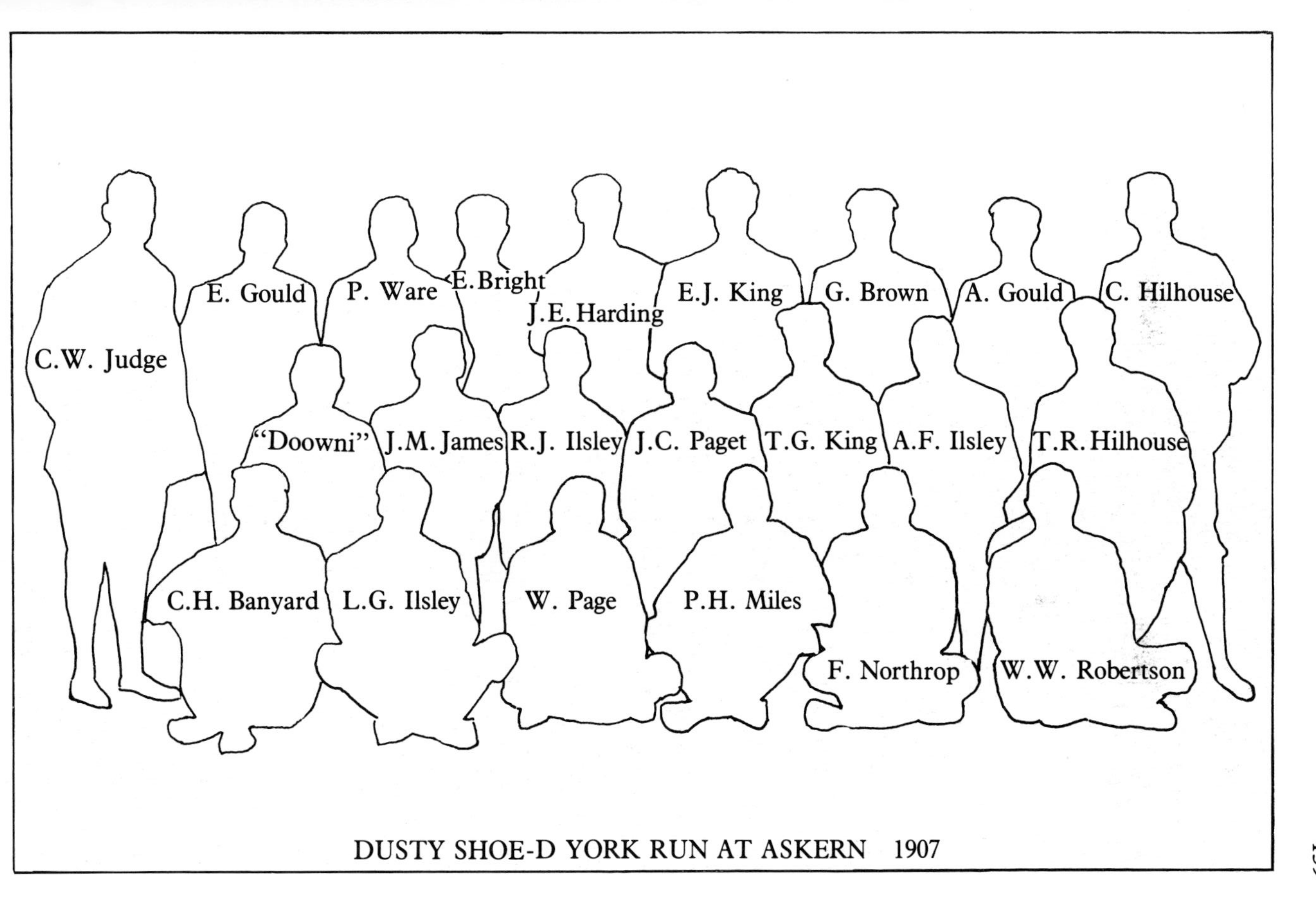

DUSTY SHOE-D YORK RUN AT ASKERN 1907

NEW YEAR RUN CROSS KEYS, ST. NEOTS 1928
F. Cole M. Mott R. Walker C.J. Cole P.H. Miles C.P. Gregory
R.S. Lloyd F.W. Nichols E. Abbott J. Owen J. Van Hooydonk
A.B. Smith J.M. James G. Brown C. Chisman W. Freeman
F. Marston L. Cockerill S. Artaud F. Thomas F.H. Inwood
F.T. Bidlake C. Couling E.G. Bullen S. Hills

AT GOSLING STADIUM WELWYN GARDEN CITY MAY 1967

Standing: K. Fletcher V. Stocker F. Birch J. Austin G. Edwards
J. Palmer R. Sewell M. Harvey G. Welsh A. Kennett
C. Hall K. Lovett B. Thorp D. Sewell P. Bury
R. Lansdown F. Thorp A. Lancaster B. Palmer
F. Sellens R. Risley J. Rhind W. Ehrman

Seated: E. Haldane J. Sewell F. Armond W. Frankum
S. Mottram H. Manwaring

The Juniors included Members: Graham Edwards and D. Reynolds

CHAPTER VII.

Club Life.

Apart from the inaugural meetings of 1885, North Road club life started on the last Saturday in February of 1886 with an invitation club run meeting at Tally Ho Corner, Finchley, and after a diversion to Shenley returned for tea and a social evening at the Salisbury Arms (alias 'The Old Sal') at Barnet. This was followed by a social evening, with music and recitation offered by members and friends to entertain the gathering and thus set the pattern for later occasions, settling as the 'Opener' and 'Closer' for the winter club run season and continuing until the reconstruction of the hotel in the 1930s entailed the destruction of the 'tin chapel' (as it was called) in the yard. Outside the Old Sal was the eleventh milestone from London, now represented by a square block in the kerb, and this, in 1922, was nominated as the southern end of the newly established Barnet to Doncaster and back ride with a cup, presented by our then Bedford member Dr. Kilham Roberts.

In the club's early years its life revolved round the races it promoted and the story of these and the names of the outstanding riders among those participating are recalled in previous chapters and particularly in Chapter II. And as the club was founded for the promotion of road racing it appears appropriate to continue recalling the men participating through the years. Consideration of space, however, limits us to remembering those who set new standards after the end of the paced era — when Joe van Hooydonk gave them 205 miles in twelve hours to beat while he remained in the club to act as master of ceremonies at many a sing-song at Barnet, St. Neots and Peterborough, despite the considerable personal and commercial interest he developed in motor vehicles and their manufacture. Seymour Cobley initiated a new era in unpaced time trialling in the first fifty of 1901 when he sped at better than twenty miles per hour for the first time — 2h. 27m. 15s — fifty years later he was the moving spirit in the founding of the 'Twenty-Four' Society within the Club. Seymour's time wasn't approached until 1906 when the youngest of the five Wingrave brothers, Frank, equalled it in the second fifty: he also brought the club 100 time just inside 5h. 20m. that year — a standard Walter Ward had achieved in Mr. King's 100 in 1904 with 5h. 14m. — surprisingly considering the course from north of

Welwyn, via Codicote and Hitchin to Norman Cross and back, Mr. King's 100 often produced faster times than the Club 100. 'Gee' Nutt was the first winner of Mr. King's 100 in 5h. 46m. — it being a rule that timing be to the next whole minute. That was in 1899 and thirty years later 'Gee' was delighting us with his company, riding a bicycle, on club weekends. The 'Boss', T.G. King, must have been pleased that his eldest son put up the fastest time on this course in the next three years, second son Eddie winning the Club 100 in 1901 with 5h. 23m. 54s. Guy Webb took eighteen seconds off the Cobley/Wingrave time in 1908 — in the third fifty — and Jack Webb brought the time down to 2h. 25m. 49s. in the third fifty of 1910, a year later winning Mr. King's 100 in 5h. 11m. when Lemprière equalled van Hooydonk's paced twelve to win the club event with 205 miles.

Then we were in the doldrums for a decade including, of course, the 1914-1918 World War years when the Club suspended sporting activities — as did most cycling clubs. Frank Armond, returning from that war, re-started improvements by winning the 1920 club twelve with 208 miles. Two years later Frank Thomas was fastest over the new Barnet-Doncaster and back ride with 20h. 38m. and in 1923 Bedfordian Cook won the new Kilham Roberts cup for twenty-five miles in 1h. 9m. 7s. In 1924 Sam Innocent took the Club 100 cup with over three minutes reduction of Frank Wingrave's time, and the next year, after I had taken nine seconds off the fifty time in the first fifty, Sam's brother John reduced it to 2h. 24m. 48s. in the second. Also in 1925 I brought the Club 100 time down to 5h. 10m. 22s. — and added quarter of a mile to Frank Armond's twelve. 1926 saw Jack Middleton make his mark, winning Mr. King's 100 in 5h. 4m. but 1927 witnessed notable improvements. Stan Artaud, coming to us from Essex Roads C.C., showed us how to ride fifties, winning the three and bringing the time down to 2h. 13m. 57s. in the third. Inspired by Stan I made a mid-week midsummer evening attempt on Mr. King's 100 and achieved the first unpaced 100 miles ride inside five hours by a North Roader — my 4h. 55m. won the Mr. King's prize. And Bill Ellis, having brought the 'Donkey' ride inside twenty hours in 1926, in 1927 showed his potential by pushing the twelve hours mileage up to 215¼ and, in 1929, to 224¼ when he also brought the Doncaster and back time down to 17h. 18m. In 1928 and 1929 Jack Middleton won Mr. King's 100 in 4h. 52m. in both years and inscribed 5h. 0m. 57s. on the Club 100 cup in 1928 — from 1927 to 1932 the club event was incorporated in the Open 100.

Mr. King's 100, as a competition over his chosen course, ended in 1932 — primarily for lack of support due to the effect of the increasing number of open events available but also the committee had doubts about men speeding through Hitchin. Also in 1930 the policy of restricting our sport to other than Sundays was abandoned — our younger members were unimpressed by the fact that the major sports of Britain avoided Sunday performances. This changed the social aspect of our club events from being related to a catering place to provide food before and after — The Cock at Hitchin, The George at Ickleford, The Old Vicarage at Shefford — to being linked with overnight accomodation, mostly at 'Fuller's' at Girtford Bridge — by then clubfolk Lou and Mrs. Ewing had taken it over from old Mrs. Fuller. From here in 1933 Bill Harrison won the club 100 in 4h. 53m. 57s. and a year later Geoff Spary was nineteen seconds faster; in 1936 Alf Marsh brought the time down to 4h. 48m. 55s. Eric Povey was then reducing the twenty-five miles time — by 1937 to 1h. 6m. 9s., when John Rhind added half a mile to the Bill Ellis twelve hours total. Les Couzens, whose father had won handicaps at fifty miles early in the century, lowered the twenty-five miles time to 1h. 3m. 50s. and that for the fifty — in the second event — to 2h. 12m. 34s. in 1938. A year later Alf Marsh chiselled another twenty-one seconds off the fifty in the third event. These two lads were among the thirty or so North Roaders who served in the Second World War when, unlike the First, road sport continued to some extent but there was another hiatus in improvements until the new members coming in during the mid 1940s, and subsequently, showed their abilities. Geoff Edwards was the first so to do, both in 1947 and 1948, when his times were 2h. 9m. 3s. in the second fifty, 4h. 37m. 52s. in the 100 and 229¼ was his twelve hours mileage. Also in 1948 Alan Kennedy took the twenty-five Cup with 1h. 1m. 59s. — a time Geoff Edwards improved by thirty-six seconds in 1949, also in 1949 Alan Blackman won the third fifty in 2h. 7m. 14s. and Bob Mynott covered the 300 miles of the 'Donkey' Ride in 16h. 6m. Alan Kennedy won a 1950 fifty in 2h. 7m. 7s. and Peter Boyes the 100 in 4h. 36m. 7s. 1951 was another Geoff Edwards year — 4h. 33m. 26s. for the 100 and 237 miles in the twelve hours while Mark Withers, in his brief period in the Club, won the twenty-five Cup in 1h. 0m. 14s. and Mynott the 'Donkey' Cup in 15h. 46m. In 1952 it was Alan Blackman's turn — the 100 miles in 4h. 31m. 59s., the twelve hours at over twenty miles per hour — by three and a half miles — and a similar speed for the Doncaster ride — 14h. 57m: Mark Withers took the Fifty Cup in 1h. 59m. 33s. Two years later Geoff Edwards increased the twelve hours mileage to 244⅞ while Alan Blackman reduced the club 100 time to 4h. 30m. 44s. and a year later achieved twenty-five miles per hour to win the twenty-five cup in 59m. 15s. In the hope of weaning our many younger members of this boom time from the plethora of open events being promoted, especially at twenty-five miles, in the 1950s we were promoting four club twenty-fives each season, in addition to three fifties, as some defence of club life, and a number of these attracted an entry of near thirty members. The increasing number of open events also created the problem of finding dates and courses on which to run club events: perhaps because we had retained one fifty, at least, as a Saturday event, it may have been easy for us to take advantage of the almost universal five day working week then in vogue to transfer most of our events back to Saturdays. Because established courses on the London-Newmarket road were more accessible from London than those on the North Road we had successfully experimented with such courses in the late 1930s. In the late 1950s onwards we tended to orientate our events to this area. Initially there were suitable catering places in the Stansted Mountfitchet area — and there was a good train service to Bishop's Stortford. Then the affluent age arrived and private transport became common among members enabling them not only to carry other members and their bicycles and/or wives and children to and fro events. As catering places disappeared the ladies took over the provision of refreshments and a new phase of club life had arrived. A number of clubs using this road had obtained — by various self help construction methods — individual country headquarters and by the 1970s the North Road was negotiating for the use of one of these — the owning club having become inactive. Ironically, since then we seem to have used the courses in that area somewhat less.

Reverting to time trialling, despite the number of club events, much riding in open events occurred (vide Chapter V) and faster times achieved, notably by George Wingfield, who, by 1961, had brought the time on the twenty-five Cup down to 57m. 48s. Ken Lovett improved the club 100 time to 4h. 24m. 45s. in 1964 and the club twelve hours total to $249\frac{3}{8}$ miles in 1965. Since then we had the misfortune to lose John Palmer in a road accident when he was showing great promise in our events. Other riders, such as David and Roger Sewell have got close to the best club event times but have just failed to improve them, except in their tandem rides.

In contrast with the Club's sporting activities are the more formal occasions — although '*The Cyclist*' said of our first Annual Dinner — on Thursday, 25 November 1886 at the Cock at Highbury — it 'made an entirely new departure in dispensing with a formal dress dinner'. At that, and a number of subsequent Dinners the principal guest was invited to take the chair — in 1886 it was Dr. E.B. Turner, president of the Ripley R.C. and a leading N.C.U. councillor. Incidently the tickets for that first Dinner cost five shillings! There was a political touch about our 1890 Dinner when Mr. Cowley Lambert, M.P. was in The Chair — he was described as a consistent and persistent upholder of all kinds of sport: this became an occasional feature of later Dinners, the most recent such principal guest being Rear Admiral Hughes Hallett when he was an M.P. and as a Ministry of Transport under secretary introduced the regulations governing cycle racing and time trialling on public roads: he was with us in 1959. By then it had long been the practice for our President to take The Chair — by chance our third President, F.T. Bidlake (alias 'Biddy') first took The Chair as President in 1914, when the First World War forced us to move out from London venues (such as 'The Holborn' and 'Frascati's') to 'The Old Sal' (The Salisbury Arms) at Barnet for a gathering restricted in numbers, and primarily, to members. The various restrictive regulations which helped us through that War prevented the holding of another Dinner until 1919. 1935, of course, was a special occasion celebrating the Club's Golden Jubilee — with our founder 'Faed' Wilson and a number of other original members rejoicing in their club's pre-eminence. The Second World War also forced us out of Central London, first to Beale's at Holloway — when secretary Frank Armond was able to offer tickets at 6s. 6d. — and then to The Salisbury Arms (rebuilt in mock Tudor) at Barnet — and tickets at five shillings as for the 1886. We had two 'Annual Dinners', in the form of Sunday lunches, at the Salisbury Arms, then in 1942 we went back to an evening gathering at Beale's — when President Bill Frankum being away with the Army, senior member Cecil (alias 'Mouldy') Paget took The Chair. In 1943 we returned to Central London venues, the risk from enemy aerial attack being regarded as sufficiently small. In the early years the after-dinner speeches and the prize presentation (in which the twenty-four winner is traditionally carried shoulder high round the room to receive the cup and his prize) were interspersed with entertainment — songs, recitations, conjuring sometimes by professional artists but more often by our talented members — and this only faded out in the 1940s. Now we wonder how there was time for such entertainment — perhaps we now talk more with our clubmates and visitors? We had a long and successful series of Annual Dinners at the Connaught Rooms, until new management decided that our habits were not profitable — a little later the Road Records Association Triennial Dinner was similarly treated. There were, of course, outstanding Dinners to celebrate our Golden Jubilee and our sixtieth and seventy-fifth years. Increasing charges eventually had the same effect as the onset of two World Wars and drove us out of Central London — in 1971 we moved back to the venue for the 1894 Opening Run and other North Road gatherings: the Red Lion at Hatfield had had a notable extension, named The Cranborne Rooms. However for our ninetieth year we reverted to central London and The Horseshoe.

Mention of an Opening Run takes us to our less formal but more numerous occasions. In 1887, linked with the Stanley Show (of bicycles, tricycles and accessories), we promoted two 'Grand Assaults of Arms' at the Royal Aquarium at Westminster — the first on 29 January was something of a failure but the second, on 5 February, was very successful — despite which we did not repeat the effort. When the North Road Club started it was already traditional in clubdom to mark the beginning and end of the cycling season with a social gathering called Opening and Closing Runs and the North Road followed this tradition. So in Spring and Autumn we gathered at venues between Barnet and Hatfield to listen to members and friends singing, reciting or playing musical instruments, to watch boxing matches (for a time there was a North Road Boxing Club based on the Two Brewers at Hadley) and 'lantern shows' showing black and white pictures printed on glass from negatives. After a time it was appreciated that the North Road club run season was in the winter — the summer was devoted to racing activities and, initially, to the social programmes of members' other clubs — so our Opening Run became an Autumn occasion and the Closer came in the Spring. In common with the world in general, with the development of radio and television, domestic self-entertainment has decreased or disappeared, with the exception of the developments in photography, giving us colour slides and ciné film for projection for our entertainment. And we should remember gratefully the men who sang to us through the years — 'Barney' Banyard, 'Harry' Cole, Mentor Mott, Joe van Hooydonk (who also provided the lantern shows), 'Mouldy' Paget and Charlie Sewell are names which come to mind.

Then there were the strenuous weekends to Shrewsbury to support the Anfield 100 at Whitsun and the less strenuous ones to villages west of Reading — with a decade of delight at Mrs. Legg's at Brimpton — for the Bath Road 100. But the most outstanding series of club runs, from London to York, an inspiration of 'Faed' Wilson and Bidlake, started on 20 June 1891 from St. Martin-le-Grand General Post Office, cheered off by a crowd estimated at a thousand. Twenty-five were booked for the run and these were accompanied by many friends over the early miles. The refreshment stops were at Hitchin, Buckden, Stamford, Grantham, Newark, Askern and Selby; the start was at midnight and arrival at York was scheduled for 10 p.m. This was the first ever organised club run over such a distance and in view of the cycles and road surfaces of that time aroused great interest, including support of Daily Telegraph war correspondent (though whether this had any bearing on the task is dubious!) Bennett Burleigh, who rode as far as Grantham and then trained on to York to see the ten survivors arrive, and to report the ride in his paper. The sense of achievement and the special joy of companionship which comes of riding through the night into the dawn and on through the day ensured that the York Run was repeated year after year. Public interest declined and the unskilled cyclists of Selby ceased to be a nuisance by turning out to ride with the party, but others joined in — Speedwellians and Anfielders — either en route or at York. And the practice grew of booking a launch trip on the Ouse on Sunday morn, postponing the return to an afternoon train with reserved coaches for

CHARACTERS OF THE 1930's

GEORGE BROWN a YORKER
of 1900's Nicknamed 'ANTI'
after 'ANTIPON' Weight Reducer.

CHARLIE SEWELL

WOODBINE HAYLOCK

BILL FRANKUM

JACK LOTEN

FRANK MARSTON

HARRY ENGLAND

'HAM' MEACOCK
First young Motorist

FRANK ARMOND

riders and for their machines. And for some the ride became a 'must', notably 'Robbie' (W.W. Robertson), who missed the first run but started in every subsequent one until the last in this series — 1916. In 1915 came the first change in the pattern of the run when, instead of riding through Doncaster, the North Road was left at Bawtry and byways via Thorne and Snaith were followed to Selby, York being reached by 9 p.m. And in 1916 the first stop was moved from Hitchin to the cottage at Roxton which, for nearly thirty years, was the weekend home for a group of North Roaders — the most successful of at least three such ventures, the others being at Chawston and Eaton Socon.

After the First World War it proved impossible to restart the Run but as one of the ways of celebrating the Golden Jubilee of the Club, albeit a year late, 1937 saw the start of a new series of York Runs, using the Easter weekend. This was the idea of new captain Hugo Paige — we started at midnight of Maundy Thursday/Good Friday at Barnet (to which the original York Run had moved in 1904), but where the original York Runners got willing service during the early hours from the hotels they frequented, we had less choice. But Mrs. Ewing, then owning the old 'Fuller's' place at Girtford Bridge, left a pleasant first snack for us. The all night café at Stilton was awful but thereafter breakfast at Grantham, lunch at Bawtry and then via Thorne to tea at Selby — the Londesborough Arms used in the original series — were excellent. Thanks to a strong N.E. wind, snow showers and the chronic unfitness of Frank Marston we reached York two hours behind schedule at 8 p.m. — and after planning the ride Hugo was unable to be with us and Vice-Captain Fred Birch was in charge — seven rode all the way, picking up others en route to make eleven at York and several others were with us for part of the ride. No plans were made for the return journey, but Ernie Haldane and I toured back through Derbyshire and set the pattern for later years — still unofficially in 1938 but appearing on the runs list in 1939. While the original York Run managed to carry on in the first two years of the 1914-1918 war it was replaced in 1940 by a very successful Easter tour based on the King's Arms at Chipping Norton, which we had found a year or two earlier and where Mrs. Barber fed us royally and with her daughter Kathleen and Mr. Barber made us very welcome. In fact we rarely missed a monthly visit there during the War and, having been evacuated to Bath, I was there able to remain in touch with the Club — and the King's Arms attracted others of our provincial members and as a prospective member, Yorkshire man Ed Green, then resident in the Lake District; while from Chipping Norton we were able to visit 'Faed' Wilson when he lived near Stow on the Wold and later at Mickleton. We were indeed saddened when the Barbers decided to retire from the King's Arms — but this is a recurrent loss we have suffered, sometimes after a decade or so, more rarely, as with the Cross Keys at St. Neots, after many years.

The York Runs restarted on Good Friday, 1946 with a programme similar to that of 1939 with a pleasant second stop at Wittering's Aero Café and breakfast at Long Bennington, en route to York, Saturday night at Monyash — a rather strenuous ride this — and Sunday night at Mrs. Copley's at Warwick. As the fifties passed the traffic slowly increased making re-routing to avoid the A1 road desirable before breakfast, (initially moved to Southwell) and entailing amusing — at least in retrospect! — routes devised by Ken Davis with R.A.F. dromes blocking our route and arriving on the bank of the River Trent with not even a ferry to get us across. In the mid 1950s instead of returning south from York we went north and west, led by Ed Green, and occasionally joined by some of the northerners he brought into the Club, to spend the rest of the weekend based on West Burton, etc. in Wensleydale, the Londoners training back from Leeds. Gradually the stretches of the A1 followed were whittled down until only Sandy to Tempsford and Alconbury Hill to Wansford were involved and all this became dual carriageway. At Wansford we worked N.E. to Bourne and over the hills, passing the old Rippingale twenty-four turn, to Sleaford for breakfast, and it became the practice for those who could not — or would not — start from Barnet to join the run there, often motoring thus far with bicycles in, or atop the car, or starting on Maundy Thursday: I did this on my last two rides, in 1967 and 1968, riding to Leicester and being motored over by Sid Mottram. Lunch was at Gainsborough and thence we twisted through the flats of Lincolnshire into South Yorkshire for tea at Snaith. The Run and the Club — and their relatives — suffered a terrible shock in 1973 when the three riding through the night were run down and killed by a large lorry, driven by a man working illegally long hours. Those gathered to meet them at Sleaford were notified by the police and completed the run in a state of shock and sorrow. After much consideration the Club committee decided to abandon the midnight start — for those who could, the run started on Maundy Thursday and slept at Sleaford where others joined in on Good Friday morn. This robbed the York run of its special quality and we know not how long it will now continue. The three killed — Peter Bury, Terry Johnson and young Robert Garrad — and particularly Peter, who had scored twenty-five York Runs — would not, however, wish us to forget all the pleasure we accrued through the years on these runs: I was on at least twenty-four of them.

Week in and week out, other than for special occasions, the Club has a Saturday afternoon tea run and a Sunday lunch run, usually with a tea venue. There have been periods of annual inter-runs with other clubs — particularly the Bath Road Club. And over many years, there was a

KEN LOVETT takes refreshment from ROY COOK: Two great workers for the Club

THE TONY KING MEMORIAL
Presented to the Club by his Colleagues, and awarded for Meritorious Service

Peterborough weekend, initially with the Speedwell B.C. and later joined by the Midland C. & A.C. both of whom had some notable songsters to join with ours to provide the evening entertainment. We also spent some enjoyable weekends with the Wessex R.C.

In the early 1950s a new event appeared on the Club fixture list. This was the Annual Christmas lunch, the first being held at High Wych. After visiting several houses in Hertfordshire the fixture settled for a decade or more over the border at Berden until the retirement of Mr. & Mrs. Smithers.

All through the years groups of members have toured together at home and abroad and their tales have enlivened the pages of the Gazette which, since 1903, has played an important part in Club life. At least one such party in southern France visited founder member Tinsley Waterhouse at his home. The Gazette was started by 'Jonah' Wilson in 1903, after several earlier unsuccessful attempts — 'Jonah' and his successors have endeavoured to ensure that members activities were recorded for the benefit of both participants and those unable to be present — and even, possibly, for posterity.

Club members have been notable for the service they have given — in the broadest sense over sixty members served in the Armed Forces in each of the World Wars of whom eight died in the First and four in the Second. In the narrower sense of service to cycling, in the early years Bidlake and William Ward were prominent in N.C.U. affairs, in particular in the formation of the London Centre of which Ward was treasurer, and for a time secretary, continuing in office until 1900 — after the Club's secession. 'Faed' Wilson took the lead in the formation of the R.R.A. in 1888 and was its President until he resigned in 1924 and was succeeded by 'Biddy' — who was on the committee for forty-three years, second only to George Stancer who scored fifty-four years, the last twenty-six as President. And of the eleven past secretaries of the R.R.A.six were North Roaders. Biddy served the pastime in many ways vide Chapter VIII and as related in that chapter Bill Frankum was deeply concerned in the formulation of the rules and regulations of the Road Time Trials Council. We have had successive representatives on the North London D.C. of the R.T.T.C. and one of these, Ted Kings, went on to become National Secretary — the longest serving National Secretary to date — after playing a notable part in an extensive revision of our twenty-four course.

The Cyclists' Touring Club has latterly adopted the secondary title of the Cyclists' Association to indicate its wide sphere of interest in protecting and promoting all aspects of cycling. 'Ever' Bright was an early member prominent in C.T.C. affairs but our longest and greatest link was Stancer who took over the secretarial duties and continued in this office for some forty years and followed other 'commoners' to become President. The first non-ducal President was Admiral Hefford, a North Roader who became a C.T.C. Councillor in the late 1930s and was Council Chairman for some years. A successor to Stancer as Secretary was Reg Shaw also a North Roader even if we saw little of him and in this period we had three members on the Council.

And through the years successive club officials — Presidents, Secretaries, Captains, Treasurers from the start and in later times Racing or Time Trials Secretaries, Captains for Open Events, Twenty-four Hours and Memorial Fifty and Hardriders Twenty-five secretaries — have contributed to club life. Perhaps the greatest of these was Alfred Inwood, alias Doowni, who was Secretary/Treasurer from 1907 to 1921, except for 1919, and Gazette Editor for three of these years: in his time the secretary was responsible for the Club's racing programme, including the Twenty-four. And such was his popularity that a 'verse' was added to that strange mixture 'The North Road Chorus' designed to show extra appreciation of a song well sung or something outstanding in speeches. To these officials the Club is ever indebted.

Although founded as a man's club the North Road has long been conscious of the contribution members' ladies have made to the Club. Initially, like the children of that period were supposed to be, they were seen (if only occasionally) but not heard. In the 1920s when women took to active cycling more extensively, they were seen more frequently helping in North Road events and the C.T.C. Hampstead Section almost became a mixed social offshoot of the North Road. More daringly in the 1930s a North Road run was labelled 'Ladies Run' and members were invited to bring their ladies to it. Twenty years or so later the Twenty-four Society invited members to bring their ladies to the Twenty-four Society Dinner and by then a Ladies Night — a dinner and social in a suburban hotel in North London — in Enfield for several years — was a well established way of saying thank you to the ladies for all the secretarial and catering work they do for the North Road C.C.

A.J. WILSON with the first Mrs. WILSON
On a HUMBER of the EARLY 1890's

CHAPTER VIII.

Our Presidents.

By Cecil H. Paget and A.B. Smith.

No club can have been more fortunate in the succession of Presidents who have led the North Roaders in the ninety years of the Club's life.

When the club was started in 1885 it was not thought necessary to include a president in the officials elected to run the club and this continued to be the view until the 1887 A.G.M. With the creation of the office there was, obviously, only one man to fill it — Arthur James Wilson, then nearing his twenty-ninth birthday.

Much has, naturally, been written of 'Faed' Wilson in the last pages of Chapter I but in amplification of those lines we can start in 1869 when he, as a lad of eleven, was riding a boneshaker. However the bad attack of scarlet fever in 1870, which left him deaf, stopped his cycling for a time and he was still a weakly lad when he resumed, developed an intense interest in the pastime and, incidentally, built up his strength. Soon he was in the Star B.C. and Canonbury B.C. and although owning only a roadster ordinary bicycle he took up racing and, before long, was winning prizes. But a bad accident towards the end of 1883, in a race on the Alexandra Palace track, turned him from bicycles to tricycles — on which his racing was even more successful and by 1885 he was a scratch man.

His successful participation in the North Road's first open event and his later leading part in the founding of the Road Records Association are covered in Chapter II and there is reference to his timekeeping therein and in Chapter III. He achieved a high reputation as a timekeeper for track and road events and records — in 1887 his cycling friends presented him with a fine 'Kew A' certificated chronograph watch as a wedding present. He was an official N.C.U. timekeeper until 1889, when he resigned that office to concentrate on timing road races and record attempts. In 1890 he was elected the first President of the R.R.A. and continued in that office until 1924, when he retired in favour of F.T. Bidlake, having, in 1920, had his year as President the Fellowship of Old Time Cyclists. He founded the Motor and Cycle Trades Benevolent Fund and was, for twenty-five years, its Secretary and Treasurer: during this time he had a succession of business activities, the last and most successful being as an advertising contractor —

an amazing record for a man suffering the affliction of complete deafness. A token of the high regard in which he was held is the number of friends and associates who learned to talk to him by the hand language of the deaf and dumb. He also achieved successes in the worlds of yachting, motor-boat racing and motor-cycling.

He felt it desirable to resign from the office of North Road President at the 1895 A.G.M. Later he was presented with a silver tea and coffee service inscribed with tributes to his services to the Club, and with expressions of the esteem of its members. He saw three other Presidents come and go and when the 1939 War drove him from his home in Christchurch (near Bournemouth) to a succession of abodes in the Cotswold area, North Roaders weekending at Chipping Norton visited him with mutual pleasure — he then had a rowing machine to keep him fit and still rode a tricycle! He died on 20 March, 1945 at the age of eighty-seven in the Club's Diamond Jubilee Year — and we remember him by naming the Twenty-four Cup the Faed Memorial Trophy.

As successor to Faed there was only one member who could possibly succeed him and, although Bidlake was also proposed, Thomas George King, nominated by Faed, was elected by an overwhelming majority. This was a tribute to the impression T.G. King's character had increasingly made on his clubmates after joining in August, 1889, when he was forty-one years old — for in the five years he had not served on the Club committee nor held office. He had, however, become a regular supporter of club fixtures and in particular the Shrewsbury weekend — for the Anfield 100 at Whitsun — and the York run.

Yet prior to joining the Club his initial enthusiasm for cycling had waned – was this a result of his amazing capacity for taking physical punishment? It was later told how he started his first holiday from the London solicitor's office, at which he began work in 1876, by walking home to Southampton in the day. Long before he reached home he was crippled — neither his feet nor his boots were adequately prepared for the eighteen hours task — and he spent the rest of his holdiay on crutches! But it didn't stop him doing the walk again until he acquired a bicycle of sorts in 1879 — some said it was a boneshaker but maybe that was a reflection on its quality — and rode down in fifteen and a quarter hours. By 1881 he owned a well made fifty-four inch ordinary and, for some years, spent most weekends plugging away for hours on end; but the year he joined the N.R. he changed to a safety. Although not participating in the Club's races he developed an ambition to do a gold medal ride and when the North Road 12 hours standard was increased to 185 for 1892, T.G. joined the Stanley C.C. also and managed 171 miles for a Stanley gold and an N.R. silver. He got his N.R. gold with 191½ miles in 1894 increasing this to the new standard of 195 in 1897 — these were all paced

T.G. KING and F.T. BIDLAKE

F.T. BIDLAKE

rides but the Boss (as he became fondly known during his presidency) did not like riding close to a wheel so the advantage he got from his willing pacers was minimal. His best twelve hours ride was an unpaced one in 1903, when he was fifty-five and he covered 185 miles for a gold medal. These rides were models of physical effort judged to last the time and having nothing left at the end. His greatest admiration was always reserved for the rider, irrespective of the time he had achieved, who was completely exhausted at the finish and groaning 'Never again!'

Like his predecessor it was as a chairman that Boss King excelled; he never made up his mind about a subject until all had had their say, weighing every argument put forward and then, but only if asked, he would state his view. A solicitor by profession, his wise counsel was invaluable to the committee and, in particular, to club secretary A. Inwood who had to write the letters to other clubs, through the difficult period of the problem of the 'makers' amateur'. This was eventually solved from 1912 onwards by inclusion of the anti-advertising clause, devised by Bidlake, in the entry forms for events and eventually adopted by all clubs promoting open events. A decade later it was included in the recommendations of the Road Racing Council. Ironically the Boss privately disagreed with Club policy and personally saw no objection to amateurs competing with professionals or semi-professionals.

In 1899, to encourage unpaced riding, the Boss instituted 'Mr. King's 100' over an out and home course between Welwyn and Norman Cross, for individuals to attempt, his prize going to the member achieving the fastest time each year. Although the course has been abandoned the prize has been retained as the fastest time prize in the Club 100.

A true North Roader in every way, the Boss was delighted when his eldest son — also 'T.G.' but known as George — won Mr. King's 100 in 1900, 1901 and 1902, the twenty-four in 1900 and 1901 and various other events, while his younger sons, Eddie and Caleb also rode well at various distances.

In his absence, due to illness, the Boss was re-elected to the Presidency at the 1914 A.G.M., all expressing the hope that he would soon recover but he died on 18 March, 1914 loved and revered by all who knew him. When Cecil Paget first knew the N.R., through his father, in the 1920s, 'Boss' King was still affectionately remembered as a great gentleman.

If T.G. King was considered in 1895, to be the only possible successor to Faed in the ensuing years Frederick Thomas Bidlake had grown in stature and become the only possible successor to the Boss. He had already chaired Committee and Annual General Meetings and the Annual Dinner when the Boss was unable to be present and was duly elected as the Club's third President.

He had been cycling for several years and was a member of the Cyclists' Touring Club when he joined the North Road in January, 1888 — his twenty-first year. At the 1889 A.G.M. he was elected Hon. Secretary, the beginning of his long service to the Club, early aspects of which are touched on in Chapter III. He was an outstanding rider, particularly on a tricycle, and his rides at various distances in road races and road record attempts are chronicled in earlier chapters: perhaps his most notable ride was his second place, on a tricycle, to Shorland in the second 'Cuca' twenty-four at Herne Hill track.

But it was as a journalist and an administrator that his fame grew until it was said of him that 'he bestrode the cycling world like a Colossus'. His name first appeared in the cycling press as assisting the timekeeper at the finish of a road record attempt in 1887. A few years later he was assisting Faed in the timing of the twenty-four, later deputising for him in the timing of Club events and finally taking over from Faed the timing of most road events and record attempts on North Road courses. The close links between cycling and early motoring resulted in Biddy (as he was popularly known) becoming involved in motor trials and thus Trials Secretary to the Motor Cycling Club for some twenty-five years: this entailed devising courses and persuading folk to act as checkers — a considerable extension of his early work in organising the North Road twenty-four! As his fame spread he also became involved in the timing of motor boat and aircraft races — notably the Schneider Trophy seaplane races in which air speed records were established in successive years.

Volumes could be written about Bidlake's activities in and services to cycling in general, apart from those to the Club.

Some of them were —

Committee man and timekeeper to the R.R.A. and, after Faed's resignation in 1924, its President — a total of forty-three years.

A founder of the London Centre of the National Cyclists' Union.

Founder and first Chairman of the Road Racing Council.

A founder and trustee of the national Cyclists' War Memorial after the 1914-1919 World War.

Member of both the Government's Departmental Committee on Traffic Signs and the Advisory Panel of Experts to the Ministry of Transport.

In appreciation of these last services and others of similar national import the Cyclists' Touring Club made him an Honorary Life Member, a Vice-President and awarded him the Sir Alfred Bird medallion.

He was a member of the Fellowship of Old Time Cyclists and its Dinner Secretary in 1925, but refused the office of President, saying there were others more worthy.

Despite the high regard in which he was held by most cyclists and, in particular, by most of his clubmates (there were some who disliked him intensely) he remained a modest man. Like his predecessors he was impeccable as a chairman, keeping his own opinions in reserve but resolving others' difficulties with kindness and humour. Not completely so, A.B. recalls a committee at which our then secretary was making a long and complicated report difficult to follow — tensions were eased by Biddy's comment 'It's an epic, it starts in the middle and goes both ways!'

After reaching his sixty-fifth birthday in 1932 he contemplated retirement and in 1933, hearing that his ancestral home at Great Bidlake, near Bridestowe in Devon, was becoming vacant he had almost completed arrangements to retire there, with his wife, in mid-October. Alas on 27 August, as he cycled down Barnet Hill, returning home from a ride, a motorist turned left across his front wheel and left him but three inches of road space. Biddy's description was 'I slowly somersaulted over my jolly old Sunbeam on to the pavement, and granitic contact has discoloured all my 'prominent parts' except my nose'. He obviously had to miss the twenty-four on 1/2 September but planned to be at the Memorial fifty on 1 October — but although his injuries seemed but superficial, complications resulted in his death on 17 September.

The news of Biddy's proposed retirement had resulted in plans for a testimonial to him and acting as Secretary/Treasurer to the testimonial fund was Bath Roader S.M. Vanheems who was ending a decade as R.R.A. secretary. A sizable fund had accumulated when Biddy died and the testimonial fund sadly became a Memorial fund which received an amazing national response and the Bidlake Memorial Trust was established. The North Road has always been represented on the Trust Committee, initially by Stancer, England and Cheveley, the first two until their deaths in 1962 and 1961 respectively and Cheveley until his resignation in 1963. Frankum was brought on to the Committee in 1938 and has been the Trust's secretary since 1948, Armond came on in 1952 and Geoff Edwards in 1975 while Cecil Paget has had the privilege and honour of serving as a Committee member since 1950.

A Memorial Garden was established at one of Biddy's favourite spots on the North Road, where it is joined by the road from Shefford, by Girtford Bridge, and known in the cycling world as Poplar Fork. In error that poplar was cut down when the Garden was being made but was replaced by three — one at the apex and one each side of the base of the triangle — a seat inscribed 'This Garden is dedicated to Frederick Thomas Bidlake, a great cyclist, a man of singular charm and culture and an untiring worker for cyclists'. A central sundial is inscribed 'He measured time' and a milestone at the apex says 'London forty-eight and a half, York 148 F.T.B. Few have known this road as he'. This part of the North Road has now been bypassed by the dual carriageway A1 road and Biddy's garden is almost as quiet as in his early years of riding.

Apart from the upkeep of the Garden, the main function of the Committee is to consider annually the award of a Bidlake Memorial Plaque. The cycling spheres considered are racing in all its forms, touring, administration, literature and inventions for, and changes in, design of cycles. Each year the Committee has to decide which cyclist has achieved the most outstanding performance or contribution to the betterment of cycling in one or more of these fields. It is to the credit of the pastime that the years in which no award was made are very few.

Quite possibly the chosen successor to Biddy surprised many outside the Club but we knew what we were doing when we elected Samuel Howard Moxham as our fourth President. Not a racing man like Bidlake or Wilson but a cyclist in every other way and one who had endeared himself to everyone by his knowledge of our game and of the Club.

Born in 1880 he acquired a bicycle at the age of fourteen, and rode regularly, subsequently eagerly following the competitive side of our pastime. As far as anyone could establish his name first appeared as a rider in the Bath Road Club's annual Bath and back tourist ride in 1911. He was still an unattached rider however, when he joined us in March 1924 and in the Club twelve of that year he covered 167 miles, this being his first ever race. In 1925 he rode the twelve again and did 178¾ miles and rode also in the second fifty when he overshot the turn and finished in 2h. 52m. 4s. just missing a handicap award; his two twelve hour rides both gained him silver medals, not bad for a non-racing man who was fast approachng the age of forty-five.

Although he had been a member for less than twelve months, in 1925 he was asked to take over the post of Hon. Secretary when C. Jay Cole retired, and held that position for three years, also taking on the Treasurership in 1927.

For years the Secretary had organised all the Club and Open races but as Moxey had had no experience of the organisation of races, it again became necessary to appoint a Racing Secretary and Frank Armond was the first of these.

Always an ardent supporter of all Club activities, Moxey was a regular helper in all races and was at Ivinghoe for the Bath Road inter-club runs, at Brimpton for the Bank Holiday weekends and at the Cross Keys, St. Neots for the New Year weekend etc. He had to retire from official work for the Club at the end of 1927 for specialist studies in his professional sphere — Insurance — but came back to the Committee in 1929.

With the approach of the Club's Golden Jubilee thought was being given

S.H. MOXHAM

H.H. ENGLAND

to its celebration and the first thing that had to be done was to ensure that all the Club records were available, so in 1933 Moxey was appointed keeper of the Club Archives; with his usual painstaking care he collated much of Club Activities from minute books, early issues of *'Bicycling News'*, *'The Cyclist'*, *'Cycling'*, and other periodicals devoted to our sport and when it was decided to publish a Club history to commemorate our Golden Jubilee, Moxey was asked to write the book. He had some misgivings because he considered that his personal acquaintance with the subject was not sufficient for its historian. The Committee, however, thought otherwise so he agreed and in the course of its preparation he unearthed a vast quantity of forgotten material. The result we all know — a magnificient book, 'Fifty Years of Road Riding', which was not only a fitting memorial to the Club but also to the fine character of its author, his passion for accuracy and his intolerance of slipshod methods.

Also in 1935, he was appointed a timekeeper to the R.R.A., a position well suited to one with his love of accuracy, unfailing reliability; and imperturbable temperament. He timed numerous road records including many of the epoch making rides by those fine Australian professionals, Opperman, Milliken and Stuart — and he is remembered with affection in Australia today by those who were concerned.

He was an admirable Chairman and his varied activities and efforts on our behalf invariably enhanced our reputation; in his last couple of years he grumbled regularly that his 'wretched screws', as he called his particular type of rheumatism, prevented him from getting to know the younger membership of the Club better. He had to miss the 1938 twenty-four because he had a heart attack followed by a slight relapse but was resting quietely at home. The result of the twenty-four was telephoned from St. Neots and brought a typical 'Moxonian' response but the end was obviously nigh and a few days later on 15 September 1938 he passed on peacefully in his sleep at the early age of fifty-eight. 'Fifty Years of Road Riding' has a dedication which says 'To all those who have striven, in whatsoever way, for the honour and glory of the North Road Cycling Club during the fifty years of its existence this history is dedicated' and none have striven more conscientiously for its honour and glory than Samuel Howard Moxham.

The sudden and rather unexpected death of Moxey put the Club in somewhat of a dilemma; there was no apparent successor although several of the older members fully deserved the honour. They were, however, not particularly active and not sufficiently in touch with the younger element in the Club whose activities would keep the name of the Club alive. Many members thought the President of the North Road Club should be one who was prominent in the general world of cycling and none of the older members was in such a position; eventually a ballot was held to decide upon the next President, with Bill Frankum being elected. He had proved during his thirteen years membership to have all the qualifications necessary — administrative ability, foresight, clear headedness and an extremely concise and methodical brain, although only thirty-two years old. However, war came, Bill was called up and in 1943 was sent abroad; he then felt that the Club needed someone who was at home and active so would not stand for re-election at the A.G.M. in 1945. This time Bill had an obvious successor to commend and Harry England was duly elected as our sixth President; the pen picture of our fifth and present holder of this office will conclude this chapter, so we will now deal with the story of another great North Roader following in the wake of Wilson, King, Bidlake and Moxham.

Henry Herbert England first came to our knowledge when appointed editor of '*Cycling*' in 1929. He was not a cyclist in the true sense of the word like his predecessors had been and he quickly realised that although a competent journalist he would have to learn all about our machines, our sport and our organisations. Biddy soon persuaded him that the obvious way of doing this was to join the N.R., which he did in December 1930 and soon brought his own brand of enthusiasm into the old game. In 1934 he was elected to our Committee and served for three years, but in 1937 business commitments prevented him from standing for re-election. Then the war came and he was back on the Committee in 1940; in the following year he took over the job of Hon. Treasurer, a position he held until 1948. Early in the war he was one of a sub-committee of three who organised our 'Comforts' Fund for our members serving in H.M. Forces and very often a cheery note from Harry went with the gift or money being sent.

Before the war he entered fully into the game of record-breaking, offering his services as transport manager/chauffeur to our men who were attempting these records; he loved the Memorial Fifty when it was confined to the twelve fastest fifty milers each year and was always in the forefront of the arrangements for the twenty-four after the war. To his great annoyance he had to miss some of the twenty-fours in the 1950s as the World Cycling Championships often clashed with our special weekend; if he wasn't with us in person his spirit was in the Fens with us.

As a speaker at Club Dinners he became in great demand, being knowledgeable and fluent; he genuinely preferred to be introduced as 'President of the North Road Cycling Club' instead of as Editor of '*Cycling*'; he was very proud of the high honour we had given him and nothing was too much if it was for the Club. He naturally served on many committees in the sport, but one in particular he liked, was Hon. Secretary of the Fellowship of Old Time Cyclists which he took on as a duty to our game; of course he was not eligible to be a member but he was prepared to serve, in the only way he could, the veteran cyclists whose numbers were fast diminishing.

In the early 1930s he toured extensively on his bicycle, or should we say bicycles, as often just before going on holiday he would have delivered a new machine glistening with plating which he would put thoroughly through its paces before giving it approval in the pages of '*Cycling*'. As far as we know he was never a racing man but there is a record of a twenty-five in 1h. 45m. 0s. in a club event, not N.R., which included climbing Digswell Hill both ways. Not in the racing sphere he did successfully complete at least one C.T.C. Triennial Veterans' 100 miles in twelve hours ride.

In the late 1950s his health began to deteriorate and although he carried on most diligently with his work as Editor of '*Cycling*' and as our President, he was sometimes missing from our activities; a cruise for some weeks to the Mediterranean alleviated his troubles to a certain extent; he retired from '*Cycling*' at the end of 1959 after almost thirty years as Editor.

At the A.G.M. in 1960 he was elected Editor of the Gazette and started to think of a new Club History for the celebration of our seventy-fifth anniversary in October. Early in 1961 however, he was forced to spend several weeks in hospital and he passed away on 9 July mourned by all who had known him.

This time the obvious successor was there in our previous President and on 28 October, 1961 Bill Frankum was duly elected for the second time. He had joined us in 1925 having learnt his cycling with the Hampstead Section of the C.T.C.; at the end of that year the Gazette remarked 'he was a promising youngster'. How well that has been proved. In 1927 he was elected to the Committee and apart from his period in the army — 1942-1945 — and a brief spell in 1951/2, when he was an inspector for the Bank in which he had a successful career, has served the Club ever since. He was Treasurer in 1929 and then Secretary from 1934 to 1938, when he became President for the first time.

In 1937, when the Road Racing Council was re-organised into the Road Time Trials Council, he was a delegate and played a notable part in evolving the rules by which the new body would work — so much so that he topped the poll for the first interim committee in 1937 and when the R.T.T.C. was fully constituted in 1938 he was appointed as its first Honorary Treasurer. He was eventually called to H.M. Forces in 1942, sent to the Middle East the following year where, in 1944, he was Chairman of the Buckshee Wheelers (Jerusalem Section) at their New Year dinner. His absence abroad had worried him in that he could not do his job as President in a proper manner. The recrudescense of massed start cycle racing on the road, banned in 1897, he viewed with concern as a possible threat to the time trial game which was the Club's main activity. He felt that it was essential for the direction of the Club, in possibly difficult circumstances, to be in the hands of someone on the spot and stood down from the Presidency in 1945. His service to the Club was not, however, finished as in December 1952, he volunteered to act as Hon. Secretary again and continued until the A.G.M. in 1955. These are his official jobs in the Club, but he has also represented us on other cycling bodies, is still on the R.R.A. Committee and the 'Bidlake Memorial Trust' Committee and was formerly on the Stancer Memorial Committee.

Because of his profession, his racing career was somewhat spasmodic; all our events in the 1920s were held on Saturdays and it was always extremely difficult to get away from his office early enough to ride. He was, of course, also studying hard to make a successful career, so that by present day standards his racing efforts appear modest. His first race was the second Club fifty in 1925 when he did 2h. 36m. 27s. and won third handicap award, whilst his first twelve in the same year saw him having two punctures in covering 180¾ miles for a silver medal. In 1926 he raced three times, a twenty-five of 1h. 20m. 55s., a fifty of 2h. 40m. 36s. and a 'Mr. King's 100' in 5h. 37m. being the result; the following year only one race a fifty in 2h. 38m. 38s.

His father died unexpectedly in 1927, when Bill was but twenty and with added family responsibilities he felt that he could not continue racing. Before giving up, however, he was determined to ride a 'twenty-four'. Thus, in 1928 he followed a twenty-five of 1h. 17m. 37s. with a good 'Donkey' ride of 20h. 40m. and ended with 354¾ miles in the twenty-four. These latter two rides also meant that he had earned silver medals at every standard medal distance.

A lover of the countryside he toured extensively at home and abroad both before and after his marriage, but still found time to help in our Club and Open events.

It is as an adminstrator and Chairman that he has given of his best to us and our sport, his organisation of our fiftieth and seventy-fifth Anniversary Dinners are an example of his thoughtfulness, the methodical way everything is planned; his equable temper is aided by a quiet sense of humour.

In 1948, when we were asked to organise the first R.T.T.C. Championship twenty-four in conjunction with our twenty-four and Cecil Paget was officially the organiser, Bill's acumen in handling the red tape of the R.T.T.C. National Committee ensured that our members had the prior right of entry to our *Invitation* twenty-four and that we must be permitted to cut detours for the slower riders.

It is a fortunate conjunction that Bill's fiftieth year of membership should also be the Club's ninetieth anniversary and his twenty-first year as President, a longer period than any of his predecessors.

W.C. FRANKUM

G.E. EDWARDS

ADDENDUM

Chapter 3 onwards of this book covered the Club story to its 90th year, but certain problems prevented it being published in the ensuing year. This addendum is designed to cover the happenings of the subsequent five years.

After promoting 27 N.R. twenty-fours Sid Mottram decided that the 78th N.R. twenty-four which incorporated the National Championship would be his last. The task of promoting the 79th twenty-four in 1977 was undertaken by a small committee led by Geoff Edwards.

Also in 1977 Bill Frankum intimated that he did not wish to stand for re-election as president at the A.G.M. Cecil Paget and Geoff Edwards were nominated as candidates for the office and Geoff was elected. Geoff joined the Club in 1944 — a good year for new members — and soon proved a very capable rider; his achievements on road and track are listed in various chapters. He has served on the committee for many years and had short spells as Secretary, Treasurer, and Editor. He was also organising secretary for the Hardriders' twenty-five from shortly after the Club became responsible for it, and for the Memorial 50, for a number of years; in 1978 he passed the responsibilities for these events to 'Newy' Nottingham and Tom Lynch respectively. After a stint of 10 years Graham Thompson asked for relief from the treasuryship and Geoff undertook the task in 1976, Graham resuming in 1977. Geoff is the first President since 'Boss' King, to ride competitively, albeit he does not now have the time to train with the intensity of his youth.

The 1977 A.G.M. was notable for another change. As in 1976 the meeting agreed to the amendment of the Articles to remove the restriction of membership to males. This decision was again challenged by sufficient members, led by Les Couzens, who demanded a poll of the Club. In 1976, while the result of the poll favoured the change, it did not do so by a sufficient proportion of those voting: in 1977 the poll proved overwhelmingly in favour of the change. For some years the presence of ladies on Club runs, primarily at tea places, had been accepted, albeit under protest from some. These protests resulted in Ken Davis refusing to be re-nominated as Captain at the 1976 A.G.M. and no other member would accept nomination. Arthur Lancaster has acted as co-ordinator of the Runs Programme; but at the 1980 A.G.M. Geoff Bruton agreed to become Captain.

So the Annual Dinners from 1977 were attended by ladies but this did not change their pattern — normally of 4 speeches with the presentation of awards after 2 of the speeches. Any desire for dancing had been catered for by Annual Ladies' Nights, latterly organised by Jackie and Alan Kennedy, and then Mary and Roy Cook, and making happy social evenings. In appreciation of their services in another sphere, in 1978 Mary and Roy were made Vice-presidents of the North Mids and Herts Cycling Association, which Mary had rescued by becoming the Secretary. Roy has long served the club as organiser of Club Time Trials.

Leading riders in the 24 since 1975,1976, and 1980 being championship years have been, with the indicated mileages:-

	First	**Second**	**Third**
1976	G.M. Bettis Bedfordshire Roads C.C. 482.656	J.D. Cahill North Staffs St. Christophers C.C. 467.912	L. Holmes Luton Wh. C.C. 461.229
1977	D. Cruse Maldon & D.C.C. 432.656	L. Lowe Speedwell B.C. 424.174	R. Usher Willesden C.C. 419.182
1978	I.S. Dow Oxford City R.C. 472.549	D. Saunders C.C. Breckland 464.218	K.M. Lovett N.R.C.C. 441.319
1979	I.S. Dow Oxford City R.C. 471.091	K.M. Lovett N.R.C.C. 446.256	R. Sewell N.R.C.C. 443.930
1980	J. Woodburn V.C. Slough 505.477	J.D. Cahill North Staffs. St. Christophers C.C. 497.337	I.S. Dow Oxford City R.C. 485.005

And the best North Roader, Tricyclist and Club Team were:-

1976	K.M. Lovett 449.439	W.H. Wootton Hounslow & D.Wh. 385.669	Luton Wh. C.C. 1323.228
1977	B.A. Hay 342.841	M. Smith Maldon & D.C.C. 307.854	Willesden C.C. 1193.310
1978	K.M. Lovett (3rd)	R. Akers Hertfordshire Wh. 386.186	Hertfordshire Wh. 1141.562

1979	K.M. Lovett (2nd)	——	N.R.C.C. 1283.017
1980	K.M. Lovett 465.188	M. Smith Maldon & D.C.C. 415.122	North Staffs. St. Christophers C.C. 1441.634

Ian Dow must be one of the youngest to win the 24, being 20 in 1978. And the third man in the N.R. Team in 1979 was Bob Mynott, winner of the 24 in 1949 and 1950.

For the first time, knowingly, the entry of a lady was accepted in 1980: This was Ann Dunk, wife of Bill and both North Roaders. Ann achieved 379 miles against Bill's 394, he had topped 400 in earlier 24s. Woodburn missed competition record by 1½ miles. North Staffs. St. Christopher's C.C. team added 27 miles to their competition record. Ken Lovett added 5.688 miles to Bob Mynott's 1950 club record.

Winners of the Memorial 50 since 1975 were:-

1976	M.T. Willcox	N.R.C.C.	1.56.01
1977	R.J. Queen	V.C. Slough	1.52.07
1978	S.O. Lovatt	Finsbury Park C.C.	1.50.34
1979	S.O. Lovatt	Finsbury Park C.C.	1.51.02
1980	I.S. Cammish	Edgeware R.C.	1.48.28

In 1978 D. Worsfold, Redmon C.C., achieved tricycle competition record at 2.4.38.

Sid Lovatt's 1978 and Ian Cammish's 1980 rides were, in turn, event and course records.

The tandem events run in conjunction with these events were won as follows:-

1976	M. Savage/R. Stirling	Glade C.C.	1.45.51
1977	A. Richards/T. Shardlow	V.C. Toutourien	1.50.46
1978	A. Shardlow/A. Richards	Oundle Velo	1.46.36
1979	P. Crofts/D. Membrey	Southborough and D. Wh.	1.44.02
1980	M. Kearney/R. Hughes	Clarence Wh.	1.51.59

In 1980 Ed Green's successor as President of the Tricycle Association, E. Tremaine, Leicestershire R.C., and D. Gabbott, Clayton Velo, established a 50 miles tandem tricycle record of 1.55.28.

The 1977 event incorporated a veterans' 50 (for competitors over 40) in which K. Armstrong of Notts and Derby Clarion C. & A.C. was fastest in 2.05.25 and A. Boutell of V.C. Slough was first on standard, his actual time being 34.32. better than the standard for his age.

THE 1979 '24' TEAM
R. SEWELL K.M. LOVETT R.F. MYNOTT

In the Club's remaining open event, the Hardriders 25, the winners have been:-

1976	A. Engers	Woolwich C.C.	1.8.34
1977	R. Downs	V.C. Olympia Sport	1.6.42
1978	R. Downs	V.C. Anglia Sport	1.8.28
1979	S. Yates	Archer R.C.	1.6.46
1980	T. Stevens	34 Nomads C.C.	1.3.45

The course was re-designed for the 1979 event to enable the start and finish to be near the Annexe to Hatfield Polytechnic at Bayfordbury, hired for the morning to provide changing accommodation, showers, and more comfort for the ladies kindly doing the catering.

In other Clubs' events, in 1976 our then member, R. Usher, won the Wessex R.C. 24 on a very hot weekend. His 425.64 miles was the only ride over 400 miles.

By the Club's membership of the Herts Cycle Road Race League, the Club's promotion of a road race and at least one annual visit to the specially constructed Eastway road circuit in the eastern part of London, the ambitions of members wishing to participate in massed start racing are largely satisfied.

There was yet another change at the 1977 A.G.M. when Ken Lovett persuaded John Rhind to become Editor of the Gazette. Ken and his wife Jackie had been deeply involved in the change of production (from printing, which had become too expensive) to 'Litho' when Henry Manwaring was editor. Ken took over when Henry died prematurely in 1970.

The change of editor coincided with increasing interest, encouraged by John, in Randonnee Events which had become popular in France, where member and erstwhile 24 rider Bill Dunk was domiciled. These events could be Club runs or ridden solo at a speed between 15 and 30 kilometres per hour. The York Run following a route mostly west of the North Road became a 300 km. Randonnée in June and a day run from Hatfield to Chipping Norton and back was tried successfully, reviving memories of war-time weekends. Encouraged by Bill Dunk, and his wife Anne, small parties of North Roaders have gone to France to participate in some of the strenuous Randonnee over the French Alps. In the centenary year of the Cyclists Touring Club a Paris to Harrogate Randonnee was organised in conjunction with a Rally at Harrogate. But the weather was wet and stormy and few completed the ride, among those who did was Bob Mynott. He has also completed the longest of these rides in Britain — the 600 km. Windsor - Chester - Windsor, which can start anywhere on the route, finishing at the same point. In August 1978 Bob participated in a Randonnée organised by the British Cycling Federation to celebrate the centenary of a ride by the Hon. Ian Keith-Falconer, a notable rider on track and road, from Trinity College, Cambridge, to his home at Keith Hall, Invererie.

In contrast, to cater for the youngsters who have come in to the Club in recent years, a series of Potterers' Runs have been organised and led by a few of the older members.

So the Club is in good fettle with enthusiasm to carry it on; the shorter Club events such as 25 miles of which there are at least 4 each yer, attract some 20 entries each. The programme of time trials includes some 9 at 10 miles, 4 at 50 miles, and one each at 100 miles and 12 hours: these last are run in conjunction with Association or other Clubs open events: in line with the general scene in cycling the longer events now attract fewer entries.

When a Club lives for 95 years it is but natural that many of the years are tinged with sadness by the deaths of members, mostly in the fullness of time but occasionally prematurely. In the latter group was Ted Kings who gradually moved from active participation — in 1957 he covered 421 miles in the 24 on a course he had been instrumental in revising. Passing through various phases of the Road Time Trials Council he eventually became it's National Secretary. Alas he died in early 1977, just before the annual Prize Presentation he had organised. He was followed by one of our Midland North Roaders, Dudley Roberts, who is primarily a Rockingham Forest Wheeler. In 1979, two who played a part in this book, Colin Buckland and Bert Dollamore, died in December. Earlier in the year Ed Green, who had encouraged me greatly, while giving Presidential support to a Tricycle Assocation 50 miles event in Lancashire, collapsed and died to widespread sorrow. These sad happenings made me very conscious of my age and anxious to see this book published. I am sure however, that they were, as I am, delighted with the healthy state of the Club as it approaches its centenary.

APPENDIX 1

Officers of the North Road Club.

Presidents

1887-1895	A.J. Wilson
1895-1914	T.G. King
1914-1933	F.T. Bidlake
1933-1938	S.H. Moxham
1938-1944	W.C. Frankum
1945-1961	H.H. England
1961-1977	W.C. Frankum
1978	G.E. Edwards

Captains

1885-1886	J.W. Day
1887	E.E. Bernhard
1888-1889	G.T. Langridge
1890-1891	G.R. White
1892-1893	F.T. Bidlake
1894	S.D. Begbie
1895-1896	F.W. Shorland
1897	A.F. Ilsley
1898-1899	W.M. Crosbie
1900	J.H. Wingrave
1901	R. Ibbotson
1902-1903	A. Gould
1904-1905	W.H. Nutt
1906-1907	J. Cecil Paget
1908-1909	C. Hilhouse
1910-1911	R.A. Wingrave
1912-1913	J.E. Naylor
1914	P.W.B. Fawley
1915-1917	W.W. Robertson
1918	A.W. Hellis
1919-1934	F.H. Inwood
1935	G.B. Spary
1936	T.E. Bryant
1936-1938	H. Paige
1939	A.V. Lancaster
1940-1945	E.W. Haldane

Secretaries

1885-1886	E.E. Bernhard
1887	C.W. Newton
1888	W.F. Allvey
1889-1891	F.T. Bidlake
1892-1895	P. Rivers-Smith
1896-1897	W. Ward
1898-1901	A. Gould
1902-1903	J.H. Wingrave
1904-1906	J.E. Naylor
1907-1918	A. Inwood
1919	A.W. Hellis
1920-1921	A. Inwood
1921-1924	C. Jay Cole
1925-1927	S.H. Moxham
1928	C.P. Gregory
1929-1930	F.E. Marston
1931	H.A. Meacock
1932-1934	D.H. Lodge
1934-1938	W.C. Frankum
1938-1940	J.M. Loten
1941-1945	F.E. Armond
1946-1947	L.H. Couzens
1948-1952	A.S. Taylor
1953-1954	W.C. Frankum
1955-1956	T.J. Baumgartner
1957	F.E. Armond

1946-1949	P.S. Bury
1950-1953	G.T. Hay
1953-1954	R.J. Way
1955-1962	K.E. Davis
1963-1965	R.A.C. Risley
1966-1967	D.E. Kings
1968-1972	R.J. Bridge
1973-1975	K.E. Davis
1976-1979	—
1980	G.H. Brutey
1958	L.E. Copping
1959	A.B. Kennedy
1960-1962	G.E. Edwards
1963-1965	K.E. Davis
1966-1969	F.C. Sellens
1973-1974	K.J. Fletcher
1975	D.G. Gates

Treasurers

1885-1886	J.H. Price
1887	W.F. Allvey
1921-1923	R.D. Cheveley
1924-1926	F.A. Cole
1928	R. Walker
1929	W.C. Frankum
1930-1936	R.D. Cheveley
1937-1940	G.B. Spary
1941-1947	H.H. England
1948	W.J. Medgett
1949-1951	N. Turvey
1952-1963	W.G. Allen
1964-1965	A.E. Blackman
1966-1975	G.L. Thompson
1976	G.E. Edwards
1977	G.L. Thompson

From 1888 to 1920 and in 1927 the Secretary acted also as Treasurer.

Editors of the Gazette

1903-1906	E.A. Wilson
1907-1910	L.G. Ilsley
1911-1912	J.D. Sangway
1913	P.W.B. Fawley
1914	F.H. Wingrave
1915-1916	R.A. Wingrave
1917	A. Inwood
1918	C.J. Cole
1919-1921	A. Inwood
1921	P.W.B. Fawley
1922-1924	T.E. Owen
1925-1933	W. Haylock
1934	E.B. Marsh
1934-1939	A.B. Smith
1940-1941	T.E. Owen.
1941-1944	T.F. Maddex
1945-1946	R.J. Jennings
1947-1952	C.V. Brutey
1953-1955	H.E. Manwaring
1956-1958	R.J. Way
1959	G.E. Edwards
1960	H.H. England
1961	A.E. Blackman
1962-1971	H.E. Manwaring
1971-1976	K.M. Lovett
1977	J.G. Rhind

APPENDIX 2

The Club Trophies.

1 The Twenty-four Hours Cup.

The twenty-four Hours Challenge Cup awarded to the Competitor, whether a member of the North Road Club or not, who shall accomplish the greatest distance in the Club twenty-four Hours Open Time Trial.

2 The Memorial Fifty Miles Cup.

The North Road Memorial Cup, in memory of Club members who died in the First and Second World Wars, awarded to the winner of the Open Fifty Miles Scratch Time Trial.

3 The Thistle Hardriders 'Twenty-five' Trophy.

A silver Challenge Cup awarded to the winner of the Open Twenty-five Miles Hardriders Scratch Time Trial.

Presented by members of the former Thistle Cycling Club.

4 Hadley Highstone Memorial.

5 The Twenty-five Miles Cup.

A Silver Challenge Cup awarded to the member who shall accomplish fastest time in the Club twenty-five miles Time Trials.

Presented by the late Dr. Kilham Roberts.

6 The Fastest Fifty Miles Cup.

A Silver Challenge Cup awarded to the member who shall accomplish the fastest fifty miles ride of the year in Club events or, in the name of the Club, in Open events.

Presented by the late A.J. Begbie.

7 The Handicap Fifty Miles Cup.

A Silver Challenge Cup awarded to the member with the best average handicap time who finishes in *all* the fifty miles Club events.

Presented by the late A.J. Begbie.

1
2
3
4

5
18
7
11
17
15
6
14
12
16
8
13
10
9

8 The One Hundred Miles Cup.

A Silver Challenge Cup awarded to the member who shall accomplish fastest time in the Club 100 miles Time Trial.

Presented by the late A.J. Begbie.

9 The Twelve Hours Cup.

A Silver Challenge Cup awarded to the member who shall accomplish the greatest distance in the Club twelve hours Time Trial.

Presented by the late A.J. Begbie.

10 The Members Twenty-four Hours Trophy.

A Silver Rose Bowl awarded to the member who shall accomplish the greatest distance during twenty-four hours in open competition in the name of the Club between 1 March and 31 October in any year.

Presented by the widow of the late A.E. Marsh and mother of the late E.B. and A.B. Marsh who were all members of the Club.

11 The Doncaster Cup.

A Silver Challenge Cup awarded to the member who shall accomplish the fastest time on the course from Barnet to Doncaster and back.

Presented by the late Dr. Kilham Roberts.

12 The Hill Climb Cup.

A Silver Challenge Cup awarded to the winner of the Club Hill Climb.

Presented by Mr. and Mrs. W.A. Palmer in memory of their son John.

13 The Founder's Novices Cup.

A Silver Challenge Cup awarded to a novice (i.e. one who has not previously competed in a race or time trial) for the best performance or series of performances in Club events during the year.

Presented by the late A.J Wilson, the first President of the Club.

14 The Junior Championship Cup.

A Silver Challenge Cup awarded to the Junior Member with the best aggregate of three rides in Club twenty-five miles events.

Presented by the late H.H. England, President of the Club, 1945-1961.

15 The Best All Rounder Cup.

A Silver Challenge Cup awarded to the Member with the best average speed at twenty-five miles, fifty miles, 100 miles and twelve hours.

Presented by the late A. Shillito.

16 The Handicap Best All Rounder Trophy.

A Silver Rose Bowl awarded to the winner of a handicap competition based on rides in the Club twenty-five miles time trials (best three to count), fifty miles time trials (best two to count), 100 miles and twelve hours time trials.

Presented by the late Mrs. E.M. Sewell in memory of her late husband, C.J (Jack) Sewell.

17 The Track Championship Cup.

A Silver Challenge Cup awarded to the winner of the Club Championship on the track.

Presented by Mr. and Mrs. W.A. Palmer in memory of their son, John.

18 Hillingdon C.C. Jack Sewell Memorial Cup.

APPENDIX 3

1889 Dinner Programme

North Road Cycling Club.

FOURTH ∴ ANNUAL ∴ DINNER,

Wednesday, 4th December, 1889.

Chairman:

SIR A. K. ROLLIT, M.P.

Vice Chairmen:

G. R. WHITE, *Captain.*

S. D. BEGBIE & W. CHATER LEA,
Sub-Captains.

Accompanist: - - MR. G. W. LLOYDS.

F. T. BIDLAKE, *Hon. Sec.*

PROGRAMME

—o—

THE QUEEN.

The Chairman

"God save the Queen."

THE NORTH ROAD CLUB.

The Chairman

Song.. .... Mr. Harry Giles

Song..................... .... Mr. Loder

Response—Mr. F. T. Bidlake.

Recitation... "The Baker St. Porter"..................

Mr. H. J. Swindley

Zither Solo..... .... Mr. Wilkinson

Distribution of Medals and Certificates.

Song.............. "Cleansing Fire"......Mr. Westcott

THE VISITORS AND PRESS.

Mr. W. F. Allvey

Song............. .... Mr. Harry Giles

Recitation....................... .... Mr. Fores

Response—*Visitors:* E. Dearman Jewesbury, Esq. and C. A. Smith, Esq.

Press: Messrs. Hillier, McCandlish and Swindley.

Song................. .... Mr. Loder

THE CHAIRMAN AND VICE CHAIRMEN.

Mr. J. H. Price

Musical Sketch........... .... Mr. G. N. Lloyds

Response ———

"Auld Lang Syne."

MENU.

—:o:—

Soups.

Scorching — Paysanne

Fish.

Turbot and Lobster Sauce — Whitebait

Entrées.

Sweetbreads in Cases

Chicken Sauté à la Marengo

Removes

Ribs of Beef and Horseradish.

Saddle of Mutton and Red Currant Jelly

Vegetables

Boiled Potatoes. — Sauté Potatoes.

Cauliflower and Béchamel Sauce

Sweets.

Record Pudding — Merletons de Rouen

Holbein's Jelly

Ice Pudding.

Cheese. — Celery

—

DESSERT.

—

The Holborn Restaurant, London

APPENDIX 4

1894 York Run Programme

NORTH ROAD CYCLING CLUB.

CLUB RUN TO YORK.

16th June, 1894.

		MILES.	
MANCHESTER HOTEL, ALDERSGATE STREET, E.C.	Supper at 10.30. Friday night.		
GENERAL POST OFFICE.	Start at 12 midnight.	—	—
HITCHIN. (ROSE & CROWN).	Light Refreshments. Arrive 3.15. Depart 3.35.	34.	34
ALCONBURY. (WHEATSHEAF).	Halt for drinks. 6.5—6.20.	67½.	33½.
STAMFORD. (CROWN).	Arrive 8.15. Breakfast. Depart 9.0.	89	21½
GRANTHAM. (RED LION HOTEL).	Halt for drinks at 10.50—11.0.	110	21.
NEWARK. (RAM HOTEL).	Arrive 12 mid-day. Dinner. Depart 1 p.m.	124½.	14½.
RETFORD. (GRANBY).	Arrive 2.45. Afternoon Tea Depart 3.15	145.	21½
ASKERN. (SWAN).	Arrive 5.20. High Tea. Depart 6.30.	169.	24.
YORK. (ADELPHI HOTEL).	Arrive 9 p.m.	197.	28.

The 5.20 p.m. train from York on Sunday the 17th, will have reserved accommodation for members and their machines.